Introducing OSCAR Therapy

A New Interspecies Behavioral-Diagnostics Paradigm
and Problem-Reversal Therapy to Restore the
Animal-to-Animal and Animal-to-Human Relationship

- or -

How *Anyone* Can Fix the Messed-Up *Mind*
of Any Animal of Any Kind

Casey Sugarman

will·ing

VOL I, II, and III

An Im/practical Manual for Learning and Employing Will-Mechanics
"Applying the Nature of Choice to Fix What's Broke"

(This book is still in draft at the time of this printing.)

Introducing OSCAR Therapy

A New Interspecies Behavioral-Diagnostics Paradigm

and Problem-Reversal Therapy to Restore the

Animal-to-Animal and Animal-to-Human Relationship

- or -

How *Anyone* Can Fix the Messed-Up *Mind*

of Any Animal of Any Kind

Published by Casey Sugarman
DBA Willing Results, LLC
P.O. Box 102
Niantic, CT 06357
casey.sugarman@gmail.com
www.oscartherapy.com
www.will-ing.com
www.willingresults.com
www.willintegrators.com

Introducing OSCAR Therapy/ Casey Sugarman. -- 1st ed. October 4, 2021

ISBN: 978-0-578-34721-9 (Paperback)

ISBN: 978-0-578-34722-6 (eBook)

LCCN-- Library of Congress Control Number: 2021923933

Book Design by Tracy Atkins
Front Cover Photo: "Artemis" photograph of unknown origin, in the public domain

Printed in the United States of America

Dedication

This book is dedicated to the animals, every last one of us.

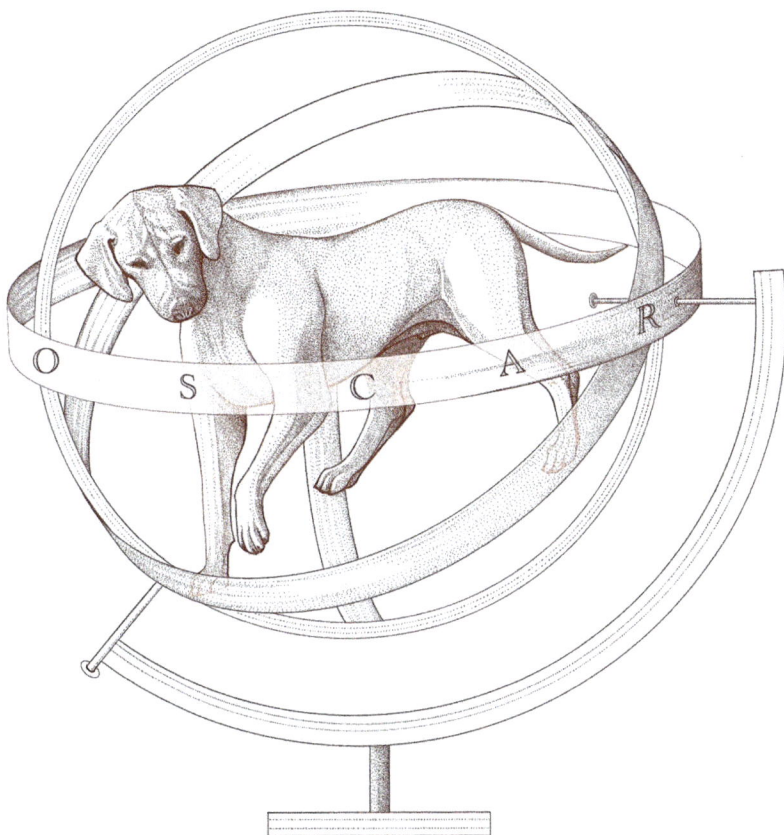

Table Of Contents

List of Illustrations, Tables, and Maps

List of Illustrations

Foreword:

Casey Sugarman's work does not force, however kindly, an individual to choose between one way to give itself up and another. Instead, it goes to the core of reconnecting the individual with the truth of itself, its Will- its right to be here. Casey demonstrates an approach to developing safe, rewarding and ethical partnerships with horses (or any other creatures), which is stunningly effective. Her approach, OSCAR Therapy, is one of the most profound educational experiences I have had in years.

Casey's work applies to any species because it's based on her years of experience *teaching* aquatic animals such as fish, lobsters, squid and sea lions to volunteer for unpleasant medical and husbandry procedures, as well as the challenge of understanding her own wild then abused alpha mare. Utilizing components of various disciplines including neurophysiology and operant conditioning, her technique is respectful, intimate, and empathetic without being anthropomorphic, sentimental, or dogmatic.

Like the horse whisperers and modern cowboy trainers, her work is based on careful observation, but it differs in that she seeks to elicit creative choice rather than manipulate the student in order to achieve a predetermined outcome. Because of this, results are not limited by the teacher's perception of the student's capabilities, and because of that, her process is more potent and accurate than other teaching methods I have observed.

A "conversation" takes place that is brain-to-brain, as rapid and fluid as thought, through which her "learners" teach themselves instead of being taught. Students of all species are voluntary participants in their own education, stimulated and supported by a teacher who understands the empowerment of creative decision making. Her OSCAR Therapy gets you to your goals by uncorking a fountain, instead of by revving the engine with the parking brake on...

Casey's human students learn to stop focusing on result and instead learn to recognize and reward intent. By releasing the need to be the alpha boss, would-be teachers learn to embrace creativity and discovery, developing partnerships based on cooperative will rather than hierarchy. This isn't always easy, but it is fun, and students of any species can trust Casey to provide a safe and even funny learning experience. Through focused, interactive, open-ended communication, fear is replaced by curiosity, resentment transmutes into desire for connection, and even phobia morphs into calm exploration. With results like these, who cares about being the boss?

—Candace K. Platz, D.V.M

U. S. Dressage Federation Gold Medalist, USDF Regional Champion AA Grand Prix

2013 US Nationals: Dressage Finals Placing Third in US in Grand Prix AA

U. S. Dressage Federation Instructor/Trainer, Torrey Hill Stables Trustee, Riding to the Top Therapeutic Riding Center, Maine Equine Associates, Auburn ME

A Collective Foreword: Two OSCAR Practitioners

The initial concept of OSCAR Therapy is something normal people can wrap their heads around... Reward at the end of a treasure map is a game any brain can play: seek the treasure and you win. The fully normal and functional animals will be able to win OSCAR's simple button-touching game within minutes and every time. But the ones that *can't* win it within minutes, those are the brains that need some more information... So that's the part that's pretty easy to understand.

What's harder to understand, though, is WHY that simple game works so well to reverse so much deep-rooted behavioral trouble. How can it be so simple as the animal just learning that it's safe for them to reach out into the social world? How can reaching out to touch someone/*anyone* be what causes dogs to stop wanting to eat the delivery man?

Most people define "training" as a dictatorship where one individual sets the rule, and if the other doesn't follow, then there is something wrong with the student. The reality, though, is that there is something wrong with the teacher.

Even positive reinforcement technique rarely gives you any information from that animal's point of view. Even in operant conditioning, we trainers have all been wired by the "training" we've been taught; but what we've been taught... is not a full conversation in any way. OSCAR is the full monty... the *full* conversation.

—Leita Hagemann, Dog Trainer, Connecticut

The real trouble comes when it just seems like the OSCAR explanation is too simple to be the real answer. Even though I live OSCAR now and see the proof every day, I still occasionally think that it can't be real, because it's just so damn simple.

I guess it's almost like having a fear of success... you just can't imagine, after trying so many things for so long, that the answer was that easy... Regular people will talk themselves right out of this answer because it sounds so simple, but it's not. For my horse, that everyone was ready to euthanize, it's been everything.

If you could ask my horse what his interpretation of OSCAR is, he would say, "Now I know where I am in space, now I know where she is in space, now I know what makes her happy, now I know that I'm not going to die when I am confused, now I know that I can win, now I know that I like winning, now I know what funny is, now I know that she gets my jokes, now I know..." And all of that is sooo much!

Most people can't deal with the truth of what OSCAR is. In their own brain, people want something they can make into a cause and effect timeline, like:

"I do x and y and then robot animal does p and q. People like things that are spelled out in a physical recipe, even when they make no sense like "kick him when" or "pull this until..." People simply cannot wrap their heads around the fact that every animal actually thinks about stuff, bringing his own ideas to the table. Working with animals seems like it should be harder than the easy conversation that OSCAR is. What people don't get though is that all of that superstition and denial is the HARDER way up the mountain—and they never actually reach the summit!

Even though my horse has done a complete 180 in his behavior, which everyone sees and is amazed by, most people just walk away when I try to tell them how we got from "him then" to "him now." When we've learned (through tradition) that certain things are impossible, that a thing is impossible to overcome... then we are blind to the solution, even when it's staring us right in the face.

But I get it. I actually played the major role (under Casey's guidance) in helping my horse recover, and the story is even hard for me to believe sometimes. I don't know why—it just is. Nobody is more shocked than me that my horse actually likes me now. Because for years he downright loathed me... for real. And I was at the end of my rope. He was right at the end of a euthanasia needle, but something was eating at me- that ultimately, it wasn't his fault, and that's when I finally picked up the phone and called the ad I had seen in the horsey yellow pages.

-Suzie Fancher, Horse Owner, Connecticut

Casey's Candid Letter to Every Reader

When I was a lucky kid with a horse, I needed the information contained in this book so badly that it became the only journey I chose in life. Every secret birthday wish led me on this path. *"Somebody*, show me the way to help her not hate my guts" was what I secretly wished.

If the path to discovering OSCAR Therapy started when I was 13 and then snaked through my life until I got the letter back from the US Patent and Trademark Office, that arc of time took 31 years. Fifteen of those years were even spent doing daily work with 750 other species from jellyfish to whales. It took just a blink of an eye, though, to write this book.

The animal that young me picked to be my partner, truth be told, I picked because I had a strong feeling that she was one who would tell me the truth, her truth, about the animal – human relationship. I needed to know more because what I was seeing all around me seemed false and make-believe. Even as a kid, I was sure the animals had critical knowledge that we humans were tamping down and forcing away into the shadows. And in so doing, we humans were losing out; our whole species was losing out. But I just couldn't put my finger on what was being lost.

Anyway, that was then and this is now. So instead of going on about the past I'll now talk to you, the reader. And to you, I'll pose this one initial question:

If your knowldege-base had a disease... how would you know?

OSCAR Therapy is not animal training. Full stop. The end result of OSCAR is so much better than anything training can produce that you can't even compare the two. And yet, so many trainers and even veterinarians are suspicious of a paradigm that is this simple. They end up seeing complexity because they expect to. Not because it's there.

There are plenty of humans of both genders that are of the "toxic masculinity" persuasion. These individuals seem too embarrassed to learn something that works perfectly well, even without having any kind of dominance at its center.

And yet, plenty of kids and farm girls and strong women and old farm hands and more have all been living proof that OSCAR Therapy is so easy to learn that some have picked it up just by watching someone else doing it even for a few minutes.

OSCAR truly is simple stuff; it's a door that's OPENING for you and your animals, not a door that's shutting ANYONE or any brain out. There are nuances, of course; there are some specific tools for when animal histories have been deeply trouble-enduring. But to think that OSCAR is overly technical and complex is to miss its point entirely.

The point of OSCAR Therapy is that any and every animal WANTS to talk with you and will work oh so hard to meet you in the middle, in *their version* of the middle... *if* you can just be curious enough to search for that middle, and *if* you can be "aware" enough to notice the animal engaging you there. That's really all it is. The most hard and fast rule of OSCAR is that NO rules are hard and fast. For example, we practitioners break the first rule of OSCAR every single day on the job. But until you understand *why* the rule is there, then break it at your peril.

With *all* things, there's the art, and then there's the science. The most *effective* things, though, those are the things that ride the line straight down the middle. If you try to make OSCAR into a straight science, you will be sorely disappointed as you totally omit and ignore the unique individuality of any receiver's brain. And if you treat OSCAR strictly as an art, you will alienate every person on Earth who considers themselves not talented; your efforts will fall on deaf ears, collect dust, and do very little good in the bigger world. So try to use a little of both.

But what I promise you is that the entire story of your animal lives just underneath the OSCAR rock. All you have to *want* is the courage to lift up the rock and look under it; *the wanting* is enough to get you there. If all you want to see is *your own* story, all OSCAR Therapy will show you is shadow. If what you seek is the truth of somebody else *and you*, then OSCAR will show you it all, and I do mean *all*.

This book will have no "students," as I am no authority who dictates truth. This book has no patients, as I am no doctor, prescribing the one-road to health. It also won't do your thinking for you, like a color by numbers recipe. To use this book, you'll have to use your brain, both sides of it. But speaking for the teenager in me, I hope this book gives you exactly what you *need*.

That means that you, the reader, get to make all of the decisions about what to implement and how to apply such tools best, to suit you and your animals' own unique settings and contexts and goals and needs. This book provides a star chart to navigate by, but it leaves the steering of your ship up to you.

And once you've got your bearings, the way to "resolution with an animal" is just "second to the right, and straight on till morning." In the novel about Peter Pan, the children are said to have found the island of Neverland only because the island itself was "*out looking for them.*" I can tell you that all of the animals I've ever worked with did and do wholeheartedly agree; they are out there looking for us, every day. By using OSCAR Therapy, *both of you* will find each other.

-Casey Sugarman

Naturalist, Will-Integrator, and Founder of OSCAR Therapy

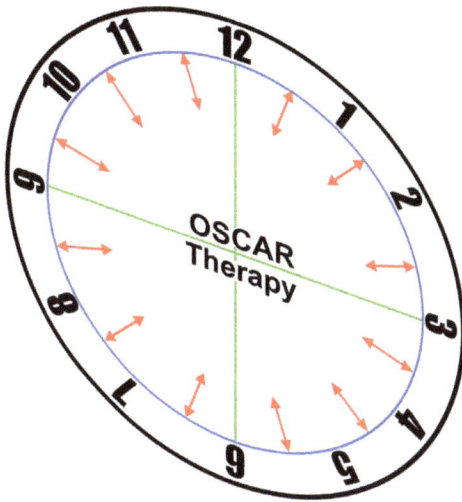

CHAPTER 1: WHAT IS OSCAR THERAPY?

What if we could think about both a body's behavior and a brain's rehabilitation in a different way? What if the end results and even the goals were something new? What if it were not about subtracting bad behaviors, and not even about adding new skills? What if it were about strengthening someone's mental, physical, and emotional *balance points* so that they could then do just about any job in the world...? And what if the most "unfixable cases" in the world actually turned out to be the smartest, fastest, most adaptable, and best partners in the *entire* crowd of competitors?

What if... the dog who used to bite now instigated *play* instead? What if animals that don't know how to play could learn *how* to play almost overnight?

What if the horse not only put his own saddle on but then also told you about the kinds of never-before-seen movements he was actually capable of?

What if the medical patients of any species including phobia-bound humans could finally be able to volunteer to "inject themselves" and be in charge of the gains and limits of their own rehab? What if another species could actually tell you precisely where it hurts, or where it used to hurt, or that they worry that it might hurt precisely there again? And what if those of us of the human persuasion could easily rewire our own brains so that we would no longer have to avoid tall bridges, snakes, deep water, dogs, spiders, bad memories, or even each other?

Well... if any of those kinds of ideas are motivating for you, then you've found the right book. OSCAR Therapy can make (and has made) every one of those ideas a reality for the brains that were "never going to learn."

1.1 Welcome to OSCAR Therapy

Welcome! We're glad you made it! Right here in the very beginning, we all want you, dear reader, to look to your left and look to your right and image every one of us who is also reading this book for the first time.

Among us all are… Younger people. Older people. "My animal eats before I do" people. "I pay my staff to feed my animals" people. Nonprofit people. University people. Animal rescuer people. Animal euthanizing people. Blue people. Orange people. Black people. White people. Veterinary people. No formal education people. Progressive people. Traditional people. Scientists, behaviorists, and especially backyard animal people are among the readers already, and we hope this wide-spectrum audience will continue to widen.

But I'd like you to be aware of this wide audience because of one very specific reason. It has to do with why I have chosen the specific layout of the information in this book. If you come to wish it were laid out differently, then join the crowd.

Having taught this information for about 15 years now, it is clear that different people take in information in vastly different ways. Some, like me, want context; others don't. Some want proof first; others want hope first. Some want the whys first; others want the who first, or the what or the how first. Some are offended by the basics that others are in need of. Some are freaked out by the advanced stuff, which others fast-forwarded to. Some read from beginning to end, some read from the end to the beginning, and many just jump around like a honey bee going from flower to flower. The digital version of this book even has a clickable table of contents to make such self-directed reading easier for anyone and everyone.

This book has been written to *cater to all* of these various types of learners and readers. That's not because I don't know who the audience is; it's precisely because I know a whole lot about the wide array of who the audience is. It's you. But it's also them. And it's also those other people. No matter who you are, I'm hoping this book will provide you with a way in to seeing the truth of OSCAR Therapy for yourself. Because… in a nutshell…

1.2 OSCAR Therapy Defined

The "elevator speech" summary of OSCAR Therapy as it applies to any species:

OSCAR Therapy is a real time "language" for helping you teach, communicate with, and navigate sticky situations with humans and/or captive exotic or domestic animals of any species and in any setting. You can use OSCAR Therapy to explain safety, training, medical, social, competition or other context-based skills to any individual, regardless of species. OSCAR Therapy employs the most primal bio-emotional paradigm- a few specific rules of social nature- to assess, diagnose, treat, and resolve, even while it points out dead-end paths.

For those who want to have "a partner who reads my mind" OSCAR Therapy is the key to that. OSCAR Therapy is fair and respectful of both you and your counterpart, helping you to find the "us" in your relationship. OSCAR Therapy is unlike ANY current training or teaching method because the choices that we promote and foster in OSCAR Therapy are based in self-expression. Because of this, learning OSCAR Therapy is like getting a chiropractic adjustment to your interpersonal skills, even your inter-species interpersonal skills for both the recipient and the practitioner alike!

The benefits of OSCAR Therapy are many:

- OSCAR Therapy is a primal teaching format based on techniques that SAFELY alter the behavioral expression and choices of animals across all species, including human.

- OSCAR Therapy is a quick and efficient way to diagnose and reverse (heal) most areas of PTSD, SAFELY.

- OSCAR Therapy is the best way to teach, educate, and/or build working partnerships with ANY species.

- OSCAR Therapy is used to create and generate both talent and skill in the learner.**

- OSCAR Therapy does not alter personality. An individual's unique, distinctive character stays in tact and is only enhanced. When the fog of confusion and distress lifts, that's when personality, style, and the individual's general charisma can finally shine through.

** The term "learner" may refer to an animal, a human, or any learning brain.

The OSCAR name is actually an acronym: O.S.C.A.R. The five letters stand for:

Operant : a positive reinforcement conversation, initiated and encouraged by the practitioner, but effectively *operated by the learner*

Social-Spatial : *the 3-D space* of social interface immediately between two different individuals (two different bodies with brains)

Cognitive : all *choices* directed only by the learner's thought, creativity, courage, and learning

Angle : the 3-D space surrounding the body, described by vectors, and defined by the learner's choice of *directional movement*

Reach & Recoil : exploration of options of *bi-directional* vectors options that are within the learner's "Social-Spatial bubble"

Operant Conditioning (OC) is simply the name of a behavior modification technique that uses associated rewards to strengthen wanted behaviors. OC has become the predominant language used to teach any species of animal in the world of exotic animal husbandry. This communication system, which was originally solidified by the dolphin-human relationships of the 1960's, has spread far and wide. It is now in use with most animal species that reside in captivity at public aquariums and zoos. Collaterally, the skills also spread to the dog world and from there it spread to the horse and farm animal world. I personally learned it as a volunteer at the NE Aquarium in Boston, MA in 1990.

Social-Spatial is a term I designate to combine the concepts of "social interface + stress." We all carry a mental picture of our bodies in "social space," 24/7. This is what I call the "interface bubble." Combined here are the two notions of a) the "personal space" of sociology and psychology, schooling fish behavior, and the "herding angles" of herd/group behavior (noticed by both the horsemanship culture and hunting traditions), coupled with b) the PTSD knowledge of human Trauma Psychotherapists. Both of these have co-mingled in this term.

Cognitive stems from the fact that REASON (LEARNING) is the main steam engine that powers OSCAR Therapy; cognition does the bulk of the work. In OSCAR Therapy, the learner's way forward is the ONLY way forward. Since extremely dangerous animals can overpower and out-leverage humans at every turn, the only way to relate with them safely is when the animal is allowed to CHOOSE to play an entirely different game, one that is not based on physical leverage.

Angle is everything in OSCAR Therapy. 3-D awareness is key to even the land –dwelling nervous systems, yet I would not have noticed this reality if not for my aquatic background. Underwater divers of all kinds must learn to be aware of the other choice-making entities in their immediate 3-D space. The sharks or whales or boat motors will be swimming in from vectors that are above, below, and behind you. Ask any submarine navigator (or any fish with bulbous eyeballs) and he'll tell you that in the underwater world, angles of approach are everything.

PTSD, Post-Traumatic-Stress (which is not at all a disorder) is a normal brain's learned survival strategy; PTSD is all about the *learned extrapolation* of an exact memory. Exact memories of "exactly what occurred" in real time and in real space become locked into the brain as highly retrievable data, and OSCAR lets you access it.

Just like a forensics department examining any crime scene, any brain holds memory of the exact angle and force that any attacker person, animal, equipment or inanimate object applied to it. In order to uncover and reverse these locked-in experiences, we delve deep into the scenes of the crimes, and identify the (reversible) "fingerprints" that are left on the actual nerves of the unwilling recipients.

Reach and Recoil refers to what the learner becomes capable of causing to happen, first in the imaginary and then in real physical space. Will they reach forth into the space implicated in the memory? Will they recoil out of that space? Or does the memory trap them there? The influence of a brilliant physical therapist (my mother) helped me see that just because a body CAN physically do a thing, that doesn't mean that a body WILL do that thing. OSCAR Therapy teaches the brain to want to reach out (when it won't) and to recoil (when it won't). Both directions are necessary options in any 3-D space.

If I were to have chosen a non-clinical name for this therapy instead, I might have called it (and sometimes I still do call it) Vacuum Therapy or Tractor Beam Therapy (if my client is a science or a science fiction fan). For the ultra nerds, you could even call it "negative space" therapy, but note that there is absolutely nothing negative about negative space. It just refers to a space where there ought to be something there, but there's not. And just like a peeled hard-boiled egg gets sucked INTO the vacuum created inside a narrow-necked lab flask when the match goes out, we suck the missing parts of animals INTO *being*.

Regardless of what you call this process, in the end, the ultimate Will of any traumatized brain is to learn precisely how to *repair itself*. This is why OSCAR is an effective *therapy*. It is merely encouraged by the practitioner, but it is performed by the learner, and *that* is where the cure, on every level, resides-- inside the learner's brain. Once the intentional brain restores normalcy to its own pathologically affected body zone, issues no longer remain. And if that same kind of awareness is applied to the whole body, the brain also becomes immune to "re-denting" again.

To be clear, by "Will" I am not referring to any sort of rebellious will; we're not talking about a "willful defiance" or purposeful rejection of what you want them to do or be. A Will is not a thing that is only had by an individual that is hell bent on only doing as it wants, regardless of the consequences.

In fact, anyone's Will is just another name for his or her wish or need.

And yet, a Will is different from "a want." These things are different in the same way that a headache is different from "it hurts to think." Your head hurts for sure in both instances, but a migraine and doing algebra are apples and oranges, as far as the experience goes. Will vs. want is as different as those two things.

The Will is a chooser, yes, but often it's a *subconscious* chooser. "I want to love you but..." and "I promise I will do the dishes..."; we all know how these scenarios end. These are examples of what your will is not choosing, even though you think you ought to. The Will is the part of you that goes against your better judgment, and also the part of you that perseveres against the odds. The Will is the part of you that is going to do what it is going to do, regardless of the risks or the reasons.

Your Will is also the part of you that makes sure you don't follow through on a plan. The "will power" you think you can't summon to battle that chocolate cake or that co-dependent issue or that addiction is a very unfortunate misnomer. It is in fact the power of your very *strong* Will which is making you ditch the plan you just made, the plan to not eat it, the plan not to contradict them, or the plan to turn over a new leaf. Your strong Will has the power to harm you, so it also has the power to fix you.

OSCAR Therapy works because it taps into these "Will channels" in the learner. Whereas other approaches to animal management show animals what they have to lose, we show animals what they stand to gain. And as far as effectiveness goes, there's no comparison. It's rotten apples verses whole groves of orange trees.

In fact, you'll find that when a brain is succeeding in an OSCAR Therapy conversation, it's mostly not because of the reward. It's because of the empowerment, the control a brain gets over its own self, even in the face of temporary confusion in the brain. The end result is that when the world moves in to touch the animal, the animal has learned to expand out, to touch the world. The implications of that are profound, and the results are staggering.

1.3 What People Are Saying: Quotes from OSCAR Therapy's Client Testimonials

"OSCAR Therapy is THE 'language' for helping humans teach, communicate with, and repair captive or domestic animals of any species, us too."

"If an animal is slated to be euthanized for bad or dangerous or unpredictable or noncompliant behavior, please, I beg you, try OSCAR. Before it's too late."

"Every rescued animal needs this, regardless of species!"

"This guy has <u>never</u> been this engaged and focused- he LOVES it!"

"It's not about 'body language'- it's like nothing you've ever learned before..."

"How come I never saw it before? It was staring me right in the face..."

"Why has no one ever described this until now?"

"The solution was right under our noses the whole time, but it took a fish behavior specialist to see it, go figure..."

"My very core is shifting. Even though our personalities haven't changed at all!"

"The OSCAR knowledge set is so primal that it's hard to describe it in human words, and yet it's so easy to learn!"

"OSCAR has made me a better person in other aspects of my life."

"If I had this knowledge back then, I could have overcome a lot of issues that happened to me in my own past. I could've corrected them myself."

"OSCAR Therapy is an invaluable 'wide view' of bio-social interaction that could not have been found in any PhD program."

"The implications are staggering... everyone needs to know this..."

"My 12-year-old son has always had a severe dog phobia. We tried everything including professionals, but nothing helped. After three OSCAR sessions, (two of those only by video chat) he asked if we can get a dog!"

"I've been unable to go in past my knees for 60 years. With Casey's keen attention to my UNCONSCIOUS behaviors in the water, eleven sessions is all it took to learn to swim, to begin swimming laps and even to have fun getting "unexpectedly" PUSHED into the DEEP END! Casey's OSCAR approach had the uncanny ability to tease out what my body's automatic reflexes have been doing to get in my way when in the water."

"The OSCAR approach that Casey has pioneered is genuinely effective and should change the way we address negative and strange behaviors in our equine friends. I hope that Casey can continue to teach this method to many others (hmm, maybe a fundraising effort for an "OSCAR Therapy School?!") so that more can benefit from this unique and ultra-efficient approach – the nomenclature, 'willing results' says it all."

"Between us, we have 9 Emmy Awards; it just figures the OSCAR we get is the DOG! We are New Yorkers, in TV, so we were hard to convince..."

1.4 How OSCAR Therapy Got Its Name, and YOUR Oscar's Name

At the barn of one of my clients, Michelle's barn, there I was teaching my "behavior skillset" to a "right brain" grandmother, her "left brain" daughter, and her seven-year-old granddaughter all at the same time so that they could all learn how to converse with their no-longer-dangerous backyard horse. I needed familiar language that all three of these human brains could relate to and easily remember. And yet, as a marine biologist, I had none.

On the hour-long ride home, I worked out the makings of an acronym in my head, a compilation of clinically accurate yet everyday-descriptive terms. And then I was immediately dumbstruck by the *PERFECT* and wholly <u>unexpected</u> name that the first letters of those words spelled out: O.S.C.A.R. And then instantly, I was worried. As a child of the first Sesame Street generation, I was immediately concerned that I would be illegally stepping on the fuzzy green toes of a certain Grouch who was a personal hero of mine.

I immediately wrote a letter to Caroll Spinney, who just so happened to live just a few towns away. You know Caroll Spinney because he has been in your living rooms for 50 years. He's not only been inside an old, dented trashcan, but more "obviously" he's been the very tall puppeteer inside the big, yellow Big Bird costume. Yes, Big Bird's alter ego was Oscar the Grouch... for the same 50 years. No wonder we never saw those two characters in the same scene on Sesame Street.

I grew up learning about the unfamiliar brains and brains of "the other" by watching Oscar the Grouch (who, as Spinney pointed out to me, is a Grouch and NOT a Monster; they are two separate species) and his love of all things putrid. And now, I could not bear to invoke anything that would in any way harm or even microscopically compete with his macroscopically good name. After explaining my work in detail in my letter, I asked Mr. Spinney, "Who presently owns the rights to the Grouch's persona?" and he directed me to get in touch with the Sesame lawyers. To this day, I have received no response to my many calls, letters, and emails to Sesame, Inc.

But what I did receive in that email conversation made me literally fall out of my desk chair and almost faint whilst on the floor. Caroll Spinney's blessing of my "well thought out application," straight from the Grouch's mouth, was in that email. I was speechless, shaking, and leaking tears of disbelief. I was so touched, blown away, and humbled by that short exchange that I see it as the most validating day in my entire life up to that point. To me, Oscar the Grouch, the persona, was the closest thing to a god that I will ever know.

Thankfully, I have been invited to invoke the memory of the Grouch's persona in order to explain what our real animals and real humans are up against. And with Oscar's trash can firmly in their mind's eye, to a person, everybody "*gets it*" right away. Here's what I explain:

Let's think back to the first grouchy individual we all remember: Oscar the Grouch! What do we know about Oscar? He's green, he's trashy, and…

He's in a can! A banged up and DENTED old can. Is he in there by choice? Or is he kinda sorta stuck in there? I think all of us kids wondered a little about that…

When a furry friend's psychological "personal can" gets dented, I've found that s/he *is in fact* stuck in there, just as you would be in the same circumstance. And then, being stuck makes *anyone*/everyone feel rotten. His/her CHOOSING to push those dents back out is the *only* thing that can turn her/him into an individual with options again. On Sesame Street, being a grouch is safe; in the real world though, being a grouch can get you killed, and in more ways than one.

If you try to yank any Oscar out of that crimped psychological can, s/he is likely to bite/kick/punch you. The reason is because s/he is trapped, trapped between you and the necessity of the learned dent. In the same circumstance, you would do the same. Yet, grouch *and monster* reversal therapy is straightforward, often quick, and indeed permanent. And its name naturally and unavoidably became O.S.C.A.R. Therapy. (Operant-Socio-Spatial-Cognitive-Angle-Reach-Recoil)

And now that we know the name of our approach, let's talk about the name of the brain we will be acting on. In fact, the name of the brain you're talking to is very important …not to you, (because you already know his/her name) but the name will be very important to this book. This book will need a *generic* name for that individual, who could be an individual of any species, any gender, any age, any size, and with any background.

For the purpose of helping the reader of this book (not the writer), I have decided that we are collectively going to call that brain: Oscar. Oscar is a perfectly good name for a brain. And yet, it may become confusing when we are talking about many different Oscars.

So… from here on out, and through the rest of this book, OSCAR Therapy (or OSCAR in all caps) will be our name for the therapy/language, and Oscar (as in the name) will be our generic stand-in name for the specific animal you are working with. In other words, when you see the name Oscar in lowercase, that means that you can read that as an underline, _____, and you can fill in that blank with the real name of *your very own* Oscar, the individual you are personally working with.

1.5 What OSCAR Therapy IS

OSCAR Therapy works the same way across all ages and genders, and across all species, breeds, and races. It works up and down all taxonomic levels too, up and down the evolutionary tree of animal life, and from invertebrate to whale to human. (Protozoa?!)

In most every brain-teaching modality, trainers teach animals (and some humans) to habituate to the normal activities of humans. And when the animals are bigger and stronger than we are, trainers usually teach the animals to respect the authority of humans by choosing to physically separate themselves from the humans by "moving away" from the spaces humans occupy.

In OSCAR Therapy however, we teach toward the opposite goal. We teach animal brains to reach out TO us, to both touch and untouch us, mentally and physically, with every single piece and part of their bodies. Operant conditioning and/or positive reinforcement trainers may label OSCAR Therapy as simply a form of target training (body targeting), and in the simplest description, it is. But this kind of body-focused learning then follows even the "incurable" animal down a rabbit hole that leads to the core of everything they are, everything they've endured, and everything they have the potential to become, even without our help.

In the OSCAR process, we trust that the animal brains know how to provide a much higher degree of accuracy *and safety* than what we humans could possibly construct by "calling it in" using traditional physical leverages. When allowed to be in charge of their own bodies, animals know much better than we do how best to create their own movements and their own body shapes that feel doable, all to generate the actions that are sought after by us humans.

To this end, OSCAR Therapy leverages both a brain's imagination and its mental focus, specifically by addressing and restoring every one of its logic-based and emotion-based roadblocks that it encounters on the way to a goal. We don't seek OSCAR Therapy because it's our only option; we seek it because it works truer and better than every other option. The result is a gained sense of co-ownership and participatory control over the things we do with, to, and for them... the sense we humans have always wished them to have with us. Oscar participates of her or his own free will.

Phobia, anxiety, chaotic unpredictability, inability to calm, and "misplaced" anger and aggression, all of these "symptoms" are merely different expressions of the very same originating root cause, but it's a root cause we can't see in a microscope or in a body tissue. We can only see the shape of this root cause as it manifests itself during a brain's willful (Will-based) avoidances, choices, and actions. The actual cause of these problems is a dented, splintered or undeveloped *sense-of-willful-control* over certain parts of Oscar's own body in three-dimensional *social* space. And observing such a case presentation in real time is astonishing, to say the least.

When certain parts of Oscar's body simply will not show up to the conversation, either not at all or only through certain angles, (even though the other side may show up just fine) this indicates a big missing piece. This major disconnect in the body-brain correlation becomes a very obvious locus of opportunity for massive improvement as we help that brain fill in that specific hole.

Regarding the "Animal Assisted Therapy" programs that benefit human chronic disease patients, human developmentally delayed patients, and human PTSD patients, all of their benefits to the human central nervous system (CNS) are fairly well understood. But consider the reverse. Where is the *human-assisted* CNS therapy for *any* domesticated animal species who has incurred PTSD, who was born with a developmental or social delay, or who has a chronic condition? Not only do a huge number of our domesticated animals need such support from us, but also... *we owe it to them*. OSCAR Therapy pays down our karmic balance sheet in huge and unexpected ways.

And especially regarding the animals that don't get a chance to socialize with others like themselves (members of their same species in the same environment) from a developing age and at every age thereafter, then how in the world can we expect them to have a normal *social interface bubble* when they don't get to practice having one with anybody but us humans, *a species who just happens to have no clue that such a "social bubble" even exists!*

Compared to how nature would build them, by and large, the animals we humans create are social pariahs. Caught between two worlds, the norms of their species and the rules of ours, domesticated species are moderately socially defective, even in how they treat us. Even with all the wide open spaces money can buy, a large percentage of domesticated animals still act as if they feel trapped inside themselves. Without an understandable social interface (and one in which they *get to fully exist*), they are in fact trapped.

And yet, recipients of OSCAR Therapy, no matter their age or background, quickly blossom into fully functional, expressive, independent teammates, who are now capable of working fully WITH us humans on any goal we have. Thus, all animal owners, experts, and professionals, regardless of the species they work with, would benefit tremendously from a working knowledge of OSCAR Therapy. And it should be noted that the *human animal* benefits equally well.

I first described Cognitive Spatial Reach "CSR" Therapy in 2005, directly after leaving the aquarium. And yet, leaving my decade long role as Senior Biologist in the Veterinary Services Department at the big, heart-of-the-city, public aquarium known as the New England Aquarium, in Boston, Massachusetts wasn't exactly my idea.

After 9/11 hit Logan airport in Boston very hard, tourists got scared, revenue fell, aquarium management changed, and the real science we had been doing up to that point got back-burner'ed in favor of ticket-based revenue building. I thought it was telling that both me and our whole learning library were shut down on the same day.

After that dream job, back in "the real world" of privately owned domesticated animals, I hung out a shingle and started taking on the extreme behavioral cases of any species that contacted me. And now after about 15 years of cases under my belt, I re-named CSR and gave it the federally trademarked name OSCAR Therapy in 2018. OSCAR Therapy is now a full program anyone can learn. And here's how the conceptual learning begins:

Just as Oscar the Grouch from Sesame Street both lives in and carries around an old dented trashcan, the brains of dangerously grouchy animals of any and all species seem to be defined by the dented "trashcans" (histories) they carry. The dents are both the learned misconceptions, confusions, fears, and also the hurts, and wounds they have experienced in their lives thus far. They are carrying around a learned "brain-to-body map" that is similarly dented, by the events in their own personal, individual backstories/histories. Commonly, this is even in cases where there has been no known opportunity for abuse at all.

OSCAR Therapy allows the brain to *learn* its way out of its own hole-riddled Swiss-cheese-like shell, literally. Occasionally it's a shell that they never broke out of (just like a weakened baby bird might have trouble in hatching) at the beginning of a life of normal nervous system development through normal life experiences and exposures. But much more often, the shell they must now break out of is the shell that they have had to construct, to protect themselves from remembering the bad things that *have already happened to them* and which, according to the brain, might happen to them yet again.

1.6 What OSCAR Therapy Is Not

The central and peripheral nervous systems of all animals, including the human animal, have yet to be fully investigated by our kind. The cross talk between the cells of our bodies, the symbiotic and parasitic organisms that go along for (and co-dictate) the ride, the operation of neural nodes and other outposts of the brain, all of it is still largely "a black box." So in the current era, these things still have to be taken as a collective whole, the bits of which will not be teased apart in this book.

The first thing that OSCAR Therapy isn't is academic. Hence, it does not require that we understand the underlying neuroscience or neurophysiology. Secondly, OSCAR Therapy does not involve, utilize, or comment on any extra-sensory systems, energy fields, or any other intricate physical-contact methodologies. OSCAR Therapy also does not utilize medium, psychic, communicator, telepathy, or spitual methodologies. *I do not believe that if you want to feel something bad enough, you will feel it.*

And yet, OSCAR Therapy does "work like magic" even though it's not magic. It is incredible how much information can be gleaned by simple observation, by deduction, and by hedging of bets. But it is even more incredible that so few of us are aware of the hearts we are wearing right out there on our sleeves. There is no need whatsoever to get all "extrasensory" about what is observable to the naked eye and ear.

Next, OSCAR Therapy does not require, affiliate with, or otherwise comment on any spiritual or religious methodologies, practices, or tenets. The candles and the essences all feel neurochemically manipulative to me. Sure, I believe that some people can karate chop through cement with the power of thought and mind over matter. What I don't believe is that the roads to enlightenment come with different colored badges that serve to delineate the value of the seeker by status. In fact, you might call OSCAR Therapy the opposite of a dogma.

Additionally, OSCAR Therapy is quite literally the exact opposite of Natural Horsemanship, "horse whispering," "dog whispering," and the horse and dog and human traditional athlete training methods. I lump all of those methodologies in together because they all rely on a power dynamic built on "relief from pressure and release of pressure," as if "pressure" were a natural state of being.

And yet pressure is *not* a natural state of being in any world but the human world, to the detriment of us humans the world over. In OSCAR Therapy, we reward the animal for choosing to come *to us*, not for going away *from us*. In large part, that means that OSCAR Therapy does not use any "equipment" at all.

Lastly, OSCAR Therapy is not of institutional origin. Only distantly related to the body targeting of the zoological and other professional animal handlers, OSCAR Therapy was created out of necessity, to work with the atypical, very injured, traumatized, and even toxic brains in any species. But OSCAR is not the first species-jumping language to be developed, not by a long shot.

Clicker Trainer (CT) is a widely popular application of the Operant Conditioning (OC) theory described by psychologists in the era of Edward Thorndike as early as the late 1800's. OC is indeed a necessary foundation of OSCAR Therapy. Food rewards, however, are not a necessary part of either OC or OSCAR; other types of rewards can be used.

In our current era, OC is the daily operating language of marine mammal trainers and other exotic animal trainers. Marine Mammals include the whales, dolphins, seal lions, seals, walrus, manatee, otters, and others. But there is a significant difference between the OC of the marine mammal trainers and the OC of OSCAR Therapy.

The marine mammals and the other exotic species that have been brought into human captivity likely had a "normal" upbringing with their own species, even if it was a short one. They were presumably not abused in their youth. Nor were they raised in foreign, socially extreme, or injurious environs, as are many of the domesticated species that live alongside, with, and because of humans.

After the acutely traumatic experience of transitioning from a life in the wild to a life in captivity under human care, life is again (typically) not terrible. The brains of marine mammals and other exotic species are complex to be sure, but in captivity they are largely treated with considered sensitivity to their biological, social, and environmental needs.

In short, exotic animal handlers aren't dealing with chronic warzone-like PTSD in their dolphins or alligators when they meet up for the first time. These captive animals live with teams of such experts 24/7. The choreographed interface with humans is an everyday lifestyle for these animals, usually from their early lives.

In fact the lives of the vast majority of the critters of all types from fish to amphibians to reptiles to the birds and mammals that live in zoological institutions are purposefully enriched with clear and respectful options provided by their human husbandry specialists. Only the occasional zoo or aquarium resident would need or benefit from the special tools of OSCAR Therapy. They might be like the ones with complicated-capture backstories or maybe the ones who were forced into chronically stressful social groups, or away from family members, yet again.

But the animals we treat in OSCAR Therapy come from meaner streets. They are primarily the domesticated species. There are both the expensively bred animals who have failed traditional training methods, and the refuges who have been passed along to many different homes. Homes can be nice enough to provide food and shelter to animals who are not safe enough to have any job other than to be companions to the useful animals. Many are rescues who now live with Good Samaritan rescuers, not trainers, not experts, not biologists, not behaviorists.

These are the animals of all ages and traumatic back stories who have been through the emotional *and physical* grinding mill, and the fact that they are still alive at all is the miracle. And yet, with so many animals going through the shelter and rescue system these days, there is no shortage of troubled brains in need of help. Helping ALL of *these* groups of animals, that's what OSCAR does.

1.7 What OSCAR Therapy Does

OSCAR Therapy is a brain rehabilitation therapy, full stop. For the purposes of this book, we will refer to both Oscar and Oscar's brain. To us, those are the same entity; we don't discriminate between them. When we refer to one, we mean the other as well, and vise versa.

OSCAR Therapy first recognizes and then diagnoses the brain-based problem, and then it will also treat/heal/reverse/cure/fix/aid/help the problem. Use whatever word you like to describe "a solution." OSCAR Therapy is a skeleton key that unlocks the imbalance when it comes to behavioral trouble or challenge.

There are more and more problem-reversal approaches out there these days, and this is just one. Yet OSCAR Therapy is a more central, core solution for any brain-to-body or brain-to-brain difficulty because it is the animal's learned belief problems that always lie at the very core of many of the behavioral problems we observe today. Unlock the OSCAR issue, and the root of the problem goes away.

The language and approach called OSCAR Therapy applies to, and so can be used with, all ages *of any and all species of animal across all taxa (the entire evolutionary tree)*, including our own human species. Using this language, the truth of the individual gets "discovered" and then the individuals fix their own problems. What kind of problems, you ask? Red problems, black problems, and green problems of course!

In OSCAR Therapy, we use the following color-coding to describe the categories of "troubles" that owners are up against in "behavior." For simplicity, we use the same color-coding for the troubles we're up against in taxes, in accounting, in our medical lives, or even in navigating highway road signs. In all things critical, we try to get out of the dangerous red and back into the safe black. But then later, we're always striving for the green *opportunities to build and progress*.

Here are the main categories of how OSCAR Therapy helps:

Behavior Troubles in the Unsafe Red: (Going from Hazardous to Not Hazardous)

- OSCAR Therapy reverses the individuals that are often euthanized or incarcerated for severe aggression, unruly, or unpredictable behavior when the trouble is left unaddressed.
- OSCAR Therapy reverses phobia, fear, PTSD, trauma.
- OSCAR Therapy removes all reasons for flighty, chaotic behavior.

Behavior Topics in the "Safe" Black: (Safe but Not Optimal)

- OSCAR Therapy creates unprecedented degrees of safety.
- OSCAR Therapy reduces/removes reasons for confusion and learning trouble.

- OSCAR Therapy reduces/removes both social anxiety and environmental anxiety.

Learning-Based Opportunities in the Green: (Going from Good to Great)

- OSCAR Therapy produces learned talent.
- OSCAR Therapy competitors advance quickly.
- OSCAR Therapy uncorks a fountain of natural talent.
- OSCAR Therapy creates the highest possible level of motivation.
- OSCAR Therapy partnerships are akin to "mental telepathy" in their clarity.

The end result is, typically, as if the originating problem never existed in the first place. That sounds too good to be true, I know. One of my first clients, a successful horse trainer described OSCAR this way: "OSCAR is not too good to be *true*; it's more like it's too *true* to be good. Or bad. It just is. It's just true." Now decades later, and just yesterday, a current client said, "Of all the ways of 'communication' I've learned, this is the best way, because it's true; it listens for the whole truth."

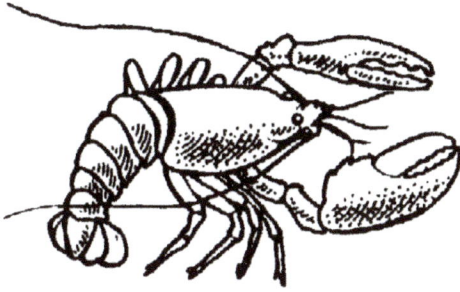

CHAPTER 2: WHY OSCAR THERAPY?

This book is going to tell you how to see OSCAR Therapy, how to do OSCAR Therapy, and how to do it well. It will even give you good access to our OSCAR community. But there is no reason to take part in any of that access if you don't first know *why* you're doing it. This chapter is going to be about the why.

For starters, let's think about an accepted norm of animal training. In almost every animal training modality, trainers teach animals to "just get used to" the activities of humans. This is achieved mainly by over-exposure and habituation to the human's dominant role. For example, we ask the animal to "go over there." When humans ask animals to "move away from us" that is seen both as a safety measure and an establishment of "a necessary hierarchy" to show 'em who's boss.

When this distanced approach cannot then solve the problems we are having with the animals, the animals who we have to or want to be in *direct contact with*, then we humans begin labeling the animal as a behavior problem. But when all you have is a hammer, everything starts looking like a nail. And when all you have is an x-ray machine, humans go peering into skeletal joints, digging in the wrong place, and looking for the roots of issues that are actually in the learning centers of the brain, far away from any moving parts.

When no skeletal cause can be found, humans start in with the chemistry experiments that are meant to alter and normalize the brain toward a more balanced and rational state. Diet and supplementation are brought up to snuff so that animal brains are receiving the optimal nutritional building blocks needed for learning. Usually, many approaches have already been tried on *all* of our cases well before they ever meet up with OSCAR Therapy. OSCAR cases have typically tried and still failed most of the traditional *and alternative* approaches below:

Equine Approaches: Diet, dental work, radiographs, traditional trainers, natural horsemanship, horse whispering, acupuncture, chiropractic, pharmaceutical drugs, anxiety medications, essential oils, alternative supplements and treatments.

Canine Approaches: Traditional trainers, alpha dog dominance models, dog whispering, acupuncture, anxiety medications, pharmaceutical drugs, alternative supplements and treatments, homeopathics, and essential oils.

But OSCAR Therapy is literally the opposite of all of these approaches. If all of the above can be thought of as "external solutions," OSCAR Therapy teaches animals to create the "internal solution" to every challenge we present to them. We teach animal brains to reach out TO us with their whole selves, physically, mentally, emotionally, and creatively.

OSCAR participants learn to choose to try hard to seek our ideas with every single part of their bodies and brains, in the best ways they know how or can dream up, even if those ways seem very foreign to us. To this end, we leverage both their mental focus and their creative imagination at the very same time.

No matter the sordid and unfortunate histories these brains have already experienced, the result of OSCAR Therapy is *always* a co-ownership and co-control over all of the things we do with/to/for them. The animals acquire almost as much good control over their situations as we have. The side benefit is an amazing relationship with animals that we've only dared to imagine in our dreams.

So to introduce each coming chapter, I will share with you a handful of our favorite accounts about how OSCAR Therapy turned an animal's life around, and in so doing, enlightened the animals' owners as well. If fact, it's mostly the animal owners themselves who will be telling the stories. But the first ones, the stories here in Chapter 2, those will be *my* stories to tell. And yet, before I do that, there is one an important point of housekeeping that must be addressed. So let's tackle this common myth, head on.

2.1 Myth: "Some individuals just don't count."

This book will NOT argue the point that babies, dogs, bosses, fish, children, cows, husbands, cats, teenagers, birds, mothers, jellyfish, seniors, salamanders, employees, turtles, wives, snakes, adults, patients, lobsters, fathers, worms, convicts, butterflies, or anyone else with that squishy organ called a brain are sentient, conscious, thinking, feeling, and planning beings. I assume that all individuals are all of these things because all animal life, by definition, dictates that they are.

If you are in a phase of your life where you are still chewing on compartmental designations about which choosing brains matter and which choosing brains don't, then this is not the book for you. The readers who follow scientific, religious, political, or academic persuasions that do not accept that this statement, "each individual is a complete being" is self-evident, they will not be readers for long.

I am not inclined to attempt to convince anyone of anything, especially the things they choose to un-see despite their first hand experience to the contrary; convincing is not my responsibility. It is also not *Oscar's* responsibility to convince anyone that Oscar uses a brain, has a will, holds beliefs, and has a history, a story, a future and a personal self. I do find it curious, however, that the people who most often use words like dumb, limited, and simple-minded to classify an individual's lack of brains, are often the very same people who use words like crafty, devious, conniving, manipulative, and sneaky when that very same "stupid" individual has *them* over a barrel.

So whether we grant that dope's gray matter the "real" stamp or not, the problems their brains cause us are real enough, aren't they? With some new conversation tools at our disposal, maybe we can use their "pretend" brains to help us solve our *real* problems.

For example...

2.2 Lobsters Foreshadow OSCAR Therapy

Invertebrates can really be the best teachers. In fact, the first beings to show me spatial cognition in its most straightforward form... were the lobsters.

Lobsters can be angry, solitary hermits, at least when they work 9-5 jobs. When they were handing out personality, lobsters were holding the door. That claw they throw up at you is just an extra thick middle finger. In the absence of pressing business, lobsters just want to be left alone. They don't fall for cheap tricks, and there's no way to sweet talk 'em. The reason I know this is because everyone around me was trying.

Woods Hole is the name of a small town in Massachusetts, but it also happens to be the original Mecca of Marine Biology in the US. As an undergrad, the people I hung out with at Marine Biological Laboratories were chemosensory modelers. They had government grants to design robots that could smell very well under water. Think Wiley Coyote buying an Acme Automatic Nose (of course, he would set the dial to a picture of the Road Runner). Now think of that device working under water, and imagine setting the dial to, say, radioactive material...

You can imagine the applications, but what you may not know is that smelling under water is a little more bizarre than smelling in air, because currents in water have different flow dynamics than currents in air. But never you mind, because as all good computer modelers are apt to do, they just look for a critter who has that talent, they watch that critter do its thing, and then they program the computer to just do the same. There's a little finger crossing too.

Anyway, that was what the very smart people were doing where I was hanging out, and since lobsters are like underwater bloodhounds, and are also easy to come by in New England, they were the critters hired for the gig of showing the scientists how to smell their way to a source in the underwater darkness. The human half of the crew spent most of its time, as is the lot of the scientist, getting rid of all the variables one by one.

The water had to act predictably, so we built a 40-foot laminar flow tank in the basement. It felt like we were building the arc, but this time, all the water was on the inside. Eau de clam (like Bar-B-Q to lobsters) was going to be the smell that flowed down stream, but of course, the computer's cameras had to be able to see the smelly stuff in the water, so we tweaked the clam juice and the tank markers so that they'd glow in a UV light.

The setup looked like a sci-fi landing strip for alien craft, and the count down counter was counting down. All the lobster had to do was sniff his way through the glowing plume all the way to the other end to show the computer how to sniff under water. In would go the lobster to his starting gate at the mid-tank mark (gate number 5 for those of you who bet on the ponies) and the race was on!

Fat chance... "#$%# you!" said the lobster, doing anything and everything except hunt... He was climbing the walls, walking in circles, and flipping us the bird all the while. Good multi-taskers, lobsters. If you touched him, "#$%# you!"; if you flipped him over, "#$%# you!" If you blocked him "#$%# you!"; if you ignored him "#$%# you!" Even a trap door setup would have ticked him off, so the rat maze gate idea was out.

I think watching the frustration build up in my friends who were very smart cognitive behavior scientists pushed me to notice that the only thing that was completely predictable about lobsters was that they always chose the exact opposite of whatever it was that we wanted. So I guessed that it just stood to reason that if I told the lobster I wanted the opposite of what I hoped for, he'd be a sport. Reverse psychology, shellfish style.

We wanted Mr. Lobster to sit still, right side up, facing front, on the bottom, at attention, no profanities. So I put a brick lean-to on the bottom at gate five, and I grabbed Mr. Lobster between 2 gentle fingers, and very slowly swum him too high, too far forward, and facing backward. And as soon as he flipped me the bird, I simply opened my fingers and let him loose at the top of the tank, free to make his own decisions.

Within 3 seconds, all by himself, and with willful purpose, every lobster we put in there reversed direction, swam down to the bottom, gingerly backed himself into the starting gate, claws folded nicely in front, and patiently waited for as long as it took us to get ourselves together, moving live electric chords out of the saltwater puddles, etc. And that was all there was to it. The experiments could now proceed without animal choice variability because the invertebrates were now playing by our rules ON PURPOSE.

What I had created was a necessary 'natural psychological environment' in the middle of our landing strip. I didn't know at the time the significance of what the lobsters had taught me, but I knew that it was new to me. Most interestingly, it didn't feel like manipulation. Ultimately, in fact, the experience was stress free for the lobsters. As for me, I can tell you that the only reason I learned the solution was because I chose to look at a lobster and see a whole person... with the power... the power to piss us off and the power to make us all happy.

Don't get me wrong; lobsters taste good. One time... don't tell anybody... I ate a patient. Some well meaning people found a 12-pounder at a supermarket and tried to Free Willy the behemoth to the aquarium. For some reason, kindhearted bozos keep "saving lobsters" without using any seawater, and though we did our best to resuscitate, he died of shock at 5 pm.

I know you're not supposed to eat your patients, and I didn't do it very often. He was for sale at the fish counter that morning, and he was going to be biohazard the next... waste not. But in a comparison of experiences, I can tell you that eating a 12 pound lobster doesn't teach you a damn thing; listening to a 1 pound lobster, however, teaches you every damn thing, especially that everyone's choices matter.

And it just so happens that the *choices* that all brains make about their own bodies in 3-D space were going to become a central focus in my world.

2.3 Some Context Behind OSCAR Therapy

The entire red to black to green continuum can happen in any single case and in every single case. Horrid, scary animals predictably go from next-step-euthanasia all the way to champion partners, *if* the owner wishes to put the time in for competition readiness, and if the owners are "too dumb to know that recovery is just impossible." If you can dream it, OSCAR can get you there.

> M's owner: "I mean I kinda feel bad winning the competition, 'cus it's not even a fair fight. Comparing performances is like comparing apples and oranges...when I can have an on-the-fly technical conversation with my horse, while no other competitors can."

Speaking of being ignorant of what's "just not possible," must have been the most ignorant one of all because on the job, we were fixing the impossible problems every single day for a decade. Some highlights from my background as an atypical medical marine biologist/behaviorist follow: I was a lobster strategist, a decapod teacher (squid and octopus), a seahorse CPR-er, a fish whisperer, a lungfish listener, and I even got my butt kicked by a mudskipper. Even Alan Alda, alongside his Scientific American Frontiers PBS television show, came to visit our aquarium hospital because what we had built was so cutting-edge.

But maybe that's the kind of background one needs in order to be flung so far out of the box that, when you circle back to "the real world," you bring back with you the most obvious things of all. And OSCAR is one of those things. OSCAR Therapy is so basic... that we all somehow missed it, even me. Not only was I never taught it in school or on the job, and not only did I never read about it, but searching for similar areas of study *still* turns up zero results. And trust me, I've been looking for anything similar among the works of my biologist colleagues for over a decade. The closest thing I have found to date is the cure for phantom limb pain in humans, which I will touch on in Chapter 5.

Not only that, but veterinarians, horse feet trimmers, and dog groomers don't even believe the stories that we OSCAR practitioners tell until they experience it for themselves. When these animal experts see an OSCAR transformation in an animal first hand, they believe it, but then even they forget that OSCAR Therapy exists, because in their worldview, "bad brains" are just an accepted norm.

Because animal brains are thought to be unfixable or at best "out of reach," there's not even a category for "brain rehab in animals" in any "animal trainer" Yellow Pages. Even behaviorists don't know about this kind of approach. And yet any layman, even someone who knows nothing of animals, would understand it right away. Such a layperson might look at OSCAR Therapy and call it "fist bump therapy" and/or "clock-face therapy." But no matter what you call it, this approach to helping brains is a game changer.

2.4 And Why Me?

Facilitators seem to run in my family. My father was a trauma psychotherapist for humans and my mother is a retired physical therapist for humans; one worked on people's dented brains, and the other worked on people's dented bodies. I seem to be a more widely applicable combination of the two. I am a biological naturalist, a teacher and therapist to animal and human brains, an inventor and philosopher, a "will-based" editor and writer, a behavior troubleshooter and a "choice-based" systems analyst, among other things. But my self-titled job description covering that whole landscape says that I am a "will integrator."

In my life I've only fed, clothed and paid the vet bills for one animal, but it was for 31 straight years. I acquired that green spitfire of a filly as a kid myself, and because of that blind-leading-the-blind combination, every birthday wish was to just understand her better and to earn my way back from her well-earned hatred of me and of humans in general. And in the process of chasing that goal, I got to know a whole slew of other animals and who they were at their core.

I went in search of the answer to what drove my mare's confusing choices, but humans never seemed to have the answer. All of this was happening long before the arrival of the Internet and well before any kind of "horse whispering" hit the public consciousness. So I dove deep into the closest field I could find: marine biology encompassing invertebrate learning, exotic aquatic veterinary medicine, and multi-taxa husbandry and behavior management.

As a senior biologist on an aquatic veterinary team that was helping to support a whole evolutionary tree of 750 wild species housed in captivity, I realized that aquatic behavior observers must learn to notice what most people don't see: behavior in three dimensional space. Observable fine angles of movement, centers of balance, rotational gravity, these are the "road signs of intentions" that are the foundation of behavior under water.

Back on land, though, where most people see only flat movement, it's the 3-D behaviorists (and OSCAR Therapists) that see clear cause and effect vectors in an animal's "interaction bubble." Just like with your own "personal space," every animal perceives that kind of bubble all around him/her. And *that* is where a treasure trove of information lies.

In fact, Sherlock Holmes would be envious of the sheer amount of recoverable evidence that a body reflects in it's own 3-D behavior fingerprint. This evidence can even tell the history about what specifically happened to an individual, and even roughly at what age it happened. For instance, if a toe contact makes the attached knee go weak, you can bet there was a history of a traumatic entanglement of that foot. If an adult animal starts (unprecedentedly) suckling on you at some point during the therapy, you can bet that a scary thing happened very early on in life.

OSCAR Therapy is a sum total approach that originated from co-mingling my professional experiences handling / interaction behavior of dangerous (poisonous/electric/sharp) and difficult fishes, reptiles, amphibians, invertebrates, birds, large marine mammals, and the labeled as dangerous horses, dangerous dogs, and known to be dangerous farm animals. And without all of those layers of animal observation, including observing the choices they ALL made, I never would have stumbled onto OSCAR.

And yet, having my unusual background of dealing with dangerous behavior is not at all necessary to duplicating my results. Around the less lethal animals, even your kids can learn this treatment and therapy just as well as any animal professional, animal rescuer, or animal guardian.

But enough about me. Instead, I'd like to introduce you to some real-life Oscars...

2.5 Horse Inspires a New Diagnostic Paradigm and Therapy

I received a call from a woman whose retired trail horse had slowly lost his vision to an eye injury followed by cataracts. With just one eye blind, Johnnie was fairly un-phased, but when he lost sight in the second eye, as his vision slipped away, so did his understanding of the outside world. People who go blind can access "re-education" services, but domestic animals who go blind have to figure out how to adapt without help. Over a few months, Johnnie became ever more trapped inside himself.

He started to panic about any and all physical contact. He used the walls and fence lines to feel his way around, but being led out to grass was too dangerous in his mind. Putting a halter on his head required a half hour of calm talking. Encouragement, praise, and repetition just don't work for an animal who is too afraid (rightly) to try things they cannot assess in the normal ways they've always relied on.

Touching this blind horse in any way was always unexpected and always made him startle, so touching him was out. Johnnie needed to be able to reach out and feel the *social world* just like he could feel the fence line, on his own terms, and *before* that world touched him.

Using the dolphin-type operant teaching I knew from the aquarium, I asked him to reach out with only two whiskers to touch my fist and reveal the carrot inside, and then to touch my *moving target* fist. (*See* Chapter 4) Once he had that concept, he was motivated to keep reaching out to find my moving target, first reaching with his nose. And then I asked him to reach out with his ribcage, then to reach out with his shoulder, and then to reach out with all four feet. He learned in an hour that he could trust us to be his eyes but also that we would still allow him time to feel his way through his world, even when we were *part of what he was feeling.*

At the end of three hours, not only did the owner have her old volunteering horse back, but we were leading this blind horse over teetering plywood, crinkly tarps and whatever we could find that might make him nervous. We would lead him up and then reward him for reaching out with his nose and feet to touch moving objects. As the horse exhaled many times during the session, it sounded as if years of compounded anxiety were pouring out of him. I spent the last third of the session teaching his owner how to take over my half of the conversation, and they had a close relationship again after that day.

One year later, Johnnie died, happy and at peace. It was an apparent heart attack, experienced while rolling in new fallen snow. In addition to the sad news, the owner included: "The work you did with us that day not only released his fears of the unknown-from not being able to see. It must have also released other fears, because he was a calmer horse after that - calmer even than when he *could* see."

What we learned from helping Johnnie is that brain-to-brain contact, especially when sharing physical space, must *always* be a two-way street, never just a one-way operation. A gentle reach from the human is less than half of the conversation. Any horse, in fact any animal of any species, must also be capable of and comfortable with *their own initial reaching out*, in order to play their part in any conversation, about every topic under the sun.

2.6 Is OSCAR Therapy *ONLY* for Animals?

OSCAR Therapy was born out of necessity, as the only available safe and effective way of helping lethally dangerous, traumatized animals learn the skills and awareness necessary to prevent their imminent euthanasia at the hands of the people who loved them but also feared them. After OSCAR Therapy, these kinds of cases all recover to *behave normally* around other animals, humans, **and even around humans who know nothing about OSCAR Therapy.**

But invariably, client after client then asks us this same question... "Now that I know OSCAR Therapy, can I use it with my teenager? With my wife? With my baby? With my patients? On myself??

The answer: *Of course you can.*

Humans are animals, plain and simple. Maybe we are animals with different kinds of bells and whistles, but our neurological mainframe is still largely the same as it was a zillion years ago. This mainframe is a shared ancestry; our cousins share it with us. So does OSCAR Therapy work with people? Yes, of course it does. It works the same way in all of us animals.

The human animal reacts to primal social triggers in lock step with the other social species, but most of us just haven't yet harnessed this predictable ability in our nature. Our primal/animal instincts are in tact; we just don't know how to consciously apply those instincts to solve our problems. Not until now.

Just the other day, I taught OSCAR games to a 12-year-old boy from the other end of the state. His mom hired me because her boy had a "severe fear of all dogs" that was precluding him from being able to go to any of his friend's houses. Therapists failed, friend's families failed, and everyone was stumped. But after just three short sessions (with only the final session being with live dogs), this kid asked his mom if they could get a dog... So does OSCAR work on humans? Yes, it does. Does the age of the human matter? No, it doesn't.

2.7 Fear of Water: Aqua-Phobic People Quickly Become Swimmers

With the help of a journalist friend, here is an article we wrote for the local papers that would give hope to local residents with a fear of water. But citing the rule that "we don't help small businesses educate the community," no papers would run it:

According to Terry, a resident of Uncasville, CT, "this surely wasn't like any swimming lessons I've ever seen. " Jack S., director of the very competitive East Lyme Aquatic and Nutmeg Aquatic and Fitness Programs says, "I am thrilled to be able to provide this unique and much needed service to the local communities, since fear of water is a real problem that doesn't get enough attention. For safety reasons alone, residents in waterfront towns should know about such a great opportunity. Also, these are people who wouldn't otherwise be able to get out and enjoy the water!"

Now that her kids are learning to swim, Terry wanted to get over her long-standing fear. "If I had to go to the beach, I'd only go in up to my ankles, and I can't help my kids if I can't go in. I've been gung ho about learning to swim before I'm 40, but my body just wouldn't do it! It's like I've had no control over my reactions to getting wet!"

For people who have tried the swimming classes, mantras, or repeated exposures and are still uncomfortable in water, their situation is actually quite common. Many people suffer from a clear but as yet un-addressed problem around water. A 1998 Gallup Poll found that 46 percent of all adult Americans were uncomfortable with the deep end of a pool. Sugarman takes students from the ages of 5 to 95. It's never too early and never too late, and overcoming a fear of water is just about the single most self-empowering thing a person can do.

Bad reactions to water are largely subconscious in nature, so we are not capable of stopping them until the brain can learn about its own *conscious* state of self-control, especially control in the three-dimensional space that is water. Sugarman's Therapy called Operant Spatial Cognitive Angle Reach (OSCAR) is a scientific mouthful describing how the basic "reptilian" parts of our brains make primal choices about how they use that space.

Sometimes sessions have to start in the parking lot, where the water is nowhere in view. Panic, feeling like you're losing your balance, feeling stiff, gasping in response to the sight or sound of water, feeling tense and unsure, heart racing, and the water feeling "foreign" are all quite normal starting places for aqua-phobia participants.

A phobia is like an emotional abscess. At the core are buried, subconscious memories of a set of un-processed negative experiences that occurred in the past, and participants may or may not even remember. Next, any phobia also becomes something like an addiction. Countless layers of evasive habits, excuses, and beliefs surround the core like layers of an onion, keeping a rotten memory hidden and walled off in order to shield the brain from further bad experience.

Terry's brain would seem to shut down just as she would touch the water, so she could never be cognizant enough to learn that she was safe. Whether the fear is of getting crowded in the water, getting pushed into the water, being underwater, not touching bottom, snorkels, or sharks!, the treatment is the same.

According to the OSCAR Therapy approach, complete phobia reversal is not only possible but the process is also predictable, and complete recovery is routine. OSCAR Therapy does not use standard "habituation" or any "mind over matter" methods, and it does not use any "body energy" approaches. It's just about micro-steps made easy. Open-ended scheduling also lets students meet goals at their own pace; sessions are all private, not in groups. And yet, progress is exponential; students are always shocked at how fast they are progressing.

OSCAR therapy does not merely teach people to "get used to it"; it teaches people to seek out the once noxious stimulus and see it in a new way, as a plaything. In fact, learners who experience OSCAR are always laughing. The treatment, which is customized to each student, teaches a game that rebuilds your normal control over your body in the fluid realm.

Any size fear of water can be fully reversed. Unlike standard PTSD therapy for returning military personnel, re-experiencing each layer of memory is not necessary in OSCAR Therapy. Also, there is no need for any flotation equipment of any kind. The only tools used are goggles. People learn best when they are lightly challenged to be creative, and creative problem solving is what quickly builds a strong, self-reliant foundation.

After just 4 sessions, Terry was playing games fully submerged, was swimming the side stroke and controlling her buoyancy with her lungs alone, even though on session #1, she says, "I couldn't get past the third step on the stairs." Terry has been able to advance quickly into standard adult swimming lessons at Nutmeg.

2.8 Why Oscar Therapy Works So Well

After they spend some time on the OSCAR side of the tracks, many people understand exactly *how* OSCAR Therapy works. And yet, many of these people still find themselves asking... *"Why? Why does something so simple work so well to completely change Oscar's behavior??"*

If the reasons are not self-evident, then in order to answer this question, I offer these two explanations / perspectives / considerations:

The initial reason why OSCAR Therapy works as well as it does is that it teaches us, the *human* animals, how to finally become aware of the other species' *own, self-directed* options, choices, actions, and challenges. It allows us to discover exactly how to support them the best way possible toward building whatever it is that each individual needs the most.

But more to the point, the main reason OSCAR Therapy works so well is because it opens up the widest avenue for real and true Will and mind recovery. The choice-directed avenue is always the truest avenue, no matter the species. So whenever this question comes up, I soon find myself describing any individual's (including an animal's) own "social imagination."

What I try to describe is that every one of us has a social imagination that surrounds each and every one of us like a bubble; all animals have this. To see what I mean, imagine walking into a party...

The very first thing you'll be aware of is your social surroundings, the potential or likely wanted and unwanted social things you'll have no option but to deal with. You are immediately scanning the room, alert for who might have just noticed your arrival. You'll be calculating what you will say to Person X if they come up to you, because you know they eventually will...

So in OSCAR Therapy, if an individual animal is learning how to safely and happily handle "one certain kind of person or thing" that comes into his/her bubble, *whether invited or not*, then they are also learning how to better handle ANYthing that comes into their bubble. In OSCAR Therapy, animals get to practice interfacing with the part(s) of themselves they've been afraid of using, (even working up to reversal of a phobia trigger). But in so doing, they also get to practice dealing with ANYTHING that might have scared them in a similar way in the future, thereby neutralizing future troubles *now*.

These animals are learning better how to learn. These animals are learning better how to interpret, how to rule things out, and how to rule things in. They are learning about winning, trying, and safely protecting themselves. Simply put, OSCAR animals are learning that they can employ *and benefit from* creative thought the same way their wild counterparts do.

Creative problem solving toward meeting new challenges, creative use of new resources and new environments, these are the building blocks of a successful species. In fact, the species that have shown a tendency toward this kind of cognitive flexibility are the species humans have ended up domesticating as they are the species that have survived in the human world well enough to reproduce there. And all of the creativity and social imagination aside, all of this recovery and trouble reversal is the real thing, all the way down to the cellular level.

When any brain becomes injured during a purely *physical* insult, like in the case of traumatic brain injury, there are physical changes to areas and structures inside the brain. With OSCAR individuals as well, there is trauma to the brain that causes similar changes, but the trauma that is responsible for leaving an imprint is somehow induced by experience. (We have no brain scans of OSCAR cases in which to look for the existence of a physical imprint from a deep OSCAR hole, but one is likely to exist.)

For example, the experience of having no control or influence over either predictable or unpredictable events can be associated with shrinkages in brain volume of the hippocampus, which is associated with memory-based learning. Such cases also see enlargements in the size of the amygdala, the area that produces and manages life-protecting fear.

Being physically abused or experiencing a bad accident are examples of situations where there is no means of escape and no means of being in control over what is happening to the self. These are just two examples of an unacceptable state for any brain. But here are some additional examples: experiencing multiple moves into and out of groups of animals, families, friends, or established social groups, experiencing prolonged hunger or illness, isolation, or life-threatening experiences. All of these leave their *physical* imprints on the brain.

When a brain experiences such impactful events, the brain changes mentally, emotionally, and even physically. The experiences become recorded in deep-seated memory, almost as if they could have happened just yesterday. Over time, affected areas of the brain organ itself have been shown to shrivel from lack of exposure to new, opposing, reparative experience.

We have a name for the acquired effects of all of these changes to the brain: PTSD (Post Traumatic Stress Disorder). But a better term might be "Persisting Trauma." Whether in a soldier returning from war, in an animal surviving a hurricane or other natural disaster, or in a small one being separated from a family (especially at the young ages that require close nurturing for survival), the effects on the brain and body are the same.

Because traumatic memory (the feeling of having no control over what is happening) is so deeply recorded, it involves all of the senses and includes even muscle memory. It even changes an organism's own internal understanding of its own body. Worse still, traumatic memory is immediately embedded in long-term memory, instantly creating a habitual response to a particular set of reminiscent circumstances, sensory experiences or awarenesses.

OSCAR Therapy, unlike other kinds of training or re-training, treats the underlying changes to the sensory system that then generate the anxiety, anger, and deep fear responses, and which are now expressed as distressing/ distressed behaviors. Through goal-oriented homework, Oscar's brain can learn new cause and effect understandings that then "re-wire" these sensory signaling pathways. This results in Oscar's ability to regain control, be able to predict new outcomes, and set aside the now unneeded old patterns of reflex behavior.

OSCAR Therapy recipients *learn their way back from* the brain scarring that was created by trauma. Oscar's brain *grows back* the choices it once had for flexibility within experience and understanding of self at the deepest sensory levels. In this way, Oscar no longer perceives his or her disturbing behaviors as mandatory for survival, and life can then go on in a more normal fashion.

Oscar's *motivation* to change is inherent because a crippling phobia is *always* an involuntary reaction that gets Oscar right in his or her Achilles heel. The Will gets offended by phobia and wants a way to bring any phobic trigger back into the realm of their control. Oscar's "I don't want this belief anymore" motivator is very strong and it works 100 percent in the practitioner's favor. If you give the warrior back his sword, if you show him the way to resolution, Oscar will shed the phobia and soak up the new rational and flexible state just like a dry sponge soaks up the ocean. What Oscar gains is not a passive state; what is gained is a state that is actively sought by Oscar and acquired.

Imagine a professional boxing match in slow motion; one sweaty guy gets off a punch that hits the head. Then the other guy throws a punch to the first guy's gut. Now imagine both of those punches happening at the very same time, in super slow motion, and while the fists are also being attracted to each other like magnets. The arcing trajectory of those punches is now going to make them collide with each other, fist to fist.

Now imagine that same co-colliding action as a softer, slower, improvised, two-person dance. In this dance, neither brain is exactly sure who is contacting whom. Each action is a co-creation. Oscar says, "Did you do that, or did I? Well whoever it was, it's fine with me." By experiencing the OSCAR language, Oscar learns that s/he can experience *and interpret* everything you do, every action, as if it's also been co-created by himself or herself, and rightly so.

The OSCAR Therapy approach is like a single skeleton key. This key creates a localized re-wiring of somewhere in the deep core of the brain. However, OSCAR *also* works like throwing a stone into a pond. OSCAR Therapy creates far-reaching ripples in the pond, and the results reach far into every aspect of Oscar's entire relationship with his or her current world.

Problem with needles? The OSCAR conversation can fix it. Problem with claustrophobia? OSCAR can fix that. Problem with aggression to people? OSCAR will fix that. Problem with spooks? Loud sounds? Medical treatment? Weird phobias? Crazy unpredictability? Aggression on others of the same species? Lack of self-confidence around humans? Lack of self-confidence in social groups? OSCAR will fix all of those too and more.

Even better, OSCAR Therapy creates not temporary change but permanent change as brains learn how to learn. They learn to assess. They learn to actively wait for both the invite and the opportunity. They learn to share solutions. They learn flexibility. They learn emotional stability. They learn to laugh through jointly owned mishaps. They learn to have faith that *things are still ok*, even when they are getting some mixed sensory signals. And when any brain learns high level troubleshooting skills like these, they don't usually get unlearned. And *that* is why OSCAR Therapy works so well.

Once you have the toolset, once you've got the tools down and have a little experience with what to do at the point of any and every eventuality, then every case is just a Peter Pan flight.

CHAPTER 3: THE SHAPE OF O.S.C.A.R. - DATA AND PATTERNS

> *"Our job may be easier than yours, Sidney... at least we [surgeons] can see where the patients are bleeding!"*
>
> - Alan Alda as Hawkeye Pierce, M*A*S*H

Dr. Sidney Freedman, played by Allan Arbus in the television series M*A*S*H, was an ARMY psychiatrist, but these days you'd call his kind of help Psychotherapy. Sidney was called in frequently to tackle the patients that were obviously in deep trouble but whose wounds were of the kind for which the surgeons and medical doctors had no tools. Most of the time, it was the doctors themselves who were getting help from Sidney, help they desperately needed in such a hellish life of endless and senseless destruction at the will of a mere few.

Every solution the fictional Sidney would come up with was actually textbook therapy from the real world, the real, effective, brain science world of the latter half of the twentieth century. Using his psychology-based, mega-balanced, deep-ballast (like a deep ocean tug boat) tools, which Sidney used like fine crotchet needles, his patients, like those of my trauma therapist father, almost always got better. Or at least they got safely out of the deep waters. As my father liked to say: "Crawling around inside someone's history of trauma would be way too depressing work if 99 percent of them didn't get all better." Amen, Dad.

Even while wading in the deepest, darkest muck of someone's worst memories, Sidney might wobble a little, but he would never fall down or even get lost. Because "trauma shrinks" use a general map of mental health to navigate by, we therapists aren't getting lost even when the patient can see no way forward. So just like with any ship in the night that would need to navigate by magnetic compass, therapists navigate by emotion-based compass. And we OSCAR therapists use compasses too, to help us locate a brain's location on the mental health map.

But the compass we use in OSCAR Therapy is more of a throwback to the traditional, physical type compass. It's a flat dial with headings on it. To make things as easy as possible, I decided a long time ago that our OSCAR compass doesn't need to be anymore complicated than the clock on the wall, just because that picture is a "map" that most of us are already very familiar with. (We OSCAR Therapists just lay "Oscar's mental health compass" flat out on the ground most of the time, instead of hanging it vertically.)

This Chapter, Chapter 3, is going to be about what OSCAR Therapy actually looks like and feels like, in real time. Chapter 3 is about what you'll be able to observe and see for yourself when you watch other individuals doing OSCAR Therapy. Whether you are there on site being an in-person witness, or whether you are watching a session on video or on the Internet or on our OSCAR Therapy YouTube Channel from the comfort of your own pajamas, Chapter 3 is about how to interpret what you're seeing in any OSCAR Therapy session and beyond.

3.1 Dog Inconsolable in Car: "The Impossible Case" Fixed in 2 Days

Account of Susan P., Manhattan, NY

Between us, we have 9 Emmy Awards; it just figures the OSCAR we get is the DOG! I'm a New Yorker, in TV. I'm hard to convince. We got our dog Charly at ARF, a canine rescue in New Jersey. She was about a year old, maybe 11 pounds, a Poodle/Terrier/Whatever mix. She was the perfect dog. House trained, she even knew some commands. And she was smart! She "got" our house immediately, but she had one BIG problem. She hated the car! We have an "every weekend" house almost 3 hours outside NYC so we figured we would just have to teach her about the car.

But Charly wasn't just nervous; in any car she'd have all out panic attacks! She was agitated, barking, crying, a mess! So we tried different things. Window open, window closed. Buckled in or let loose in the car. Sitting on my lap, sitting in a doggie car seat, in a pet carrier. Thunder Shirt, soothing music, dog-calming CDs. Pheromones, essential oils, and different diet. Treats. Tasty bones. Get the picture?? Nothing worked! We were finally forced to try the Doggie Downers. I can't even remember how many drugs we tried, but I do remember resorting to Xanax, which had the opposite effect. We finally found a drug that knocked her flat but she became a drugged out mess- it just wasn't fair to this happy, active dog.

We called many trainers. Some said the problem was untreatable. Some never called back. Others came up with great ideas like blindfolding her. One day as I was Googling I came upon another dog who had a fear of cars but was cured by Casey and her OSCAR Therapy. I immediately got in touch. Casey got right back to me. I explained the problem. She said, "Sounds like an OSCAR dog, but the trouble is, we can't do car work in NYC because the streets are too crazy there, too many stoplights!" But the thought of driving THIS dog 3 hours through blizzards with the windows open to get to our other house was not a fun thought so we waited till spring.

Casey arrived at our country house at 9 PM on a Thursday night. She said, "This is the moment of Truth: in the next 10 minutes we'll know if this is a weekend OSCAR job or a months long phobia job." Casey plopped onto the floor with the dog to play a short game and got back up: "Thankfully, this looks like a textbook OSCAR case... After this weekend she'll be a different dog."

I must admit, I wasn't too hopeful when for the whole next Friday morning; Casey sat on the floor with Charly and played more of "the game." But then Casey stopped and said that she had gotten in to the core problem. "Really..." I said, "but you haven't even seen her in the car yet!" Casey drew me a "map" of "Charly's body, according to Charly." But the left side of the drawing was missing. "Exactly," she said. "Charly doesn't know she has a left side, a common problem in rescue dog brains." I started imagining how my wife was going to kill me because I hired some crazy person who says my dog's "left side is missing!!"

But then Casey showed me how Charly will only spin in one direction but not the other, how she will only lay a certain way and had lousy coordination on that side. Casey: "Ever heard of "left side neglect" in stroke patients? Charly has like an emotion-based brain trauma instead of a physical one." Crazy, right? Casey did some exercises with Charly to get her to "discover and try out using different parts of her left side on the floor and then on the slope of our lawn furniture. I was still not convinced, as I had no frame of reference for this storyline.

On Saturday, we all piled into the car for the first time. In the driveway, Casey taught her to use her new pivoting ability on the sloped car seats. We went 5 mph; Charly seemed ok. Then we spent an hour going 15 mph but only doing right hand turns. Then we added in left turns, which were harder, but Charly was learning she could balance herself. Then we drove around town. Charly was still good but I still had my doubts about highways. Still, every evening Charly was sleeping like the dead. Like she had really exercised hard, standing still. Go figure.

Finally, on Sunday morning Casey said, "Time to go for a real ride." So Charly hopped into the car and we took off for the highway. I floored it at the entrance ramp and next to me was Charly (still in her seat belt harness), "surfing" on the console! No barking, no crying, no agitation, just sniffing the ocean air. This dog looked normal. Casey said, "Charly is digging this." And she was!

The 3-hour trip back to the city on Sunday afternoon was a joy for all. And a year and half later, she still loves the car. Not only are WE happy but Charly is a happier dog and is less nervous all around. Casey really rescued us from our rescue dog! And for the entire weekend, Casey charged us LESS than the weekend doggy "farm retreats" our friends send their dogs to, where they come back no different.

Casey's Addendum Two Years Later:

For two years after Charly's OSCAR Therapy weekend, she was good with car trips... always a little keyed up for the first 10 minutes, but then always settled down. But a week ago, something changed in Charly and for 4 consecutive car rides, she was inconsolable. After a 30-minute video chat, and some quick OSCAR tips for the RIGHT side of the dog this time, she went instantly back to normal and the 3-hour trip back to NYC was great !

3.2 Anxiety Permanently Reversed in 4 Sessions

Account of Cindy P., Chester, CT

My lovely 6-year-old Oldenburg mare was incredibly anxious any time she could not see my gelding in the next field. She would run the fence line, in an almost OCD trance, until she was lathered and then, literally frantic. It wasn't uncommon to find her missing a shoe, with lacerations from banging the fence, and in such a state that I was hesitant to have anyone but me bring her in from turnout.

She would panic and become desperate even in the stall if the gelding was out of her line of sight. But then, a day later, like a flipped switch, she would be calm, non-plussed, and happy as a clam. Even under saddle, some moments she would be lovely and other moments unglued. It was a Jeckle and Hyde existence. Three accomplished trainers all had the same experience with her, so the rider was definitely not creating this problem.

I met Casey at an Equine Symposium and immediately appreciated her humor, intellect, and desire to help horses in distress. She was giving demonstrations of her "fish science-inspired" therapy. I'll warn you, what she says may sound a bit quirky, but she is incredibly smart and intuitive and got amazing results from her equine volunteers. It was really a "no-brainer" to ask her to come to my farm to evaluate my mare.

Casey observed the mare and did an assessment in just 5 minutes. She informed me that my mare was probably just using the gelding to ground herself because her thinking brain was blocking out the entire left side of her body. "She had no knowledge of half of her body in space." I had never heard of such a thing.

While skeptical, still, it started to make sense to me, particularly given the dropping of her left shoulder and her rule of thumb to ignore my leg on that side completely. I pictured something akin to the movie sets of old westerns, where there was a town on one side of the street, and then a flat, plywood fake town on the other side. My first thought was, "oh great, a single-sided, 1700 lb., 17 hand, psychological wreck..." Now what?

I honestly don't purport to know what Casey does with her OSCAR method (my husband asked what all the clucking and hand near *but not on* the horse, was all about...) although I can wrap my head around the theory. But as I watched every minute of the therapy, what I do know is that the mare was clearly riveted and enthralled for the entire length of each of her four 90-ish minute "at-liberty-in-stall" sessions.

Casey actively engaged the mare's own willful choice, allowing her to find her own path to the "OSCAR game" solutions. (And to feel so very good about it!) The mare looked obviously lost in space sometimes as she was, herself, trying to rewire or newly wire her own brain to include her entire body, not just the one side. By the end of every session, my very smart mare was visibly mentally tired.

Thanks to Casey's respect, and her brilliant ability to see what others haven't yet seen, I have a happy, content, and eager to please horse, going on eight months now. The transformation was remarkable, immediate, and permanent. It was frankly so inspiring that I plan to have Casey work her magic (she insists it is brain science though) on another horse who has a physical neural issue... Then, if she is still game, she can take a stab at my own brain map as well!

Update two years later: "Mare is still doing awesome with no problems!"

3.3 Dear Oscar, Your "X" O'Clock Is Missing...

Just off the top of my head, in recent memory, I've met a dog with a 12 o'clock missing, a horse with a 1 o'clock missing, a painter with a 2 o'clock missing, a dog with a 3 o'clock missing, a computer programmer with a 4 o'clock missing, a llama with a 5 o'clock missing, a dentist and a CEO with their 6 o'clocks missing, a school teacher with an 8 o'clock missing, a competitive equestrian with a 9 o'clock missing, and a pony with a 10 o'clock missing. I can't think of anyone recently who has had their 7 or 11 o'clock missing. So either my 7 and 11 radars are on the fritz, or I just haven't seen these problems lately, or... the universe is having a bit of fun at my expense.

When I say that someone is "*missing their x o'clock,*" I mean that they have a localized lack of Presence (not just a lack of awareness) at that angle off of their own body. Here's what I mean... If you were to draw a clock circle on the ground around you, and if you stood in the center facing straight ahead, let's say that your chest would be pointing to 12 o'clock, so your butt would be facing 6 o'clock, and so on with the numbers as if they were points on a "*clock-like compass.*" If you are "missing" one of those numbers on your clock, we mean that you react with the world in an abnormal and *unintentional* way when the world (anyone or anything) *interfaces with you* at that specific angle of yours.

I know that will sound implausible, absurd, and absolutely nuts to many people, so I'll use one animal example to describe this phenomenon in generic terms. It's easier to see things objectively when you get away from your own familiar, subjective experiences. That said, observing such a presentation in real time is still astonishing, to say the least, for any and all who are around to witness it.

What's even more astounding is that the actual cause of these problems in any one of us animals is merely a splintering of our *sense-of-willful-control* over certain parts of our own bodies in three-dimensional *social* space. *It's the social interface parts of the space we inhabit that seems to be the smoking gun.* Animals can usually still use the body parts that are on stage in a social scene; they just can't *think* about them at all. Roboticism has taken over.

So a super smart, professional and competitive, 3-day eventing, cross country jumping horse had a brain and a face that worked quite well when he was at work, jumping over hill and dale on the course that cut through the woods. And yet back in the barn, when his face was around people putting his bridle on and taking care of him, he seemed odd. It would take 30 minutes to put his bridle on, which is usually a 30-second job. And when I assessed him, he was indeed odd, but only about the right side front half of his body in general, and his right cheekbone seemed to be the weirdest part of all.

For example, this horse was normal in how he related to me if I stood anywhere on his left, whether behind him or in front of him on his left. But if I stood on his right, and specifically at this 1:30 angle, *offering a handful of grain*, not only would he not take the grain coming in at 1:30, but he also couldn't touch me at all if I was there.

If I stood at his 1:30 on his clock, his brain, including his eyes and sense of smell *and touch* seemed to just blink off line, like when your electricity flickers off during a storm. Sensory input received by that zone of his body seemed unable to get to the "conscious" main frame of the brain's computer, like there was a short circuit in the wiring to that part of his brain. And his weird "hole" was not happening just in my eyes. The hole *of missing normalcy* was plainly visible to his owner and the other people who were standing a few feet away during my assessment.

And yet, the astute owner would have never noticed this anomaly over the whole five years that she owned this horse because the horse always did what anyone with a "blind spot" would do... He would pre-emptively rotate his feet in relation to you so as to "move you over" ever so slightly, either to his 1 o'clock or his 2'o'clock, and that quick adjustment on his part would quietly and immediately resolve his trouble. But since I was moving my feet right along with him, keeping myself right there in the 1:30 slice of his pie, he would just shut off like a light bulb... eyes, ears, nose, whiskers, they all went offline and stayed gone.

Now, what to do about the missing 1:30? Well, the answer is to just fix it. Repair the hole. That's what you do in OSCAR Therapy. You use all of the teaching tools described later in Chapters 4, 5, and 6 to encourage and reward Oscar for exploring, imagining, building, and using that missing slice of his or her pie of "spatial will." How? By playing a simple fist-bump game.

You just hold up your hand or a safer target of some kind (if danger is a factor), and you start rewarding the brain's approximating efforts. When they can reach into said angle of social space, *with said body part coming through said angle*, to bop your hand (like a gentle high five) with that body part, on purpose, rationally and slowly, while still breathing normally, then that's when Oscar's "pie slice rebuilding work" is done. Once s/he has a newly re-wired brain-body map that can now learn about his or her work-a-day world in normal fashion, s/he's good to go.

Any brain (of any species) that has unfortunately had to learn at some point that reaching out to touch another living being (or object) is likely to cause their own distress, demise, or something akin to demise, is at a stark disadvantage. But unlearning this hard-won knowledge will not be the first choice any brain will make. For instance, it would take a lot to convince you that fire doesn't burn.

And for this reason, I'd like to clearly state my official opinion thusly: the very real fear of reaching into social (or active mechanical) contact space *should be classified* as a sub-category of posttraumatic stress disorder, or PTSD. It is presumed that social-spatially affected brains have acquired their problem due to either starkly under developed (via lack of exposure) or traumatized (over-developed via over exposure) brain-to-body mapping knowledge. And just like PTSD is, generally, these socio-spatial phobia problems are fully reversible.

Of course, the horse above was later checked for a right eye vision abnormality by Boston's equine ocular specialty veterinarians. He had a full equine eye exam that showed nothing wrong. But I didn't need to hear that result because it only took about two hours to "rewire" him to bring his 1:30 o'clock back on line. Once I taught him (or reminded him) that he could safely "exist" there at 1:30 o'clock with me, he came around to using that space normally again, but not without a noticeable re-calibration adjustment period.

The horse's owner, a very smart and observant professional horsewoman, asked me, "Should I do anything special to help whatever the hell you did to him stick?" I told her that the best thing she could do was to leave him be for about a week or so and just watch him. The next week, when I showed up, she gave me an update on her big adult horse:

"For a few days, he was spooking at things that he's walked by every day for years. Like the white fence. Honestly, I tell you it was like he had never thought about it being there before. When things were on his right side, the fence, his blanket, his buckets, the same furniture his eyes had "seen" every day for years were suddenly being experienced as new, like he had not actually consciously registered them being there before. And of course, his bridle problem is now entirely gone."

Many of the cases I see, across species, have "shut down" the conscious wiring to parts of their bodies, which makes the other parts of the body have to work that much harder to compensate. When a body part shuts down, the result is usually that said body part is under-expressive like in the horse above. But an OSCAR-positive body part can also be over-expressive, like a flag that's flapping haphazardly in a chaotic wind. But whether too quiet or too loud, these OSCAR affected parts are always acting irrationally. A horse ignoring oats on the right side of his face is seriously irrational. (More on the over-expressives later.)

Now, the 360-degree, spatially aware readers, like the athletes or the airplane pilots, might be wondering about this clock face around a body and wondering about how elevation fits into it. They might be asking, "If an individual can regain his awareness about whatever is at 1 o'clock on the horizontal plane, what about the space that is high up over 1'clock, like Oscar's reactions to the things coming in at them from the sky, or things coming up from below?

Indeed, *what about* all of that other possible interaction space? Can a brain be missing those pie slice areas too?" As a SCUBA diver myself, I immediately asked the same question. (Divers have to try hard to be aware of things like sharks or boats coming in from way above and behind their heads.) I fully expected to find individuals with elevation issues, but what I had found instead is that the answer is "mostly no," in the cases I have seen to date, with the exception of very small animals.

The lateral (side-to-side/flat) interface clock is the dominant OSCAR clock for us gravity-bound land dwellers. The vertical clock gets affected for sure, but it is usually secondary. It might be quite different for birds with PTSD or fish with PTSD. Way back when I was dealing with over-handled, gun-shy fish, I didn't know enough to notice. But here's a horsey answer to this question.

The very tall horse above, the one with the 1:30 o'clock missing, had a tall tree in his paddock; it had leaves he liked to nibble on. One day, during his week off after OSCAR treatment, his owner was convinced that some other horse had been mistakenly placed in his paddock, because the horse inside the fence looked foreign to her. His craning of his neck around to the right (instead of his typical left approach of the last five years) to reach up to munch on the high tree leaves is what made the horse look, newly, like a mirror image of his usual self. It took the owner by surprise because her eyes had never once seen that image/shape of her very own horse before.

This horse's spatial awareness at an elevation high overtop of 1:30 had been fixed. And yet, I would have had to be 9 feet tall to teach this guy how to do this leaf-eating trick in this new way. So I presume that giving him back his 1:30 o'clock interaction angle just a few inches from his face is what allowed him to experiment with the same idea at any skyward angle of elevation.

I have seen this phenomenon happen time and again with many cases, many owners, and with my own eyes in my own animals. A body interacts with the outside world from its core. What it cannot do at its core, it seems to not be able to do at *any* elevation or extrapolation of itself. But when it gets fixed at the core, the fix radiates out to all levels.

3.4 OSCAR Maps, Shapes, and Trends

Phobia, anxiety, chaotic unpredictability, inability to calm, and misplaced aggression, all of these "symptoms" can be merely different expressions of the very same root cause, even if it's a cause we can't see in a microscope or a body tissue. Maybe we can only see the shape of this cause as it manifests itself during willful avoidances, choices, and actions. When physical problems have been ruled out as causative, as frequently happens, we must look to the *brain* as the originating driver, and/or the purposeful non-driver. A body cannot do what it can't, *but it is the brain who will not do... what it won't.*

When certain parts of a body simply will not show up to a simple color-by-numbers game, (even though the body's other side may show up just fine) this indicates that there is either a major disconnect (or cut off connection) in the brain-to-body correlation. Some of these disconnects are congenital (since birthing or in utero), and some are caused early on from imbalances in the adult. For example, if a mother only allows nursing on one side, a baby may develop right or left-handedness in a front quadrant.

Some disconnects are learned later in life from relationships with and/or exposure to other very "sided" conspecifics (members of the same species), or relationships with OSCAR-"sided" humans. Many seem to be correlated with abuse, but I doubt that abuse is the original cause behind much of the OSCAR-positive animals. On the contrary, I believe that OSCAR-positive animals are the animals who often *become* abused, as their inherent imbalance gets passed along to more and more dire living situations.

Chronologically, it would make the most sense to say that the animals who are born into imbalance show "abnormal" presentations for good reason, then their "irrational" presentations scare people, and then those scared people proceed to employ increasingly drastic "expert measures" to force a square peg into a round hole. Many if not most expert training methods are well known to attempt to *over-power* both animal and human brains, especially the brains they do not understand.

For all we know, being born with a positive OSCAR map, that is, being born missing a slice or two or even a whole side, might actually yield an evolutionary advantage to the wild species. When large swaths of an animal's spatial map are missing, that animal tends to relate to a neighboring animal through only the side they DO have. If I am a dog missing part of my left side, I will want other dogs to be on my right side, where I can understand what we do to each other.

Teams of driving horses, teams of sled dogs, and even teams of human rowers in a team boat are well know to be organized by the rule that the individual team member makes their own choice about the side they like best. If you swap someone to the side they don't feel comfortable on, all hell brakes loose.

So I can also imagine that if your herd feels "Velcro'ed together," that herd as a whole might escape predators more often. I can further imagine that maybe these missing and sticky "Lego-like" holes in the sides of a pack of wolves might make them better at working as a team. "Surrounding" a loan stray prey animal inside an ever tightening, collectively derived noose of neurally-enhanced pack adhesion.

But back in our world, at the end of the day, the *fault* behind anyone's current predicament with a dangerous or irrational *domesticated* animal brain either lies with the humans or it lies with no one. Trainers don't know about what they don't know about. If they'd rather not learn about how to reverse and fix the diagnosis that we call "Cognitive Spatial Pathology," then the best thing a flummoxed and frustrated trainer can do is to leave any perplexing animal's brain alone. Don't euthanize. They should just assign someone else to read this book and solve the puzzle. Once you know the game, any brain is incredibly easy to solve.

3.4.a Normal OSCAR Maps

Plenty of our domesticated, captive, companion, working, or otherwise partnered-with-us animals are perfectly normal in how they relate to their own bodies, how they solve problems, how they relate to other animals, and how they relate to the humans in their midst. These animals are largely just fine as they are.

And yet, just as this statement is true: "not every animal is nutritionally deficient, but every animal can benefit from good nutrition," the same logic applies to the following statements:

> *Not every animal is an OSCAR case (having OSCAR pathology), but most animals would benefit from Oscar Therapy. And certainly every animal can benefit from the OSCAR <u>language</u> and the topics we discuss with it.*

What OSCAR Therapy is most interested in is the animal's use of the full three-dimensional space immediately around its body, with special attention to the spaces that both initiate *and react to* direct social contact. And it just so happens that we humans imagine and diagram any three-dimensional space along the idea of the coordinate axes that many of us learned about, or attempted to learn about, in algebra class.

In 3-D space, we measure the *horizontal dimension*, which is the right or left span of something along an imaginary, flat, "horizon" line that we call the x-axis. In that same 3-D space, we measure the vertical *height* of something along the imaginary up and down (gravity) line that we call the y-axis. And some of us may not remember that in the same way again, we measure the *depth* of something along an imaginary "skewering" line that we call the z-axis, which tracks how far away from the x,y plane something is.

All three of these imaginary dimensions are important and of use to us when we are describing the three dimensional shape of how the brain uses its own body as it relates to and bounces off of other bodies. However, in OSCAR Therapy we use even more familiar everyday compass points, ones that can very roughly describe these same x,y,z locations, so that we can leave the academic, mathematical references back on the schoolroom shelf. At least for the children of the analog generations, the people who know how to read a clock on the wall, our very simple mapping system is a little easier to imagine on the fly than any of the East – West – North – South directions or any of the x,y,z coordinates stuff.

3.4.b Images of Empty OSCAR Clocks: Two Orientations

Because humans don't have a shared, common understanding of how to map all points of the irregular, lumpy "sphere," that is an "animal body," and especially since we are without 3-D holographic modeling equipment on everyone's desks, we have to all make do with flat, paper approximation maps. Our maps also have to be easy to jot down notes on, quickly, outside, and in the rain and snow and mud puddles where the animals live.

The first part of getting ourselves oriented is about deciding what we mean by right and left. Just like when you synchronize your watches to get ready for a bank caper, all of us humans must synchronize what the heck we are referring to when we use the words right and left. So for this entire book, when we say right and left, what we mean is *the animal subject's* right side or left side, AS IF YOU WERE THE ANIMAL.

If an Oscar is facing you head-on, and you start talking about what's on your *right hand*, this is the part of the picture that's closest to the animal's *left* side. Do not get confused this way. Your own right and left eyeballs don't mean a lot when we talk about OSCAR maps (unless you yourself are the brain we are attempting to map.) Oscar is the main topic here, so we collectively decide that Oscar's own body orientation, the one we are going to be talking about in detail, takes precedence over yours.

On our OSCAR Therapy maps, the numbers act like very familiar compass points, the green lines block out body quadrants, and the red arrows represent the normal reach and/or recoil ability we want Oscar to have. Here are OSCAR Therapy's empty / blank maps:

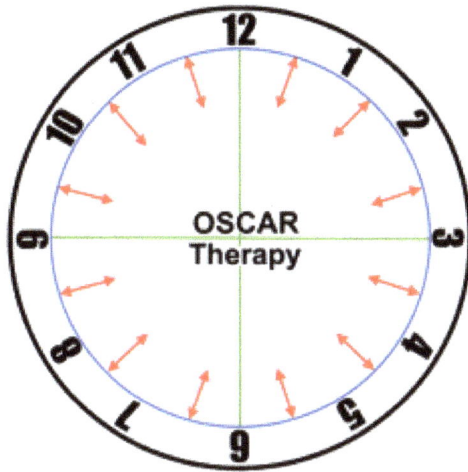

Figure 1. The "OSCAR CLOCK" is the map we use

The map/clock we use most is the bird's eye view "compass" of a clockface, where you could imagine this clock laid out on the ground around where you stand.

When Oscar is straight and not bent, the chest always point to 12, and the tail base is always 6.

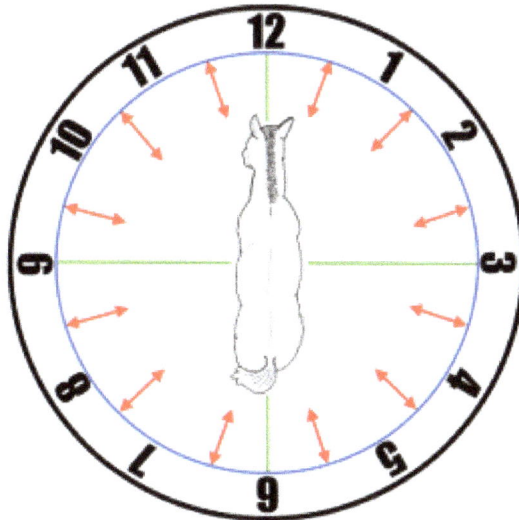

Figure 2. OSCAR's Horizontal Clock Face

Sometimes helpful is the vertical map/clock, where the location of 6 would be underground, and 12 would be the dorsal, topline parts, basically whatever faces the ceiling.

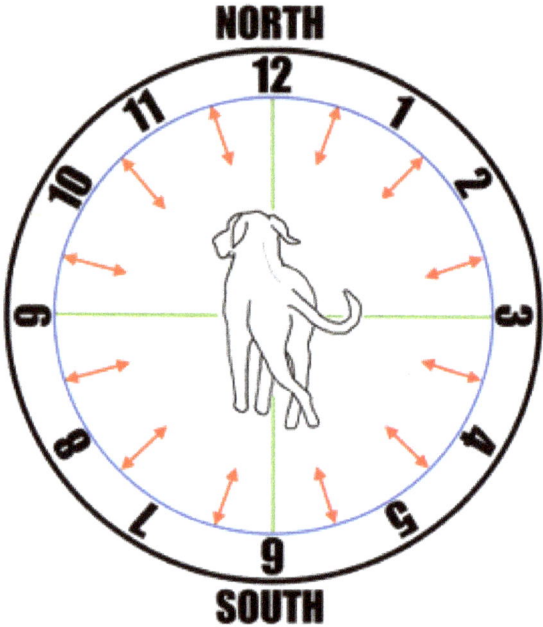

Figure 3. OSCAR's Vertical Clock Face

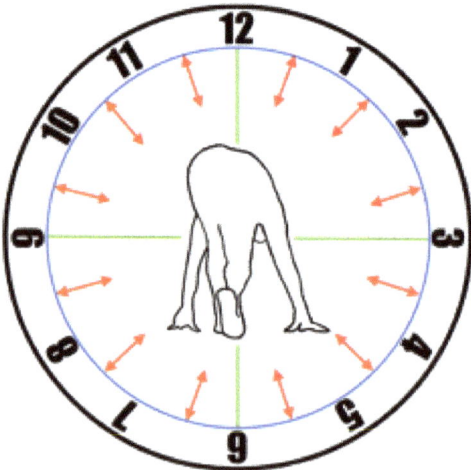

Figure 4. The Human Animal's "OSCAR CLOCK": Part Vertical, Part Horizontal

The two maps with animals in them above take care of the x and y-axes. The last axis, the z-axis (depth of field axis) is where we OSCAR Therapists just start referring to body parts, like hip or shoulder, eye or last rib. And regarding that depth of field dimension, we just have to remember that we humans are an atypical species. Use the diagram above, the outline of a track runner at the starting block, to see how we are both 2-legged and 4-legged creatures at the very same time.

We humans are four-legged animals that just so happen to walk on our hind legs most of the time, just like prairie dogs or kangaroos. We have the same neural wiring as all four-legged animals, but sometimes we have to bend over at the waist a little bit in order to remember that the OSCAR shape of us is just like the shape of our animal partners.

So even when we're standing up straight, the compass points on this clock still apply to us. If we are lying flat on our stomachs, the compass points still apply to us. If we are laying flat on our backs, the compass points still apply to us, but those clock numbers would be upside down. The point here is to understand that you can instinctively empathize with what Oscar is trying to learn because you can demonstrate it all in your very own body using the very same map.

Note also that animal bodies have parts that stick out and joints that allow those sticking out parts to rotate back and forth somewhat, swivel somewhat, and work in tandem to boot. This way, animals are designed to be able to reach into almost any kinds of spaces. Heads can go in almost any direction; so can legs, and so can tails.

Just as a chiropractor looks for freedom in a body part's *passive* range of motion, we OSCAR Therapists look for the freedom of an *active,* willful range of motion. For example, where the foot will place itself and then re-place itself on the ground is pretty good evidence of the angles a leg and body frame "think" they can move toward and balance on. So we map all of those appendage body parts too. Yes, even the tails tell much about what a brain *thinks* a spine can and cannot do. They are tell-tails.

OSCAR Therapy's Maps of Each Leg:

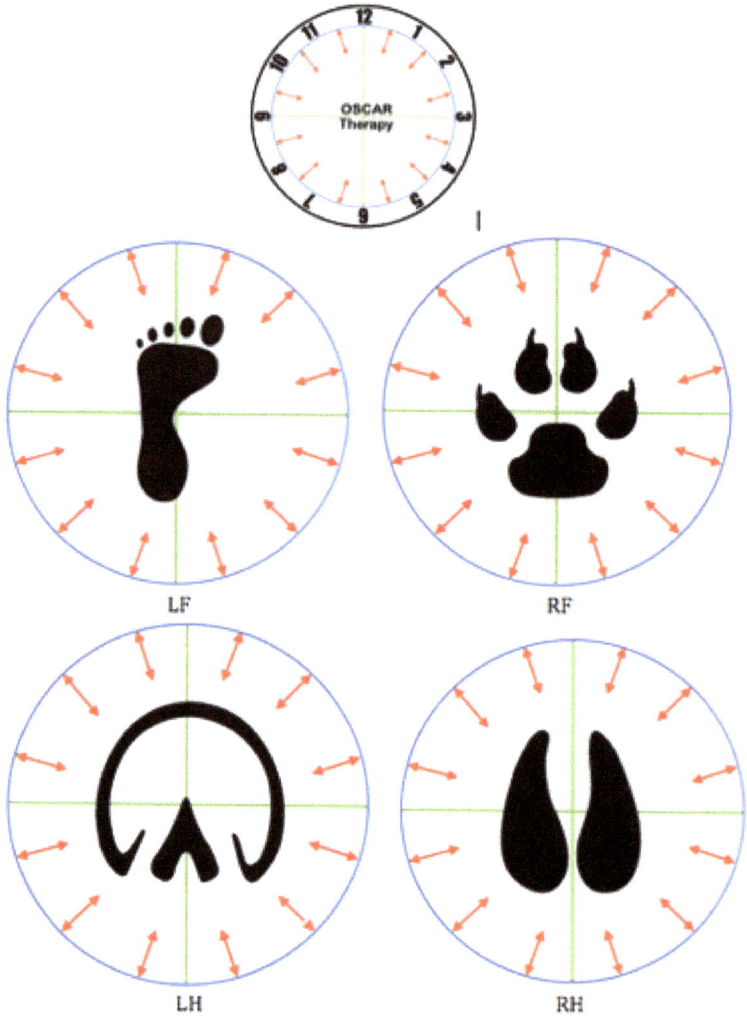

Figure 5: Think of each leg as having its own OSCAR clock.

3.4.c Abnormal OSCAR Maps

Somewhere in the first emails from new clients, the vast majority of animal owners make the same mention: "I've had animals all my life, but I've never come across an animal like this one before, not in any species." They've already tried everything and nothing is working, so they finally have no choice other than to start looking outside the box of familiarity. And as soon as I start communicating with them on the phone, they know they've landed on a shore that is well beyond their known horizon.

From the get go, I explain that we humans may have preferences or abhorrences about our own rights and lefts that we can talk about rationally (like our preferences in holding a pencil in one hand or the other). Then I explain that OSCAR issues go far deeper than preference. In an OSCAR problem, the brain has a clear fear, and often a full-blown phobia of even *attempting* to use certain zones of its own body, especially in "social interface." I explain that a positive OSCAR finding should be classified as a true pathology and not Oscar's fault.

But since first time callers have never heard someone talk about such things before, let alone have they seen anything like it in real time before, even the most savvy and experienced animal owners have no clue what the hell I'm talking about. If it were not for the detailed and lengthy testimonials on the Willing Results website, and the fact that I sound largely coherent and even funny on the phone, new clients would never actually invite me to their homes, farms, and estates.

Oscars can be very afraid of social "body part use" at a *visceral* level, so much so that whenever they are required to try to *actually use* that part in daily social life, (even before they've ever met an OSCAR practitioner). These animals typically look like an explosive "automatic reflex" is hitting them like an electric shock, almost coming from the "insides of the outer body," as if their distal lymph nodes or lower spinal vertebrae were directing the peripheral nerves to jump, without consulting the thinking brain at all. (This is not nerve damage; this is visceral phobia.)

What the owner sees, and is at the mercy of, is only the strange, unpredictable, and dangerous outbursts, often strung together in a series, as the animal attempts to grasp at straws, trying to manage an unmanageable situation coming from no identifiable source. Owners are the unwitting recipients, but the animals themselves are often just as surprised as their owners, if not more so.

Odder still, gaps in "social space" interface bubbles may even look to be normal when the animal is alone. For instance, an animal can be comfortable using a body part to touch *itself* as in self-scratching behavior, scratching on furniture, or interacting with inanimate objects. And yet that same body part can be quite incapable of purposefully touching a living and breathing *individual*, no matter its species, because *living things* sometimes make unexpected moves that an Oscar won't be able to then react to.

The worst and strangest part of the OSCAR brain is that in many, many cases, humans can reach out and touch the animal on all of his or her parts all day long, with not so much as a peep, a hair out of place, or a step out of line from the animal. Many Oscars appear normal *when they are being touched* or groomed/ tacked/handled by others. So when a veterinarian starts digging for physical cause to aberrant behaviors in cases like this, the sincere vet will tell you that they find nothing physically wrong in the bones, in the muscles, *in the nerves*, or even in the behavior.

But the keen behavioral observer will often see that these same animals display odd choices even when they are away from all social interaction. For instance, OSCAR issues are often at the root of "interactive anomalies with the normal environment" like around water puddles, clothing, furniture, or even around lines drawn in the sand! Some brains even cannot initiate interaction, play, or creative use of certain parts of their own bodies in space, until OSCAR Therapy teaches them that it is safe to initiate.

Any animal can learn to build herself or himself a better brain-to-body map, but at any given time, their map is their map. A brain's OSCAR map is like their personal fingerprint of their identity in social space, no matter whom they are near. Only with the focused attention that OSCAR treatment brings (or after years of risky over-exposure) do those fingerprints change.

When a brain shuts down its sensory-cognitive pathways, the result is usually that the body part is "under-expressive," as in the 1:30 horse discussed in the first section of this chapter. But the body part can also be over-expressive, or not able to be "in quiet contact" with another body. Whether these "abnormally wired" body parts over-react or under-react, these portions of the animal are always behaving irrationally in contact-based interactions.

Conveniently, (otherwise all of us OSCAR Therapists would surely and appropriately labeled as nutjobs) any map abnormality that is diagnosable will always be a finding that is independent of the individual who is assessing or interacting with Oscar. OSCAR maps are not influenced by the identity or the belief of the assessor. You can swap out the people doing the testing, and the abnormality in the animal will always present the same way. The abnormality is in the animal itself, not in the evaluator, and not in the airspace of the interface zone. This is the main reason that we can solve and repair cases via live-streaming video, in any location around the globe.

3.4.c.i Positive OSCAR Findings: Predicting Specific Troubles

Facing Fear is a technique that many in the cowboy culture use to teach a horse to engage a scary thing in order to make that thing stop offending. For instance, a running chainsaw stalks the runaway horse. As soon as the horse stops, turns and looks at the chainsaw, the human switches off the machine, and it goes quiet. That teaches the animal to investigate the trouble (the mental stress) in order to get control over it and "shut it down." OSCAR Therapy is the opposite.

Quite opposite of that, the diagnostic process and the "stress/heat absorbance" capacity that OSCAR Therapy teaches goes much deeper, and it goes much further. We teach Oscar not to shut down something outside of them but to *turn on* something *inside* of them.

When OSCAR diagnostic testing discovers, unearths, or comes across an abnormal finding, we call that an "OSCAR Hole," a part where Oscar is missing a "number on her clock" or a "slice of his pie." OSCAR holes are like scarred-over but still frightened localities of the brain's "wiring" that become dysfunctional in certain scenarios (often many scenarios) because those parts of the body are anxiously interpreting all interaction as a "likely to be toxic" experience.

The difference between a normal animal's "I don't know why I should touch that" and an Oscar's "I can't touch that" is readily obvious to anyone who has watched animals before. On their socially normal body parts, every animal will engage us within just a few minutes and after just a few asks. They both investigate and inquire to suss out why we are approaching or mildly encroaching on them in a strange manner and from strange angles. But when we come to an abnormal body part, there is no investigation at all. It's as if Oscar's previous inquiries, hesitations, and educated guesses about that zone have gotten them in trouble in the past.

What we usually see is a learned, under-reactive "stone statue" response. These body parts have learned to shut down like the iconic three wise monkeys: see no evil, hear no evil, speak no evil. If they can perceive nothing, then they can have nothing to say about it. The brain has learned that if it has *no reaction*, then it can never be punished for being having a "wrong" reaction. If someone then tries to pile on any layers of "learned skill" on top of such an "off-line" zone is a fool's errand; there's nothing at all there to add on to!

An equally common initial finding is a body part doing one of these two things:

a) The South Pole Magnet: It treats your hand as if it's a repellent magnet. Imagine two refrigerator magnets that a kid is trying to stick together, but instead, the same-poled magnets forever push each other away. (A south pole will stick to a north pole, but it will NEVER stick to another south pole.) An OSCAR hole will often treat your button hand just like that repelled south pole magnet. The body part (that your hand goes near) leaves... at the same rate of speed.

b) The Smear: The body will not only crash into you, but it smears itself all over you as if you are a non-scratchy scratching post. This body part is craving rational cause-effect contact, but it has not a clue about how to proceed.

But if the degree of "confusion stress" coupled with physical stress (we call this combined stress "heat") that is experienced escalates further, these same under-reactive and unaware animals can reflexively lash out, explode, and become extremely dangerous immediately, even while they are *still unaware*. In fact there is always a marked absence of inquisitiveness both immediately preceding and immediately *following* every flight or fight response from an Oscar's brain.

I have met individuals with OSCAR holes in ribs, eyes, ankles, shoulders, hips, noses, throats, hands; you name it. And the holes are almost never bilaterally symmetrical. The normal side usually presents as very courageous and able to tolerate almost anything while the abnormal side is largely willfully useless to the animal. Such a brain experiences its social life as would a plate glass window incarnate. It's a very one-sided, two-dimensional existence, even though the machine of any body was built to be used in three dimensions.

For example, if a brain's body map is abnormal on the left side ribcage, they are usually hyper flexible both mentally and physically on their right side ribcage, because while half of them is "off line," the other similar body parts must compensate for it. Like if you are deaf in one ear, your other ear and swiveling neck are going to be doing double duty as much as they can.

The animal that has OSCAR holes on both sides of the body has even bigger problems. The individuals with the highest numbers of OSCAR holes are the animals that come across to humans as the headstrong, offensive, or aggressive individuals. Because they can't absorb social "heat" very well at all, they have had to create a large, far-reaching, "stand-off" bubble of rude and offensive "bully" displays. These are designed to stop you in your tracks well before you get close enough to them to find out about their internal body-to-brain shortcomings and "Achilles heel" liabilities.

Almost immediately, OSCAR Therapy will make it obvious to you that these individuals have almost no faith that they can survive any of the world's insults/attacks/onslaughts, a mildly pointing finger, or even someone's mere gaze or existence in close proximity. Brains with a high percentage of OSCAR holes often put up a big front, but it's just so that no one will challenge them on these terms. And that's where we come in.

OSCAR Therapy provides predictive, behavioral diagnostics that are second to none. The individual shows us the tell tale signs that point to the root cause of a myriad of "unpredictable" reactions and intention-based behaviors. It's all so predictable that we can even map out common findings on a generic Oscar's body map...

But before we do so, in order to all be on the same page about OSCAR maps, we have to all be on the same page about generic anatomical body parts. So... whose body shall we think about? Readers of this book will likely be coming from all walks of "animal life," in their main interests anyhow, so we need to be talking about a "generic body" that can stand in for the specific bodies we all work with in our daily lives. Now, just where could we find such a generic body map...?

At the butcher shop, of course! In the absence of other familiar images that are fit to meet our needs, let's go with "Mr. Bully." The following drawing is a perfectly good generic animal body.

Figures 6 and 7. The outline of a generic mammalian animal

3.4.c.ii Table of OSCAR Holes and Corresponding Trouble

Have you noticed a trend in any of your personal animal's Oscar-related "unfortunate accidents"? Do they have the same shape to them? Do you have injuries from situations that oddly ended up being all on the same side of your body? Does the animal always bolt away in or attack from one certain direction?

A social interaction hole (an OSCAR hole) is something that can't be observed very well on a still photograph. [Although I challenge myself this way all the time; I'm dying to know whether I can observe OSCAR holes in photographs. So I make educated guesses from initial photos to compare to later findings, and I'm getting better at making accurate predictions.]

Usually, eyewitness accounts or video recordings are what are required to document the existence of social interface avoidance at all, let alone its particular abnormalities. But after having seen a slew of these holes over decades, patterns begin to emerge.

What follows here is a list of our own personal experiences with problem cases we've treated, and the corresponding OSCAR hole(s) that seemed to be at the root of them. And since we are just talking about a rough sketch of a generic animal, these spots are rough estimates of the anatomic locations on any particular vertebrate animal, meaning any animal with a backbone, a right side, and a left side. But since we don't need to duplicate this long list, we will only delve into the right side of the body below.

Roughly, when there is an OSCAR hole at numbered location "x", that's when you are likely to come up against the corresponding (and common) display(s) in behavior. This is not an exhaustive or definitive list; these are merely the trends we have seen from years of OSCAR casework. Brains are extremely complex organs and learning pathways can be generated for many atypical reasons so take the following list as a guide, not a rule.

OSCAR holes DO NOT typically originate from incidences of normal life wear and tear, like from an accident or acute injury. An OSCAR hole seems to be only generated after an animal's brain tries and fails to resolve a scary situation, *thus learning* that it has no easy way to remove itself from a trauma-inducing experience.

If a brain tries to free its body from harm and *learns* (even over just a few seconds) that it cannot free itself, the brain can and will shut down/sacrifice the information it receives from that particular zone or part of the body. In order to maintain focus on protecting the remainder of the body that is still functioning with control, the unfortunate sacrifice is made. (This is similar to a wolf chewing off its own foot to get out of a trap.) But remember, not all OSCAR holes stem from obvious trauma.

The originating etiology for each OSCAR hole, how it came to be there in the first place, is information that is of note, especially in prevention planning. [Please always remove animals from all abusive influences. But more importantly, remove ALL abusive influences from having access to animals!] Yet, knowing the originating cause is NOT at all necessary to the recovery of the case. It doesn't matter how or when they got this way; since we can fix it, let's just fix it.

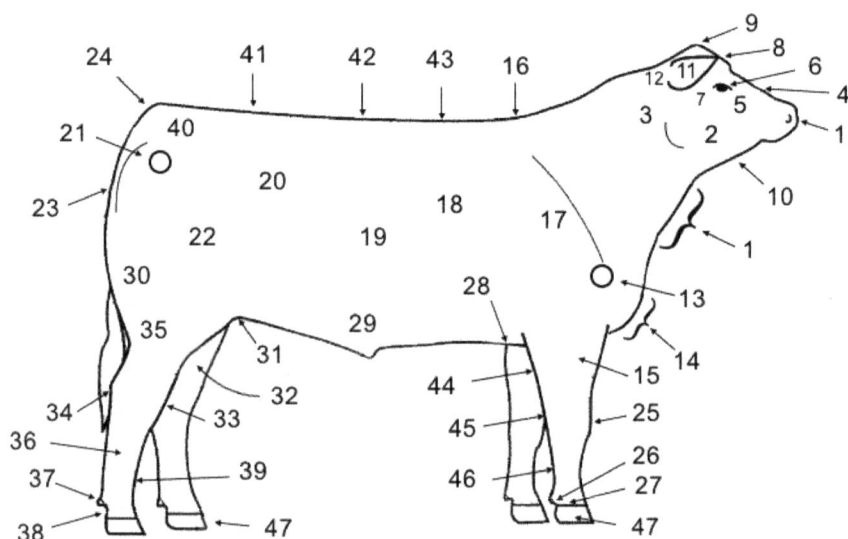

Chief Complaint About Animal in Italics (Unearthed Issues are in **Bold**)	Deep OSCAR Hole Found at Location #...
Biting everyone, Separation anxiety, refuse toys	1
"Wrecking ball" head, common in large animals	2
Fear of needles, clippers, head equipment	3
Human abuse by striking implement	4
Can't bridle or halter	5
Right shoulder and right eye are linked	6
Fear of humans, **Afraid of hind field of view**	7
Suckling accident/injury	8
Rearing, **Ceiling or suckling accident/injury**	9
Pain at 12	10
Ear phobia, Ear twitch device is abuse	11
Fear of head leverage equipment	12
Fear of ALL front ground objects, puddles	13
Fear animals/people, **Runt's fear of littermates**	14
Rears up, **Fear of hobbles and tie downs**	15
Fear of saddle, barrel or shoulder impingement	16
Fear of tripping on ground hazards	17
Fear of humans, Fear of all handheld tools	18
Separation anxiety, **entire Right body**	19
Separation anxiety, sound phobias, **entire Right**	20

Table 1a. Generic OSCAR Hole Locations

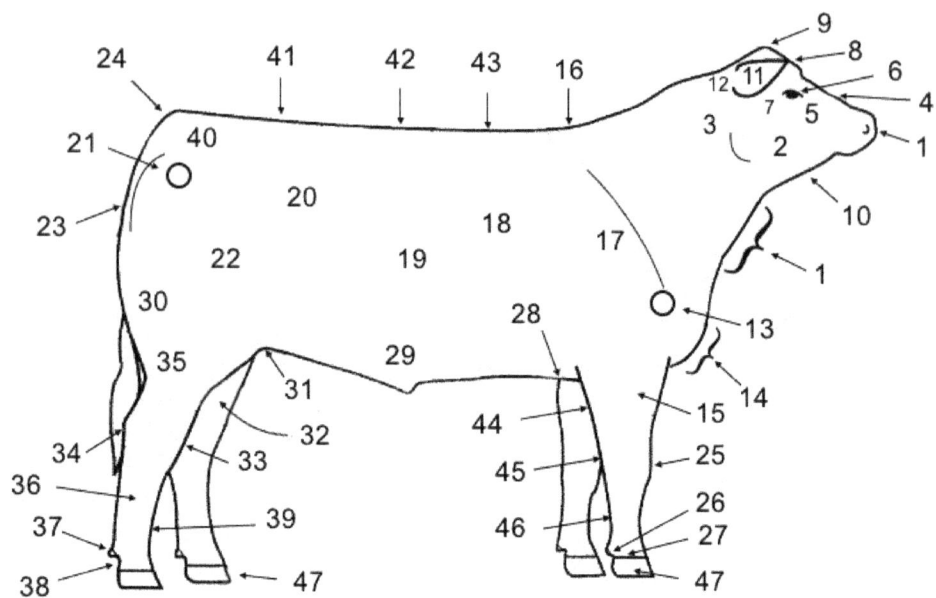

Chief Complaint About Animal in Italics (Unearthed Issues are in **Bold**)	Deep OSCAR Hole Found at Location #...
Separation anxiety, Bite strangers, Sound phobia	21
Predator attack, Impaling accident	22
Fearful tail removal, bone break, entanglement	23
Leg entangled in large equipment, predator	24
Knee pathology	25
Bad for foot or nail care, Fear entanglement	26
Bad for foot or nail care, Fear entanglement	27
Fear of girth strap, pressure	28
Fear of human abuse by kicks to the gut	29
Claustrophobia in small spaces, attacking	30
Claustrophobia in small spaces, attacking	31
Claustrophobia in small spaces, attacking	32
Visual phobias, **Leg entanglement**	33
Fear of tight confinement walls	34
Fear of butt bar restraints	35
Leg entanglement in wire	36
Bad for foot care, **Fear of entanglement**	37
Bad for foot care, **Fear of entanglement**	38
Entanglement in Wire	39
Separation anxiety, **entire Right body**	40
Fear of dominant animals	41
Fear of blanket, clothing	42
Fear of humans in general	43
Club foot issues, whole-quarter, tight arcs	44
Fear of sprayed liquids	45
Jellyfish tentacles, needles	46
Hoof knife or hammer phobia	47

Table 1b. *Continued.* Generic OSCAR Hole Locations

3.5 Oscar's Presentation: The "Abnormal Response" Will *Escalate* Over Time

The humans that walk into any psychotherapist's office come from all walks of life and every stage of mental and emotional collapse. And animals at any and every stage of those same kinds of trouble show up on my virtual doorstep. As Forrest Gump might say, "A brain is like a box o chocolates; you never know what you're gonna get" walkin' through your office door.

The way I explain this to my understandably skeptical (and yet still desperate) clients is this: If it were possible to give your animal a pencil and a blank sheet of paper, and if we could say, "hey Buster, take this pencil and draw something like a chalk outline of your standing-up self on the paper," they might draw something akin to this peculiar but true and very common self-portrait:

Figure 8: Example of an OSCAR dog's "self-portrait"

And yet, after enough brains and their (witnessed) back-stories have come through the door, patterns begin to emerge and the back-stories that led here begin to become predictable. Reconstructed histories and their timelines prove that *the longer* an OSCAR problem is ignored, and/or the more Oscar is punished for his/her "choices," the worse the story will be in the current day.

Issues that stem from an originating OSCAR problem(s) mean that Oscar's responses to every day scenarios *will predictably* ESCALATE over time toward the following progression pathways, roughly. Just like an unaddressed disease shows you early issues, then advanced issues, and then late-stage issues, this is the general progression that Oscar will be pushed toward, until they reach the very bottom of each of the symptoms/behaviors lists below:

3.5.a Front End OSCAR Holes Cause These Issues
Front end OSCAR holes tend to generate the more dangerous responses. The more angles that are missing in front, the more dangerous Oscar is.

- Won't walk into, through, or over things? Objects? Water?

- Which leg goes first? One leg "tries" first and one leg NEVER tries first?
- Claustrophobia of being inside four walls or even just three walls
- Rearing
- "Wrecking ball" head actions
- Striking
- Biting
- Stomping
- Attacking other members of their same species
- Hunting/stalking attack
- Vision "abnormalities," can see but won't see, or refuses to look

3.5.b Torso, Barrel, Trunk, Lateral Body (Side of Body) OSCAR Holes Cause These Issues:

An entire side is often missing, everything to one side of midline. This animal seeks to "borrow" or "mentally lean on" a normal side of "another animal's body," as you would lean on a crutch. When you or another companion leaves the room or the area, Oscar becomes frantic, feeling like "their supporting half" has disappeared. Oscar feels very vulnerable as a result and launches into a full-on panic.

- Misjudges space alongside others
- Insufficient peripheral vision awareness
- Will only pass through a narrow space (i.e. doorway) on one side of you even though the only open space is on the other side of you
- Fence pacing
- Acts "smeary" on human laps and legs
- Separation anxiety
- Herd bound, pack bound
- Runaways, hopping fences for escape
- Unpredictable explosions
- Situational dizziness, loss of balance
- Tail usually only bends or wags one way, to R or L side

3.5.c Hind End OSCAR Holes Cause These Issues

When "hind end" outsides are missing (dorsal surfaces), animals tend to stay away, are distant, and can't be touched. When "hind end" inside angles are missing (ventral surfaces), animals are claustrophobic, cannot swivel on hips in one or both directions, and thus have balance problems *seeming* like vestibular problems, but inner ears are not the cause.

- Tail usually bends or wags only one way, only Right or only Left
- Cannot spin/rotate in one direction, either clockwise or counter-clockwise.
- When animal spins, they usually leave the UNKNOWN / UNAWARE / UNUSED quadrants to their OUTSIDE. They "can't" or "won't" rotate themselves easily in the opposite direction.
- Prefers sitting or lying on ground, instead of standing
- Chronic sitting, slinks or oozes down to ground
- Cannot perform a "sumo step" with hind legs.
- Unhappy in a vehicle, trailer or car, often refusing entry
- Claustrophobic behavior even in wide open spaces
- Sideways elevated "pop ups," like spooked cat or jack-rabbit springing
- Cow kicking toward the front with hind leg
- Single Shot kicks backward
- Double barrel kicking backward

3.5.d Given Time to Worsen, OSCAR Holes Often Create a "Squeeze Toy" Affect on an Animal

Have you seen those stress reliever toys that look like animals whose eyes bug out or whose claws or teeth appear when you squeeze 'em? These squeezey toys show us a similar idea to what often happens to OSCAR holes that have not been addressed, and are festering over time.

They go from something like this UNsqueezed (pressure-balanced) toy...

Figure 9: Unsqueezed toy at rest

...to something like this SQUEEZED (pressure-imbalanced) toy...

Figure 10. Squeezing toy makes some parts larger

When the animals add on years of normal life exposure, which to them, are always somewhat frightening and definitely confusing, they learn over time to start guarding against these noxious and scary social experiences. At animal assessment visits, I often find myself drawing a two-part picture for the owner on the back of the intake sheet that goes from the initial situation on the Left to the later situation on the Right. Animals learn over time to hide and protect these chronically exposed "holes" behind preemptive, *offensive* measures. In this case, the teeth do the job that the missing shoulder cannot do for itself.

From this...

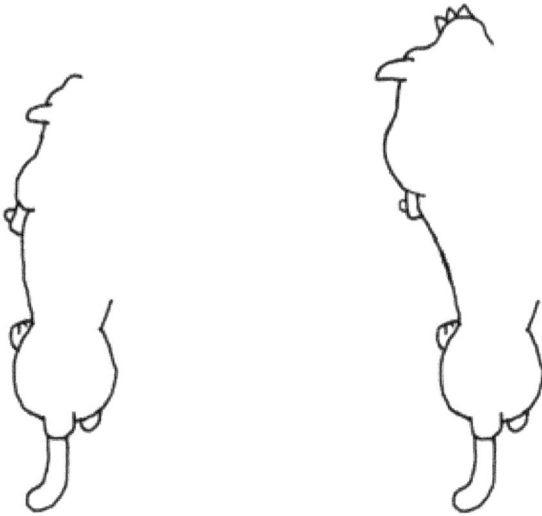

to this fighting biter!

Figure 11. OSCAR holes in dogs get protected by their other parts.

Or from this OSCAR hole horse....

...to this *offensive*, STRIKING OUT horse

Figure 12. OSCAR holes in horses get protected by their other parts.

3.5.e Observed Associations

Here are some unexpected, not-so-obvious overall trends we have noticed over years of rebuilding OSCAR maps. This is a short list, but it's a list that is still growing. I include them here in hopes that they might help future practitioners save some time in diagnosis.

- Whatever part(s) of the animal "wishes it could pass through a wall/floor/ceiling," that part usually is the one with a big OSCAR hole in it.

- When around-the-eye zones are missing, they are often tied in to a same-side shoulder that is over-present.

- Skittishness, spookiness, and jumpiness can indicate ANY missing quadrant, but more often what's missing are a few points of the middle torso, or barrel. Don't forget inner angles of front armpits near the heart. The side with the OSCAR holes will usually (not always) be left to the outside of a voluntary spin/rotation.

- If a leg, south of the knee, has an OSCAR hole, it's often caused by a history of entanglement in hazardous material. Look closely and you will often find the dermal scars. Note: A human who is "holding on and not letting go" is experienced as an entanglement.

- When behavior is horrible for foot care, it's often due to some angles of the ANKLES and wrists that are missing, not the knees. Also the opposite hip may have an OSCAR hole and cannot purposefully rotate to find it's one-legged balance.

- Surgical restraints seem to be able to leave an OSCAR hole in their wake. I don't know how this arises in the brain, but it can arise. Is it possible that there is some part of the peripheral lymph node tree or nervous system that is not entirely asleep during anesthesia?

- When one eye has been surgically removed, the hip on the same side seems to not have exterior lateral and forward angles.

- Claustrophobia? There is often one way they can't spin without getting "jammed up" by their OSCAR hip. Instead, they splay out like a cat held over a bathtub.

- Sound phobia? Often, one side of the hind end is missing. In extreme sound phobia, both sides of the hind end may be missing.

- When 80% or more of the body locations are missing in the brain, the animal can be described to be largely shut down. (80% OSCAR)

Figure 13. Big OSCAR holes are usually left to the outside of voluntary rotations.

They often will not (or cannot) rotate in the other direction.

The only way Oscar can defend such a hole is with a preemptive attack (bite or kick) because Oscar cannot do the reverse recoil that would protect/guard the part with the hole.

Figure 14. Oscars often leave missing parts to the OUTSIDE of voluntary rotation.

Chirality. Pronounced... "kaɪ'ral I tee." It's one of my favorite words. It's been a favorite of mine ever since I learned about it in high school chemistry class. Chirality is a version of the Greek word for "hand" or handedness, and it basically refers to the idea that some shapes are left handed shapes and some shapes are right handed shapes.

If two "identical" things cannot be superimposed on each other (stacked in an *identical items* stack) no matter how you flop them around, then those two things are said to be chiral things. Meaning that they have a right or left (R or L in English) (D or L in Latin) (D or S in French) (clockwise or counterclockwise in clocks) handedness to them. Such things are literally mirror opposites of one another.

OK, so a great thing about bodies is that they are foldable and bendable. And normal, bilaterally symmetrical (2-sided) bodies can fold themselves up into a right side (right goes on the inside) type pretzel, or they can fold themselves up into a left side (left goes on the inside) type pretzel. Animal joints are made to handle either direction of folding so that you can fit yourself into small spaces.

Tucking into tight places, like a squirrel backing into the crux of a tree branch or a fish curling into crevices in the reef where a fish might sleep at night, is a body shape that helps all of us animals find protection. Canines need to fit into corners of a small family den. It's less true for wild equines but baby horses still have to fit into squeezed spaces between the larger animals in a collected herd.

And even though many veterinarians and behaviorists alike consider claustrophobia (the many and varied types of fear-of-small-spaces) to be largely an incurable problem, I've discovered that all it really is is a phobia of Oscar's own infolding pretzel shape. And this phobia is easy to reverse.

OSCAR Therapy is my name for the ability to purposefully reach out into the physical space that is around you and touch something or someone that is out there. If that thing touches you first, that doesn't help you; you have to be the one to touch IT first. When "Oscar" cannot reach out and touch something or someone, that's evidence of missing Presence at the angles they can't reach out through. But the *claustrophobic* Oscar has the equal *and yet opposite* problem. What this brain is missing is not the reaching outward; what this brain is missing is the reaching *inward*, what we humans would call a "tuck." So the solution to any claustrophobic "Oscar" is to teach her/him some CST.

CST stands for "cognitive spatial tuck," or, folding yourself up into a tighter ball, in the clockwise direction, AND/OR doing the same in the counterclockwise direction. All bodies need to be able to do this interior angles tucking on both sides. And many of us don't like to. When you sit on a couch and cross your legs, that's normal. When you try to cross the OTHER leg over top, instead of the one you're used to, it suddenly becomes abnormal to you; it feels weird, and you'd rather go back to doing it your original way. That's due to some imbalance in what we might call your "ambidextrous chirality."

Now, what does it mean to be "chirally screwed"? Well, it means that you so much prefer one direction of fold to the other direction of fold, probably because you are staunchly avoiding the other one. Maybe it's because you don't like folding that way, but more likely it's because you believe (rightly or wrongly) that you *can't* fold that way, so you refuse to try. You then get married to only the side you know.

For instance, take a power drill with a screwdriver bit in it. I like the cordless ones myself. We humans have decided that all screws that spin clockwise should dig deeper into the wood. Hence, when that screw spins counter clockwise, the screw should back out of the hole. We could just as easily have developed an opposite industry where left-turning screws could dig into wood, but we all had a meeting one day a long time ago and decided not to do it that way. We decided that right makes might (righty tighty lefty loosey).... a totally arbitrary decision.

So imagine that you are a screw that is self-drilling; you run on your own power... like a spiraling, burrowing worm. Now imagine that you only know how to spin in one direction; you don't have a reverse button. Now, imagine that you have screwed yourself into something very thick, like a tree stump. Now imagine you wanted to exit back to the surface and go someplace else.

How would you get out? If you only know how to spin in one direction, you'd be stuck. Forward is the only way out; but if forward is not an option, then you might start to panic. In your panicked state, you might explode and blow the walls out of the little place you're stuck inside. If you can't exit the hole, maybe you'd blow through its roof. Every choice you'd make would be logical, based on what you believe to be the facts of your situation.

Welcome to the nightmare that is animal transportation. And when we can't follow this chiral phobia logic, that's when insane-seeming outcomes will surprise us. Animals end up doing backwards somersaults, pouring themselves through tiny, forward facing windows, going through the roof, breaking down doors, and pushing through the sidewalls, blood and broken bones be damned. The decisions these animals are making seem crazy to us. That is, until we can put ourselves in their same spatial shoes to realize that *in the same circumstance, we would try the exact same escape*, and choose the exact same way, even if our physical strength didn't allow it.

Many of the animals who can't deal with being in a small space are only that way because they are literally screwed, just like the worm... They are *screwed in there*. Because they don't have the knowledge of the opposite folding direction in their own bodies, they don't know how to "unscrew" themselves to get out. They can't even imagine how they could possibly get out, and that's what scares them most of all.

Until you can rotate yourself in a tight ball in <u>both</u> directions, you can't feel like you can *exit* the space you are in. And when they can't feel comfortable, most brains will push their wills, brains, and bodies against the OUTSIDE of that same space... pushing on the walls. What walls? Any walls. The walls of the crate, the walls of the elevator, the walls of the car, the walls of the trailer, the walls of the stall, etc.

Animals who can't feel safe indoors are often chirally screwed. People who can't cross bridges are often chirally screwed. Dogs who cannot chill out in a crate or in a car are almost always merely chirally screwed because they feel that they can't reverse their rotation, especially overtop an alternate rotation *of the car*. Even the aquaphobics, the people who can't feel safe in water, are often chirally screwed like this; it's the root of their problem. They just need to learn how to *get themselves un*-screwed.

You can even ask the aquaphobic humans who say, "Swiveling my torso in the other direction cured my fear of water!" Whether it's a person or an animal who can't be IN something, invest the quick time to find out if <u>Oscar</u> is "chirally screwed" into the small space you want them to be able to go both into *and* OUT of. It's not that they can't do it, it's that they can't UN-do it. *That* is the root cause of the problem. And the commonality of the chirally screwed human is what brings us to the next fascinating discovery about us humans!

3.6 Humans Often Have Their *Own* "O'Clock" Issues

I'm not exaggerating or using metaphor when I say that we humans have missing compass points too, at least as commonly as our animals do. These missing slices of our own pies are often missing Reach angles (where a human body won't show up) but they are just as often about missing Recoil angles, (where a human body won't *let go*). The presentation that is often easier to identify is the hole in their Recoil bubble. Animals are the same way; biting problems are easier to identify than stone statue problems.

Finding these holes in human brain-to-body maps is equally as weird and unexpected to most of us as it is in the animals. And yet these holes are just as real, as troubling, as reproducible, and as treatable as those missing slices we find in the non-human animals. *And they freak the humans out, no end.*

For instance my grandfather, a professional illustrator for forever, was getting on in years. He asked me to go through the 300 drawings he had amassed in the cellar and put a sticky note on the ones I might like as gifts for the holidays. One afternoon, I went through the whole lot. When I went back upstairs, he said, what did you find?" I said, "I found out that you really like people who are facing to the right." "Huh?" he muttered. "Of all the drawings down there with people in them, at least 90 percent of those people are facing to the right." "You're crazy," quoth he. "You're putting me on." Me: "Cross my heart and hope to die, you never draw a person's left eye, not much anyway."

After making fun of me some more, he changed the subject. A week later, my father told me that his dad had reported to him, "Son of a bitch...I had to go through maybe 50 drawings before I found a left-facing person. In 70 years of drawing, how come I never noticed that about how I draw?"

I also pointed out that a professional bicyclist-photographer I know has a propensity for the same exact road. The median lines, in the middle of his photographs of the open road, are always pointing toward 2:30. In every single shot. The cool part about the human cases, though, is that we can actually TALK about where the gap(s) in their own spatial awareness could have come from, history wise. Whether it be from congenital anatomy, injury, emotional memory, or maybe from avoiding memories of emotional trauma, those are things we can gingerly survey.

Actually, I spoke too soon. In fact, the very coolest part about searching for spatial Reach or Recoil gaps in humans (noting also that many people have no gaps at all to be found) is that when I locate one, and I say "you do not exist at 4 o'clock", they often say, "You're full o' crap. If I don't exist, then what are my clothes hanging on?" I then give them a rope and we both hold about 2 pounds of pressure on that rope, with me standing at say their 4 o'clock angle. I say, "Now take a step toward me." And that's when they fall forward toward 10 o'clock (opposite to 4) with a perplexed look upon their face.

I then ask them if they can step to me if I'm at 8 o'clock (the mirror image of 4); they do it fine. We try 4 o'clock again and they fall forward to 10 again. Trying 4 again, this time in slow motion, I say "Slowly lift a leg off the ground and slowly step it toward me. They say, "I can't." "You can't step toward me?" I ask, expecting some balance trouble in their spinal vertebrae. (I was trained as a veterinary biologist, after all.) And then that's when they usually come back with this (seemingly nutty) answer:

"No. I can't lift my leg off the ground. I want to, but it won't go. Holy crap. Can I try it without holding the rope so I'm not in contact with you? " I say sure; because remember, ropes don't matter when it comes to the Will. (And that's what we're doing here; we're looking for holes in the Will.)

So we drop the rope, and we try it again, and they say, "Wow, it's not the rope, it's me. My leg still won't go. It's like I can't become myself in that direction, if ya know what I mean, but I don't even know what I mean. You must think I'm crazy. Am I broken?" This is what it's like to finally see your own OSCAR outline (with its gaps or divots or dents in it) for the first time. It is pretty weird, but it's really just more surprising than it is scary or uncomfortable.

Most people don't get to the age of 20 or 40 or 60 and remain unscathed by life. Everyone has some old injury that might explain why the gap is there, but it hardly matters, because within minutes or hours, even a human animal's OSCAR gap can be largely restored. Spontaneous resolution of *tissue pathology*, of course, does not occur. For example, vision does not just show up where there was none before. But if a zone has been shoved down into the subconscious at some point in the past, it can be brought back out to see the light of day without too much trouble.

Some of these missing OSCAR angles are due to unhealed physical injury. For example, if your right knee doesn't work correctly, you're less likely to interact with the world through your 3 o'clock angle because that knee would have to act as a balance point. You'd be more likely to turn around and do the same job using your good knee on your left.

But many if not most of these missing compass points are due to unhealed *psychological injury*, an injury caused by our looping memory circuitry, which seems to be always on-call. You may have been (unconsciously) too spooked to use that part of you ever since the time you repeatedly got attacked there, or were trapped from there, or almost drowned by being stuck under water through that point. Even though any physical damage to that location healed a long, long time ago, the "experience" of having no control is still locked inside our nerve memory.

Unresolved spatial OSCAR gaps fester over time to become a subconscious state of mind. The narrower the missing angle, or the smaller the slice of pie that someone is missing, the quicker it is to come back, as the neighboring normal areas help it along in its recovery. But even so, even the biggest of these missing zones can be regained, recovered, and reinstated with some OSCAR Therapy phobia reversal work in that zone of the body.

And once we get all of our compass points back on line again, we have many more tools at our disposal, as far as how we can balance ourselves both on our feet, fins, and wings, but more importantly, in our state of mind. When we can finally imagine precisely how we would now handle habitual stressors, we do a much better job of it.

3.7 Doctor OSCAR: Rule Outs, Rule-Ins, PT, OT, and Disabilities

It's not surprising that the potential overlap between OSCAR Therapy and the medical world might be and could be vast. In this section I will lay out three different "Medical OSCAR" areas in order of their "remarkableness," if I can invent the word. The areas I will cover first are the ones that are easiest to wrap our heads around, and then we'll proceed toward the unknown.

But let me state from the outset that it if OSCAR Therapy and teaching animals to unlock and use body parts did routinely, frequently, or even sometimes... cause a physical breakdown in joints or body tissues, I would not have ever gone down this OSCAR path in the first place. In the beginning, I strongly expected that it might, but in case after case, I was proved wrong. To *FIRST, DO NO HARM* is a foundational concept, especially in the exotic animal veterinary arena, and it's a foundational concept of OSCAR Therapy.

First, OSCAR can often *rule out* a possible "medical cause" because a body part that "can't be used" today CAN often be used normally tomorrow, after OSCAR Therapy. Persistent fear of remembered pain gets reversed with OSCAR; non-use can become *use* overnight.

In this way, we can often rule OUT a "hidden or subtle" ligament or nerve issue that is suspected because healing of physical injury to those tissues never happens within hours. And yet new capabilities after OSCAR Therapy are quickly evident. A body part that can be used "only mildly" before OSCAR may go through a window of time of non-use *directly after* OSCAR Therapy for a few hours (because of being exhausted by the emergence process). But by tomorrow, previously "nonfunctional or dysfunctional" parts can be working much stronger than ever.

And then oppositely, we come to the second topic. OSCAR Therapy can rule IN or suss out (identify) the deep malfunctioning body parts that a doctor might never think to look for or even be capable of diagnosing due to technological limitations. Many animals or their parts are simply too thick for effective diagnosis by radiograph, or too large to fit inside CT, or other 3-D imaging machines designed only to accommodate us bite-sized creatures.

When a brain tries to use the physical body to make the shape it's imagining it wants to achieve will show themselves more readily, in the twinges and tripping and cockeyed postural structures inherent in misalignments. Physical disabilities that no one knew about before can show up like a sore thumb, when Oscar's body cannot exactly achieve the shape his or her mind imagines it can. Example: broken pelvic structures that have healed wrong.

Following are opportunities for *radical* patient participation via OSCAR Therapy:

OSCAR Promotes Patient Participation: Occupational Therapy for Animals

- Accept medical treatments of all types i.e. needles, topicals, eye drops
- Serial injections and blood draws
- Safer re-orientation in anesthesia recovery
- Anesthesia-contraindicated cases, or when anesthesia is unwanted
- Hospitalization and post surgical management
- Reversing phobia of an action-induced injury, during rehab

OSCAR Assists Disabilities in Animal Cases

- Blindness is augmented by reaching and spatial skills
- Deafness is augmented by social-spatial awareness skills
- Physically Challenged cases gain quick control over equipment aids
- Spinal surgery rehab would be especially aided by OSCAR Therapy

OSCAR Assists Physical Therapy (PT) for Animal Patients

- Injured / rehabilitating patients
- Builds *active*, self-initiated physical therapy for rehab cases
- Acceptance of *passive* physical therapy for rehab cases

If a body part has been long healed, physically, but Oscar is still anxious about using it, then that part won't be used, ranged, and strengthened, *even if the body drags it along.* A helpful Physical Therapist on the team might prescribe exercises requiring 100 percent follow through from the patient, following strict "DO THIS and DON'T DO THAT" rules, but the reason for trying has to come from Oscar herself/himself, and if s/he is too afraid to try, then the case may have a lesser outcome.

But when the patient does participate fully, the results can be remarkably positive. I worked an OSCAR case all the way through a mare's pregnancy; her owners feared that her mean streak would put the baby in harm's way. Not only did OSCAR recover her rational brain, but also, after her completely normal pregnancy, the foal was born to be an instant extra-normal champion, right out of the gate. The mare was an attentive mother who was not at all afraid of her baby.

The primary thing to know about OSCAR Therapy is that, by definition, it is SAFE. I have never seen it cause a permanent worsening in any case of psychological, physical, or even physiological pathology. And yet, OSCAR's streamlining of health-promoting treatments by creating patient participation is not even the most interesting way in which OSCAR Therapy can intersect with the "medical world."

3.8 OSCAR Nerves: A Physiologic Wave Passes Through

Now, to the last and weirdest area of "Medical OSCAR." The "medical-electrical" topic I will cover in this section will not only sound *implausible* to the uninitiated nonbeliever, but when it happens, it also leaves *me* scratching my head in near disbelief. If I had not seen these things with my own eyes, I would have a hard time accepting their validity, as I have been well steeped in a lifetime of methodical observation.

OSCAR Therapy is about helping a brain go through the re-experiencing and the "re-learning to have control over" previous psychological states and real memories of real events long past. As such, *all* brains that are undergoing OSCAR Therapy will go through stages of deep sleeping, serious dreaming, and reliving events.

I have seen both dogs and horses "crash" into deep REM sleep, immediately after and *even during* OSCAR sessions. All species will not only run in their sleep but also be quite vocal in their sleep, even animals who have been non-vocal for their entire lives to date. My silent horse started vocally chatting to/with me at age 17, after 15 years silent. Dogs will start being vocal around owners after 5 years of silence. OSCAR allows vocal expression to come back on line, and that switch is observed by owners to be thrown during sleep. Big dogs even seem to be using their high pitched puppy voice in sleep.

But what is much stranger still, and much more shocking, literally, to the human witnesses who happen to be watching the early sessions of a case, is that many animals experience an internally-derived "electric shock" that hits them like a lightning bolt. The jolt can be so large in its affect on the animal that it can almost knock you, the practitioner, onto your knees if you don't let what you're seeing just pass through you and not surprise you too. Electricity is not passing through, and there is no visible spark, but visually, you'd swear that Oscar must have felt one; the whole body looks like it got zapped one time with an electric gun, even though the body had been standing still.

These kinds of lightning bolts are *very* common in the OSCAR pathway, but they only happen about two to three times in a row before they are gone, never to return at any other spot in the same body. They usually show up during Oscar's first reach out, to voluntarily touch the practitioner. The choice to do so must be so anxiety-inducing that every nerve in their body jumps at once upon contacting us. Sometimes though, these shocks will show up much later in a case.

In a very important case of a 90 percent OSCAR-missing Gelderlander horse brain, this huge, failed "carriage horse" was thinking about taking his first ever right-foot-first step over a straight lead rope laid out flat on the ground, something that "should be" easy for any animal of any size. And he was really thinking hard about trying it, for the first time ever.

As he was focused in on his intention to attempt this single step, I unfortunately let a few pellets of food rattle in my pocket like coinage sometimes will. That tiny noise came at a bad time because Oscar's "busy with imagining" brain perceived that rattle sound as if something had "touched him."

This very tall and grand nearly 18-hand (6 ft. tall at the shoulder) horse standing next to me was instantly nothing but hoof in my field of vision. The entire horse jolted up, 7 feet straight up above where he had been standing just a split second earlier. When he came down basically in the same spot, with only his front feet past the ground rope, he was a lot more surprised than I was, as he immediately looked all around for what had just caused whatever he had felt.

Some spooky stuff does occur in the OSCAR process sometimes; you'll know it when you see it. Make a note of it when it does; write it down, but don't be overly concerned. All species can feel these mental electric shocks when their missing slice of pie is either about to try or actually tries to reach out for the first time, maybe ever. For a few minutes, anything coming in from the sensory world can just overload the newly used circuitry *and it arcs*. But back to the practitioner's role here:

Of paramount importance regarding OSCAR's lightning bolts is that...

EVERY NEW ANIMAL YOU'RE WORKING ON MUST BE AT LIBERTY.

DO NOT ATTACH ANYTHING TO OSCAR. DO NOT "HOLD ONTO" A NEW OSCAR IN ANY WAY, BECAUSE IMPOSED, EXTERNAL PHYSICAL LEVERGE PREVENTS FREE EXPRESSION. Any and every piece of equipment attached to Oscar will make a lightning bolt scarier or worse yet, it will prevent its expression *and not let it come out.* If a lightning bolt sized anxiety resides in your animal, then... *better out than in,* we always say! OSCAR Therapy is designed to tap off the unseen yet dangerous pressures inside the brain's pressurized teakettle.

That said; try not to let it freak you out that you're standing right next to a lightning bolt when it happens. Part of Oscar's brain still knows you're there, and that you're an empowering partner. No part of Oscar's brain is aiming to hurt or even affect you. Sideswipes don't usually accompany lightning bolts, as those shocks are not a mechanical/physical reflex. They are electrical in nature. Just learn to let the energy waves pass right through you, and you'll be safe. It's amazing. (If you feel at all unsafe, you must employ a fence between you and Oscar.)

But even more amazing to me, some very unexpected "*physiologic* memories" will also crop up alongside the psychological ones. Still-unresolved physio-neural echoes of previous insult or physical injury will sometimes surface and make themselves known in the process of rebuilding the awareness-to-body connection. During the excavation process, Oscar can become temporarily "medical."

And the presentations of these out-of-nowhere "medical events" are obviously connected to the OSCAR Therapy, if you take their odd timing into consideration. They can begin as early as 24 hours to 3 days after the onset of OSCAR Therapy. Owners and participants should be forewarned that they might see and/or have to manage some temporary changes and physiologic shifts.

OSCAR Therapy can alter, improve, or temporarily cause some "worsening" to both the normal physiologic states and the chronic conditions. In short, OSCAR Therapy can bring on immune system changes. And no, these observations have never been diet related, as the food used in session is usually the same food(s) the animals regularly eat. (Only emergency sessions may use yummy, bad-tummy junk foods.)

In a moderate percentage of cases where we see some physiologic "jazz" dredged up by OSCAR, the changes temporarily run alongside OSCAR Therapy for a time (about a 2 week duration), until the wave passes through and is gone.

We support the system with probiotics, gut binders, and other GI and anxiety supports, but calming psych meds are not usually allowed in OSCAR Therapy. The patient must be able to feel all of the emotions that bubble forth, in order to reintegrate the memories to body and brain. Here are some examples of the medical changes we've seen:

A dog rescued years ago in Puerto Rico passed bloody stool then loose stools then had incontinent bladder, all in three separate phases. The whole lot resolved within 3 weeks. Luckily I have only one seen OSCAR affect the guts of a horse, but in dogs, we have seen it more. Worms get expelled, and the gastrointestinal system coughs up weird stuff that's been stuck inside for a time. The one colicky horse had no impaction and was back to normal the next day but was hydrated just to be on the safe side.

The tall Gelderlander horse that sprang sky-high, he had always had anhydrosis; he lacked the ability to sweat. After a few months with OSCAR Therapy, he began to sweat like a normal horse for the first time ever, in any season. He now showed normal sweat patterns in all the normal places. Nothing else had been added to the case; Oscar was the only addition that could have caused the change, which was permanent.

A few days after building a new anatomical zone, a Pit Bull dog broke out with nerve shocks in her toes, hitting her like real-time lightning bolt "bee stings" on her toe (tingling?), which she began to lick raw. This morphed into nerve twitching in her inner thighs, and then even included evidence of some mild hip strain and frog-dog posture. And yet, each new symptom mysteriously disappeared, morphing into the next symptom just days after it made itself obvious.

And as if all of this topic were not weird enough, consider my suspicion that OSCAR Therapy somehow involves the mirror neurons that neuroscientists have discovered in primates. A mirror neuron is a neuron that fires when an animal acts, but ALSO when the animal observes the action performed by another. They play a part in how individuals learn by observation and by empathizing.

So why would that same system not *also* be able to act just like a set of jumper cables to jump-start a defaulted circuit in a conspecific (same species) member of your social group in a social species? That's not a far leap of logic. But what seems to be a cross-species capacity, *that* is the part that makes this idea really weird. I have witnessed some weird brain-to-brain physiologic effects, especially from animal to practitioner (me and others).

In my humble experience, it seems that a physiological stress can jump from brain to brain. Exactly at the moment that an animal's awareness "expands into a new 3-D zone," my legs often get momentarily wobbly, like I'm all of a sudden on the deck of a boat, even though I'm standing on hard ground.

Even before Oscar has made a single move in a new direction, that involuntary wobble in me is my "tell" that lets me know they've arrived at a new awareness, and that their very next try is going to hit the bull's-eye mark for the first time. Reliably, right after I get wobbly is when the animal touches a button for the first time, a button they've never been able to successfully touch before. And remember, I don't knowingly have anything to do with any energy fields of any kind. I merely urge animals to try things, and I pay attention to what's happening as they try.

Weirder still, utilizing the "wrong arm" of our body as the OSCAR button and jumper cable always makes the connection worse, causing a map-building Oscar to "become lost" instantly. Using the correct side of our bodies though (our 12 o'clocks must be pointing the same way as Oscar is pointing) always gives Oscar clear information they can then leapfrog off of and learn from. It's weird that crossed wires in you… can cause crossed wires in another brain. But more on that in Chapter 4 in the section called *First, Get Parallel.*

But the weirdest brain-to-brain jump yet was with a Paint mare horse. After facing her to rebuild her left eye and the surrounding skull with OSCAR, my right eyelid would not open for the next 30 minutes. It's never happened before or since. Weird, right? Especially as I have no unusual pathology of any kind in my right eye.

3.9 Seeing How Oscar Sees Is First About "Seeing Spots"

Painted horses are fun to look at. It looks like someone dunked them in a bucket of paint, oil, and water. Whether the coat is brown, red, or yellow, it looks like some Greek God on Mount Olympus took a big eraser and erased huge swaths of the color from the body, both hair and skin, leaving just white hair over pink skin, where the normal color used to be. These animals end up looking like the continents on a globe, or like the black and white cow on your milk carton.

And although I had done OSCAR Therapy and treatment on all of the painted horse and dog color variations before, it took working with a white and *black*

Oreo cookie looking horse in a darkened stall for me to literally be able to see the light. And it kills me to have to write this… because I know how Looney Tunes this story is going to sound, but I wasn't the only witness.

Spaz is a rescue of untold scary history. He was also just "any old horse" who happened to be coupled with me during a weekend long equine wellness fair at a local nonprofit rescue farm. My role at the fair was to educate passersby about what OSCAR is, how it works, what it reveals, and that it cures. My role at the fair was *not* to totally fix whatever animal happened to be laid out before me. There wouldn't be time enough for that.

But for reasons of logistics, Spaz kept being not only available for demonstration, but there were also more people who kept showing up, asking me to show them OSCAR Therapy even though I was "offstage and on break." Spaz was hanging out in an antechamber stall nearby, so we ducked the lights of the arena and went to the more dimly lit stall.

I was rebuilding Spaz's left flank and answering the questions of the one person watching; I was talking my way through. When I was talking I also remember muttering under my breath, in a very exasperated way, "Ohhh nooooo, horse– please don't tell me this… They think I'm crazy enough as it is…"

I was tired. It was the end of Day 2 of schmoozing and hearing and relating long winded stories and breathing dust and eating left over hotdogs and the melted m&m's I teach human Oscars with. Spaz was earnestly trying to investigate his newly discovered body parts in his darkened stall with me, but I was on autopilot. I just didn't want to believe the wave that seemed to be coming in over my bow.

Spaz is still alive today, surviving the mean streets of rural America, because he is one of those ultra expressive brains. If he spoke English he would be an orator or he'd spit rhymes in rap battles. When he's proud he looks it. When he's scared his eyes become saucers. When he's angry, he reaches out with a back foot and taps you in the ass. That's just who he is, for better or worse.

But in any regard, the rescue-dog rescuer who was watching from outside the stall, someone who knew nothing about horses, said right out loud the thing I was observing but wouldn't let myself believe: "So do horses' brains act differently depending on the color of the hair you're asking them to touch you with?"

I shook my head in disbelief. I did a lot of exhaling before I answered her very observant question.

I said to her, "For my whole life, up until this very minute, I would have told you (if I had ever heard of it before) that such a notion would be completely crazy. I've never seen this before, consciously anyhow, but Spaz is making it pretty damn obvious that what you just said is… true, *isn't he.* I'm too tired for this right now. Are you freakin' kidding me, horse?!! How can such a thing be possible…" (But when brains are too tired to *actively* ignore facts, they often, *finally*, see some new light.) It took an environment of dim light in the stall to let the black hair fade into shadow and to let the white zones really pop. With such a stark contrast available to my usually oblivious eyeballs, here's what we saw:

Even though the dividing line between white and black was a mere ¼ inch wide, Spaz could reach out with his white part, but he could not reach out with the adjacent skin and muscles that were under his black part. Until 10 minutes later, when OSCAR Therapy and his own exhaling helped him to make the leap, to bridge the gap.

And then, Spaz was fine at using that very same black zone... until... I bumped up against his next dividing line. He could not then cross over into the next (north, east, south or west) white patch. His brain got stuck at the color edges like a retreating army gets backed up against the sea. He acted like he felt instantly lost in space at each precipice.

This was way too mind-blowing for me. I needed to go to sleep now.

Literally months later, Spaz kept popping into my head. I felt awful that I had left a horse in a barn somewhere only three-quarters built. He didn't ask for this, just like he didn't ask for any of the other raw deals he was dealt in his life. Spaz needed to be finished, and gratis, on my day off. And wouldn't ya know, a perfect opportunity arose. I was teaching OSCAR Therapy to a very open-minded human not far away; she was looking for more OSCAR experience, more cases. We decided that I would walk her through the last remaining 30 percent of Spaz.

I didn't tell Dana anything about him because assessment is an integral part of the OSCAR Therapy process. I left it to Dana to tell me what she was finding, as I looked on and watched Spaz's thought process. About 30 minutes in, Dana said, "ummm... this might sound crazy... but what the heck is going on with these colors? This horse is either racist or he hates racism or something, but he's like a different animal as soon as his OSCAR brain hits up against the next black patch! Like he shorts out! What the heck!!!??"

During this session we were outside on a cloudy day, in Spaz's paddock with him. Half way through rebuilding his Right side, Spaz tapped Dana in the ass, lightly, with a hind hoof. She said, "Hey!" mostly laughing. I saw the kick but from where I was outside his fence, I couldn't see what body part Dana's hand was near.

I said, "Yikes, where are you right now, I can't see." "I just came up on the other color again!" said Dana, followed by "Ok, what about this other white to black over here, dude?" Spaz tapped Dana a little too hard this time on Dana's butt. Not safe. It was time to move this conversation to the fence line to do the rest of the rebuild across the protective barrier of the old wood, split-rail planks. Both individuals could lean on that strip of fence and use it as a buffer, protecting each body (each a perceived threat) from the other.

Spaz, as with all brains in Operant reward conversation, was very, very willing to voluntarily (no halter or lead) pack his body in laterally, within one inch of the actual wooden planks of the fence. He needed to get as close as he could to where we were in order to continue creating these contact points and discoveries about his own body in space that he desperately needed and wanted to make.

Many exhales and a few hoof shots to the ground later, Spaz was in full possession of his whole hind end now. His whole body map was finally intact. Later reports said that he was a) much better as a school horse teaching riders, b) no longer moody with unpredictable outbursts on the ground while grooming and tacking, and c) no longer afraid of the sounds overhead, the sounds of snow falling off the roof in winter.

Nowadays, I make it a habit to look both ways before I cross the color street on every species of paint swirled animal. Nutty Jack Russell terriers, anyone? Got sproingy Springer Spaniels? And I even looked back at the photos and the OSCAR maps of paint horses and dogs I have OSCAR'ed in the past. And sure enough, there was a color boundary line running right through the bull's-eye in the majority of the zones that needed to be rebuilt, according to their records.

And although it still makes me exhale too much to know this now, I don't blame myself for not having picked up the pattern of neurologic mapping evidence earlier, before I saw it in black and white. When looking at the globe of the Earth, noticing where the continents were was something we humans historically did ok, but who the hell noticed the fault lines and the plate tectonics way back in the days of Magellan or the Lewis and Clark expeditions? Who was looking at the Earth's behavioral transition lines under their feet? I sure wasn't. To me, "parts was parts," no matter with what color they were splashed. Now I know better.

For whatever reason of developmental neurology, the colors and lack thereof are not integrating and/or triangulating on each other. The shape of the animal is getting lost in the animal's own brain, preempted by color (and presumably nerve development) patterns. If you cross-reference the topics: Coat Color and Genetics and Neural Pathology, you will find some interesting discoveries of late.

But damn.

You really have no shot at a clue about what any individual Oscar is experiencing until you really are ready to perceive the world as that particular Oscar is perceiving it. Maybe Oscar is seeing the letters of words in reverse order or better yet, as letters running all over the page like ants. Maybe Oscar is seeing 3D objects as having only two dimensions, making walking down stairs and driving on the highway a real challenge. Maybe, as biologist Oliver Sacks observed, some brains even experience the passage of Time as going by too quickly or rather slowly. I have certainly noticed the same variations even in re-normalizing animal brains.

But if Oscar either will not, cannot, or is not capable of telling you outright that they perceive what they perceive, then the question becomes: can you still find out? *Can you see or infer what <u>Oscar</u> perceives?? Can you see it?*

If Oscar is suspicious of you, can you imagine his or her real, and not fake, reasons for that? Must we condemn those reasons? Or can we see our way to helping our Oscars connect each dot so that they can find out that the side we are actually on.... is Oscar's side? Can you help Oscar get there? Can you follow Oscar's CRAZY and unique breadcrumb trail all the way around the baseball diamond of recovery in order to show them that it leads eventually back home to reason and safety, every time?

You might not know the way forward with your Oscar. You might not know the way to get Oscar's brain all the way home. But I'm here to tell you that there is only one way to get there: Oscar's way. And if you've lost sight of where Oscar is coming from, then it's because you have not gone out far enough on Oscar's walkabout trail, out far enough on that far-flung (you might even say detached) tree branch, to find out just what it is that Oscar thinks is true.

But when you won't go out there, when you won't go way way out there, to where Oscar has gone, it's highly likely that it's because you don't actually want to know what Oscar actually perceives. Likely, it's because it's too weird for you to hear about what Oscar actually perceives. Maybe it's because Oscar's perceptions (his/her reasons for what Oscar actually believes) is searing into your brain. Maybe it's because you are actually afraid of Oscar, which is why you are afraid to see the world that Oscar sees.

Even though all of this is true for most of us, please don't be afraid. Our fear of Oscar is the last thing that Oscar needs right now. Remember, Oscar is usually more afraid of you (and her or his own nervous system) than you are of him/her. In OSCAR Therapy, *that* rule of nature is always, always true.

Try to use the eyes that Oscar sees with, *even if they are not your eyes*, to help connect the spots and dots that Oscar still needs to connect. Just because you don't perceive something doesn't mean it's not there. Nor does that mean that Oscar's devil (or disconnect) is not real. Generically, if Oscar sees a devil, then you must (safely) invoke that devil in order to meet and greet that devil. But if you can't or don't want to even know Oscar's devil at all, then you won't be much help at all to Oscar.

A Final Note to Chapter 3:

In case this is the only OSCAR book I ever publish, I should take this opportunity to describe the only truly spooky OSCAR-weird situation I have come across, as I've now seen a few different instances of it now. Even though I have no way to explain the following, I'm reporting it just as an observer who takes notes.

There is no part of me that has ever collected information that would support the existence of ghosts or spirits of any kind. But because it is my job in this book to introduce the whole spectrum of my experience with OSCAR Therapy, I must include this weird bit.

All of OSCAR Therapy is about understanding the use of the spaces around and between the central nervous systems of living organisms. And yet, I have been called to a few cases that butt up against a different flavor of spaces altogether. Be they due to reasons of lingering chemical smell or the subconscious influence of human memory or for some other reason, I have witnessed two different horses that would adamantly not cross the pieces of ground where a previous horse died.

These were horses at different farms in different towns, and who had never met and had never even seen the horse who died. Both unfortunate horses had been put down immediately after tragic, painful accidents. It was as if the deceased horses somehow left a mark on the weathered earth in that spot, a mark lasting for months... When the new horses arrived months later, they fastidiously avoided those pieces of ground.

So maybe in the rare instance it's actually something odd about "the space itself" that influences whether a brain will reach into that zone or not, even when no one is watching. I don't know what else to say about these observations.

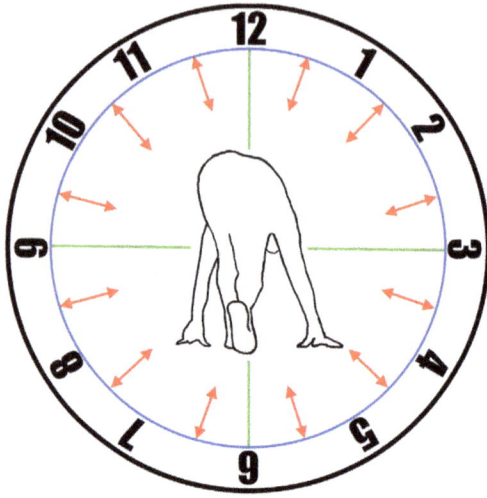

CHAPTER 4: OSCAR THERAPY ANYONE CAN DO!

Recipients of OSCAR Therapy, no matter their age, their gender, and no matter the intensity of their hideous background story, all blossom into functional, expressive, independent teammates who are now capable of working fully *with you* on any goal you have, no matter the sport, no matter the job, and no matter the challenge.

But Oscar can't do it alone. Your Oscar lives in the real world, so s/he is going to need to hold your hand for most of the way through this learning, until s/he doesn't need to anymore. You are the one who will be providing Oscar with each "for instance" opportunity during day-to-day life. You do not have to be an expert, a professional, a student, an apprentice, or even an adult to help Oscar turn it all the way around, but you will need to be the other *equal* team member, the other oar in a two-person canoe.

OSCAR Therapy requires communication, collaboration, a truly level playing field, and sharing of responsibility. And if you think back, way, way back, to what you loved about these kinds of life forms when you first laid eyes on them, their potential for those particular skills is what probably drew you to them in the first place. This is your opportunity to see all of that felt potential come to life. Your life. But the question remains: will YOU choose to be an *equal* instead of a leader?

Fixing a major imbalance in somebody's (some animal's) body-brain connections obviously provides an opportunity for massive improvement. As we help Oscar fill in that out-of-balance hole, literally everything about Oscar's choices and lifestyle then proceeds, all on its own, to right itself. Even regarding the really scary animal cases, the simple brain equation that explains them goes like this:

(a missing hole) + (PTSD from mismanagement of missing hole) = aggression

This chapter, Chapter 4, will be a description of all of the skills and tools we teach to all new learners of OSCAR Therapy. Whether they are owners of difficult cases or people that will only spend a weekend clinic with us, Chapter 4 covers the critical information to all new human learners of OSCAR Therapy. In an OSCAR Therapy clinic, it takes only a few hours to learn them. Just like riding a bike, and just like learning any new language, it takes a little practice to get into the groove, but before you know it (and usually even by the next morning) it has become second nature.

4.1 The Pre-Game Theory: Casey's Class I, II, and III

I think it's strange that I am burying reference to the following golden treasure chest so deep into this book, but t/here it is. The fact is that I have written a separate opus/tomb/proof on the topic of how to get any brain ready to teach anyone anything. It's a nearly 1000 page, 3-volume monstrosity, which you can also use in its app form called BichFish.com. But for the purposes of *this* book (and when I teach it's nuts and bolts to clients) I have to boil the theory down to its physical essence, which I call my three-class triumvirate. Amazingly, each equally important class is only two hours long.

Class I gets people really good at operant language- the why, when, and how of saying what you say. Class II is about physical leverage and learning how NOT to use it. (Sometimes we also call this class *How Not to Be an @$$#%!&*.) Class III is about the ancestral essence of what I call Social Pull. All of these one-session classes drill anyone's brain down to the essence of what it means to actively use social interface.

As noted, if I were to explain what is learned (by all different kinds of people) in these classes in writing, it would require 1,000 pages; this book is not that book. But I mention these classes here in order to explain that OSCAR Therapy is the practical blend of all three topics. If those three are the ingredients, then OSCAR Therapy is the recipe. OSCAR Therapy provides the easy way to shortcut you into the benefits of all three essential classes, no matter your age, gender, or background.

This chapter, Chapter 4, covers everything you'll need for your "do it yourself" OSCAR Therapy recipe. If it turns out that you are a natural in this kitchen, a natural at picking up the OSCAR language (and many people will be) then the roughly 9-part recipe below is really the only instruction you'll need. If you get hung up someplace, just search through the essays in Chapter 5 and Chapter 6 to get yourself un-stuck. [All tool-based essays in Chapters 5 and 6 of this book are largely excerpted from *Will-ing*, my book describing the philosophy that generated OSCAR Therapy as an offshoot.]

But if it turns out that you are *not* a natural at picking up OSCAR Therapy, Chapters 4 through 6 will help you connect all the dots and fill in the gaps. If you understand most of OSCAR Therapy and are just stuck at particular points along the path of a typical or even a challenging OSCAR re-build, I wrote all of those essays *in the order* in which you will need to add those tools into your mental (and emotional) toolbox.

4.2 Reasons to Adopt OSCAR Therapy

It seems to me that you would not likely be holding this particular book in your hands unless you already were up against some trouble that you really wish you were not up against. I'm guessing you already have a list of problems you would like to fix.

But on the off chance that you don't already have such a list in mind, here are some examples of some OSCAR troubles that are had by three different common household species. Any of these problems are fair game. And if your favorite species is not mentioned in the following chart, then just fill in the blanks below. Your Oscar will help you reverse any of the items on these lists:

Species_____: Issues to Be Fixed by OSCAR Therapy

Fear problems: _____
Phobia problems: _____
Handling problems: _____
Husbandry problems:_____
Aggression problems:_____
Social with Same Species problems: _____
Medical problems: _____
Teaching problems: _____

Human Issues Fixed by OSCAR Therapy: (All Ages, All Abilities)

- ✓ All Phobias:
- ✓ OSCAR Therapy specializes in Zoophobias (fear of animals)
- ✓ Aquaphobia (fear of water)
- ✓ Spatial Phobias
- ✓ Medical Phobias (diagnostics and treatment procedures)
- ✓ Body Related Phobias (memory-based neglect)
- ✓ PTSD, mild to moderate, and possibly severe as well.

4.3 OSCAR Therapy Reverses These Common Canine Problems

All species and breeds of animal are welcome to participate in a clinic at the Host's discretion. Equids, Farm animals, Canines, Pack Animals, Felines, Reptiles, Birds, Fishes, and Exotics are welcome! But here are *just some* of the dog-related problems that are reversible with an OSCAR Therapy approach.

Attitude	Jobs	Trauma	Seasonal
General Attitude Unpredictable Aggression Anxiety Bullish Dominance Unfocused Patterning Chaotic	**Medical Patient** Exam Positioning Can't anesthetize Needles Eye Drops Range of Motion Wound care Foot and nail care	**Accident/Abuse** Previous car accident Outdoor accident Previous torture Inhumane Restraint Memory of Pain	**Spring** Needle Phobias Fear of Vets Fear of Men Nail Clippers Rain or water Car loading
Safe Manners Drop it/ Possessiveness Biting Leash Harness	**Vehicles** Car Loading Car Unloading Car Riding Riding Alone	**Physically Challenged** Blind Dog Deaf Dog Injured / Rehab Patients Accept Medical Treatments Anesthesia-Contraindicated Hospitalizations	**Summer** Recall Won't stand for Groomer Fear of Equipment Fear of hosing water Fear of spray bottle Body clipping Vacuums Loud Noises Thunder
Social Safe around other Dogs Be Kind to other Dogs Separation Anxiety Environs Crate-Claustrophobia	**Ambassador/Companion** Hospitals Visiting and Therapy Dogs **Assistance Dogs** Readies "fail" dogs Improves blank slate Quicker job learning	**Environment** Electric Fence Social Fencelines Elevators Daycare	
Phobia Environs Stairs Weather Sounds Social Vehicle	**Sport** Agility Sports Traditional Sports *We will not teach hunting of live or dead prey **Chemosensory** Search/Sniff Ability	**Phobia** Environs Stairs Weather Sounds Social Vehicle	**Autumn** Loud Noises Windblown objects **Winter** Enclosed Arena Noises Clothing

Table 2: OSCAR Therapy reverses these common canine problems

4.4 OSCAR Therapy Reverses These Common Equine Problems

All species and breeds of animal are welcome to participate in a clinic at the Host's discretion. Equids, Farm animals, Canines, Pack Animals, Felines, Reptiles, Birds, Fishes, and Exotics are welcome! But here are *just some* of the horse related problems that are reversible with an OSCAR Therapy approach.

Attitude	Jobs	Trauma	Seasonal
General Attitude	Medical Patient	Accident/Abuse	Spring
Unpredictable	Exam Positioning	Previous trailer	Needle Phobias
Aggression	Can't anesthetize	accident	Fear of Vets
Anxiety	Needles	Trail/Outdoor	Fear of Men
Bullish	Eye Drops	accident	Clippers
Dominance	Range of Motion	Previous torture	Rain on trailer roof
Unfocussed	Wound care	Inhumane	Trailer loading
Patterning	Foot care	Restraint	
Chaotic		Entanglement	Summer
Cribbing Endorphin		Memory of Pain	Won't return from
Addiction	Competition		pasture
	Won't Stride		Won't stand for
	Won't Collect	Physically	Hoof-care
Ground Manners	Sport Skill	Challenged	Fear of Equipment
Biting	Won't Track R or L	Blind Horse	Fear of hosing
Pushing	Pain Triggers	Deaf Horse	water
Kicking/Striking		Injured / Rehab	Fear of spray bottle
Rearing/Bolting		Patients	Body clipping
Cross Ties	Equipment	Accept Medical	Vacuums
Single Tie	Long Line Diagnosis	Treatments	
	Bitless Conversion	Anesthesia-	Autumn
	Will-Based Riding	Contraindicated	Loud Noises
Trailers	Harness	Hospitalizations	Windblown objects
Trailer Loading	Carriage		
Trailer Unloading			Winter
Trailer Riding		Troubling	Snow Falling Off
Riding Solo	Equine Assisted	Histories	Roof
Butt Bar Spinal Injury	Therapies	Anxiety	Enclosed Arena
	Therapeutic Riding	Bullish	Fear
	Special Needs Mount	Dominance	Blanketing
Social Skills	Safety with children	Unfocussed	Trailer Hauling
In-Herd Aggression	Safety around side-	Patterning	
and Pecking Orders	walkers	Chaotic	

Table 3: OSCAR Therapy reverses these common equine problems

4.5 Do Remember to Video Original Problem(s) *Ahead* of ANY OSCAR Therapy:

I have very few regrets in life, but there is one whole category of regret that I ALWAYS kick myself for not having done, because there's no going back for a do over. Take it from this regretter: whenever it is relatively safe to make the request, get video proof of many of the problems an animal displays BEFORE you start the case. Because even very soon, and definitely later on, you *will want* video proof that the animal was ever abnormal in the first place.

I have a "bad" habit of launching right into the fix for the problem right at the assessment. Because I have much information the animal needs, *I just plain give it to them* from the very first moments. But then, after the case is a few sessions in, every owner ends up telling every onlooker, "No really! Just last week and for the last 5 years, s/he was NEVER as good as this.... I am kicking myself that I didn't get the bad stuff on video, because it's not like there was any shortage of opportunities since every day was pretty bad!"

Hearing that for way too many years, and even saying it to myself way too many times, I finally came up with a mandatory video rule for all new cases. That said, I promise that you WILL forget to get video ahead of time. So the wise practitioner will have the owner take the video even before they meet you. Here is my video request form:

ALERT: IN ORDER TO INITIATE ANY NEW CASE WITH WILLING RESULTS, A VIDEO OF THE TROUBLING BEHAVIOR MUST BE SUBMITTED PRIOR TO BEGINNING CASE.

EXCEPTIONS:

> 1.   Cases where eliciting the troubling behavior puts the animal, handler, or camera person at risk of physical injury

> 2.   Behaviors that are "impossible to catch on camera" are also exempt.

But when you end up missing the shot, running out of battery on the video device, or just plain forgetting to hit the record button, as I do all the time, all I can say is, "Join the club." All of us OSCAR practitioners have the same self-described disease called *no videosis*. We've all felt its pain all too frequently. You'd think that we behavior reversal specialists would have solved our own bad behavior problem by now, but no such luck.

4.6 In All OSCAR Cases, Everyone's Safety Comes First

First, do no harm. As the therapist, achieving and maintaining safety must always be your top priority. You have to protect you and the other humans on the scene, but you also have to protect the animal from being mistakenly euthanized by its humans who are just trying to protect each other from the "incurably unsafe" animal you are there to repair.

One time, I was there to fix a horse with a trailer issue (I think.) During the first half hour of my OSCAR Assessment Exam, the owner said, "Oh, ummm, you might not want to be dealing with his ears." "How come?" I asked. Well, it wasn't his fault exactly, but the last person who dealt with his ears, he killed."

I stepped back. "Like dead killed?" "Yes, he broke her neck." I think it was just some kind of a freak accident reaction on his part, but..." "Ok, good to know," I said, "I know you were just trying to protect him by omitting that tidbit at the outset, but is there anything else interesting in his history that you might want to share?" There was nothing else.

If things had gone south again (and all because of a simple reflex) this animal would have been euthanized instead of being the great horse that he turned out to be. This client was terrific and a dedicated learner. But let this be a lesson: get all of the information you can, ahead of time. The animal's life *literally depends* on you not getting hurt by mistake while you are doing these repairs in Oscar's brain.

4.6.a Self Preservation 101: Acknowledge the Danger You Are In

Having electric eels and poisonous fish as patients in our animal hospital taught me once and for all that if you perceive the danger and do nothing to seriously lower your risk of getting killed, then your own ego and shortsightedness are just begging for Nature to teach you a lesson, and she will. Eventually, she will. So in this section, I'm going to be blunt. Life depends on it.

It just so happens that as a tool to stop the onslaughts of the eventualities of Nature, "hope" does not work all that well. If the thing you are relying on (to get you through the next part without injury) is *hope*, then that is hard evidence that you have skipped at least a step or two in your process. If you so much as imagine the words "I hope," then teach yourself to always follow that with, "What step have I skipped?"

If you routinely subject yourself to Oscar's fear and exasperated, frustration-induced chaos or anger, and if you don't get hurt or killed by Oscar's explosions, it's not because you are generally lucky or talented. If you didn't get "killed" by Oscar's dangerous actions, it's just that your number wasn't up on that day. Be convinced that your own safety is as imperative as Oscar's safety. For without you, who will be around to give Oscar the help s/he needs?

Yet injury is just one of a myriad of examples of how an Oscar can pose a danger. Think of your own Oscar. What real or potential dangers does Oscar face? What real or potential dangers do the people nearby face?

During an OSCAR conversation, you may become aware of problems you were not aware of in Oscar's past or in your own past; buried things bubble forth that need to be addressed. Through all of this, an unsafe You will also make Oscar very nervous, making it impossible for Oscar to learn much. Getting killed does not help the communication process at all. Neither does getting hurt.

Moreover, setting a dangerous example for observers to "learn from" is downright negligent. Every OSCAR Therapy practitioner must always have a way to safely *stop* engaging Oscar at any moment during your conversation; this fail-safe kill-switch or backdoor exit is not negotiable. If you don't have a safe and clear exit at all times, you need to stop what you're doing and create one so that you'll have it at the ready. Getting in (to a body or a brain) without being able to also get out, whenever you need to, is an extremely bad idea.

We teach OSCAR Therapy to anyone who wants to learn it, but we do not perform phobia reversal for any client without first giving these strict orders, "do not try this at home." Phobia reversal can be quite dangerous to you and to Oscar and to anyone who has not yet learned to practice it. In phobia reversal, the action goes much too fast and is much too hot for the novice person to attempt. I make no bones about it; phobia work can be dicey.

In the dangerous cases, punting, canceling, regrouping, and do overs are the tools that save lives. At Willing Results, LLC, I mandate that we all employ a three-strike rule. If any one risk has a likelihood of sinking us, then having two is pushing it, and having three is downright asinine. It's asinine because risk is avoidable.

In my experience, when the deck is stacked three "maybes" against you, you can no longer actually do the math on calculating the likelihood of a session going bad. When three main factors are even *potentially* working against you, the likelihood of it all working out in the end with forward progress is no more than 30 percent. It's more like 20 percent. And those odds are just stupidly low.

If lives are not really in danger yet, but you still press forward with bad odds, then you just can't call yourself an expert; you don't know how to plan better to prevent eventualities. Even if you are not putting others at risk, you'll be risking the safety of the rescue crew who has to get all involved in the stupid thing you've created. On your tombstone it will say "stupid, shortsighted, selfish" and no one will ever be calling you a hero. If you ever were a hero previously, your good name will very likely be overwritten and updated. Literally, you're only as good as your most recent safety measure.

In my work, I don't even qualify the risks; I only count them. Bad wind? One strike. Bad footing? Two strikes. Bad reflexes on the part of Oscar? Three strikes. And I call the game on account of strikes, even without any rain.

Here's another example: challenging patient + my own recently sprained pinky finger + owner in tears. That is enough to postpone a session. The owner is capable of doing something rash, and I'll only have one hand to save them. The commotion makes Oscar nervous and now shows up with teeth bared near someone's eye, and even though it was just an accident, a perfectly warm sunny day turns lethal. It doesn't matter what KIND of strikes they are, it just matters how many unwavering "poor steady states" you can count.

And when you are open-minded, you'll be able to count them. Murphy knew something about dangerous animals: "Whatever CAN go wrong WILL go wrong." But if you have no experience in this bad physical or social or medical "weather," when you can't even tell the difference between a rock and a hard place, then may your God protect the drunks and fools. But even when you really don't have any ability to qualify or quantify the immediate risks that are happening around you, then you only have one final angel on your shoulder... you have your blink reflex.

No matter what all is happening, no matter how safe you think you are or will be, I tell you now, that if your eyes are not blinking normally, if you are wide-eyed, if you have a steady stare in any way, then what is about to go down in the immediate future is NOT going to go as you have calculated it to go. If you are not able to pause enough to blink, then you are not able to pause enough to accurately assess. And if you cannot assess, then may the force be with you, because nothing else is going to be. Nature does not care at all about your plan.

If all else fails, you'll know when you are in too deep by your heart rate. Any thumping at all and you are truly, and quite objectively, asking for trouble. If your heart rate is elevated, (even when you think everything is safe and easy) it's because you are about to get hurt, and your heart rate is the big red flag trying to stop what you're doing. It's trying to force you to use a different approach.

So just stop what you're doing until your eyes are blinking again and your heart rate is not elevated. A huge exhale will pour out of you soon after. And then you'll see the thing that was just about ready to hurt you.

Finding yourself in too deep is going to happen now and again, but don't let the same "almost" happen twice. There is always a way to ensure that you don't get trapped that same way again in the future. Find it.

4.6.b Attendant Wisdom: Before Assisting Others, Fix Your Own Map First

As the airplane flight attendants are wise to point out, you really will not be able to help others put on their own oxygen mask if you are bereft of oxygen yourself. In fact, your hypoxic flailing about will probably do more harm than good. And the OSCAR Therapist's role is no different. If you yourself cannot personally take a big step to your left, for instance, then how will you be able to help somebody else learn to step to *their* right, to meet you there in the middle? (We face the same way that Oscar is facing, like in basic line dancing or cheerleading, explained later in this chapter.)

A hopefully obvious aspect to being an OSCAR Therapist is that if you are going to use your own body in space to teach another brain about their own body in space, then the body you're using should be one that is fairly neutral, balanced, forgiving, and especially, not offensive. There is no point in trying to build somebody else's Oscar map when your own map is out of whack. Because if you are measuring with an out-of-balance measuring tool, then all the measurements you make with it will be wrong.

The best way to find out if your own clock is out of whack is to find another Oscar therapist and ask them to test you out. Remember, if you are looking through warped colored glasses, then even your own assessments of your own map will be wrong. But when any missing pieces of your own pie are pointed out to you, you'll see it right away.

If you have gaps, bulges, or wrinkles in your own OSCAR clock, you'll be spreading those biases all around, either seeing them in places in the world where they do not actually exist or not seeing them when they do. Do everything you can to get rid of every bias you have; unlearn them. And do not take on a challenging OSCAR case until you are fairly well balanced yourself.

The hard fact is that you will need to be able to instantly step out of harm's way when you are near OSCAR's flailing, learning body. And if you cannot do that because there are certain directions in which you are anxious to move toward, then the next injury caused by this disadvantaged Oscar may just happen to your very own body. Even though you think you're the teacher, you could wind up the victim.

It is important to note however that OSCAR Therapy is brainwork, not bodywork. So it is *not* necessary to have a good functioning *body* in order to be a good OSCAR Therapist. What *is* necessary is to be able to *imagine using* the good functioning body, *in you first*, and in Oscar second. And if you are directing a proxy person to do the Oscar rehabilitation work you cannot physically do yourself, then your imagination has to be even more tuned in and well-balanced.

4.6.c Be Able to Exit from STAGE RIGHT and STAGE LEFT:

When you need to move away from someone else, in order to get your own self to safety, you have to be able to exit *or leave the scene off of* Oscar's left side, and you have to be able to exit or leave the scene off of Oscar's right side. Just like actors coming from and going back to different sides of stage, we animals need to be able to do this same thing around each other; otherwise, we find ourselves *feeling* socially "cornered," regardless of whether Oscar is actually trying to threaten us *or not.*

And you'd think this would be a no-brainer, but it's not. Just yesterday, I was teaching this Disengage skill to a client, and we were in my favorite place for this kind of work, a big empty dirt floor indoor arena under a roof. (In here, there are no shadows cast by the sun to confuse matters.)

On this huge dirt floor, it was very obvious to me that this woman was much weaker on her Disengage to the left. Her Disengage to the right was very strong and very effective, but her disengaging from me off of my 10 o'clock was pretty unconvincing. I had already spent a few minutes explaining her missing piece and showing her the effects of it, but she still quite couldn't feel where it was going wrong.

After we had been out there a while, from the side of the arena, comes trotting in a tubby orange tabby cat, the kind of barn cat that is always bored with chasing mice... Barn cats are usually sort of ignored by people too, so they are often looking to be part of things. Anyway, this barn cat came over to see what we were doing, as if he were sort of sucked into the game from afar, and I suggested that my client just walk away from him to tell him not to bother us. What a dope I was, because I almost missed an amazing opportunity.

As she walked away from the cat off of the cat's right, he followed her, as if attached by a leash. When the cat was "in tow" about 10 feet behind her, I asked her to swap sides and walk away from the cat on the cat's left. As soon as she crossed past the angle in line with the cat's 12 o'clock, the cat would stop walking, and sometimes sit, or sometimes walk away from her. This random cat, who showed up to this conversation of his own accord, was now playing my role for me, and showing my client that the left side of her is what attracted another brain, while the right side of her, had no "social Velcro" at all.

The barn cat was curious enough about this person long enough for about 25 side–swap Disengages. She proceeded to lose the cat off of her own 4:30 o'clock just about every time. I was grateful for the demonstration of the fact that "this is not something I invented, it's "a confounding effect" you have on anyone in your midst, but only on your right-hand side."

This client did have a chronic injury in her ankle on her right leg that affected her balance somewhat, but it had healed long ago, and I wondered... Did her "out of balance" stem from her old injury? Or, did her old original injury to the right side of her originally stem from her being out of balance in her body's expression of her own Will on that side? Accident-prone people are often just brains that are *motion-triggered* and OSCAR-dented.

4.6.d Begin With a Barrier Fence and Other Safety Tips

Regardless of how physically fit and/or spatially balanced you are, always remember the reason that you have come to meet this individual in the first place. It's because people are afraid to be around this individual, or this individual is afraid to be around people, or around himself/herself in certain contexts, and with very good reason. Oscar cases usually have become quite toxic, leaving desperate owners to go looking for help. And when most kinds of sought help have been tried and failed, Oscar's individual brain can become even more wary of new strangers. This all leaves the owner that much closer to throwing in the towel.

Far and away the worst day of any Oscar case is day number one, session number one. The suspicious new client has no frame of reference for what you do or what OSCAR Therapy is. At the beginning of many cases, even the new Oscar is looking at you with fire behind their eyes. Not only does your timing have to be more than perfect but you also have to be splitting your focus. You need to be verbally explaining everything you're doing so that the owner has a chance to understand the problems you are (or are not yet) spotting.

The reality is that no individual will be helped if you don't get called back a second time. That's why it is very important to make session number one, and all early sessions, as risk-free and as productive as possible for all participants including owners, onlookers, Oscar, your helpers, and yourself. So even for the animals that are reported to be non-aggressive and generally safe, on day one we have to take nothing on faith.

As soon as we begin asking Oscar questions about Oscar's ability to understand the normal array of interface angles, suddenly the truth comes out; very often, they can't. This can immediately summon nips and snaps or kicks and strikes that are "totally out of character." The real fact of the matter is that the owner cannot see what may be lurking just under the surface in the anxious Oscar brain. An Achilles's Heel can be exposed to the light on Day 1 in just a few minutes, so the animals can feel newly raw, like a big secret is now "exposed."

Because it's just plain better to have the first few sessions be totally under control, and because we need to be able to hit the pause button on the action quite frequently in order to explain the unfamiliar OSCAR approach, I often need the Oscar brains to be physically separated from me, on the other side of a fence I can reach over or through.

The fence separates us up until the time that the animal thinks of me as a new best friend. Usually that only takes a session or two to achieve, but some animals have a look in one eye or the other that is just so dead and spooky that I have to remember my rule about my own heart rate. If anything about this animal is making me exhale deeper than usual, the fence stays up.

Fences are your friends. Whether they are cement walls (note that cement can be unforgiving when kicked hard), thick barn board, split rail, chain link, baby gates, flimsy stall guards, or even a rope or a clothes line strung across the threshold between you, it's extremely helpful if not essential for both Oscar and the therapist to feel protected from the other. I have even stood behind a few trees in my time, because it's incredible how much even the biters do not want to bite into tree bark.

One horse I worked with had to slam her shoulder into a 4 x 4 vertical roof-supporting beam for 10 minutes straight in order to realize that she was inadvertently falling into an imaginary hole at 11 o'clock on her OSCAR map. I was so glad that the hardwood was there to take the brunt of that action, so that I didn't have to. That's the other big reason we give Oscar a presence-absorbing barrier. Not only does it protect us from them, it also protects *them* from the *eventual* us, meaning the euthanasia wrath we humans tend to unleash right after someone has been inadvertently badly hurt by a reacting animal.

But all of these fences bring with them one obvious problem: from behind the fence, now it's harder to reach out toward Oscar. And if Oscar cannot reach you, then the game is over even before it gets a chance to start.

So this is the time I pull out my handy dandy toilet plunger, the one that each new client has been staring at in horror ever since I arrived. No, not the one from my actual bathroom, but the one I bought (I promise) at the hardware store in the plumbing aisle. For just a few dollars, you too can own your very own perfectly weighted target pole not unlike the tools seen in dolphin and sea lion training session videos. But my cheap one is one that no one, and I mean no one, will ever want to steal. Get ones with a wooden handle. Not only are they easier to grip, but also OSCAR animals need to chomp these things sometimes, and biting on plastic handles just doesn't work.

I hold the stick end. I hold it so that the plunger end is aiming right near the owner's hand, at about 1 inch from their hand. When they happen to bump into the rubber bell on accident, I give them some of what's in my pocket. Not rocket science. After the owner understands the game, I offer the same game to the animal, and all animals figure it out within a short minute.

If your target pole isn't long enough then fashion something on an extender pole. Regarding the rubber bell end of the plunger, I find that this pliable but firm, large object is the best and safest way in to a freaked out Oscar brain.

At the start, it's hollow center offers just a wide "circle of sort-of-contact" that is better and safer to use than anything smaller, pointed, or hard. At the outset it's better for any nervous system to let Oscar "paint with a wide but empty brush." The more non-specific the contact is, the better; because any contact from Oscar is scary enough already, to them. (Don't actually paint anything on anyone.)

There are some additional safety tips for OSCAR sessions. For instance, unless and until its presence is extremely mandatory, all equipment on Oscar's body will work against you in any OSCAR session. Blankets and coats are never allowed in session, leg wraps have to go. Leashes, lead lines and leverages of any kind are never allowed. Hair over the animal's eyes also needs to be pulled back into a braid, clip, or elastic band. The animal's brain has a hard enough time without having to also triangulate around all this junk in the way.

The same goes for extraneous stuff on the part of the therapist. Long hair that is not tied up seriously gets in the way of your field of view, especially in your peripheral vision, which is critical to your success in OSCAR sessions. Floppy sleeves and flapping jackets get in the way. And anybody who works with animals routinely knows that jewelry, especially earrings, is an accident waiting to happen. A tight wristwatch may be ok, but bracelets would have to go.

Cages and small, confined areas usually work against the process; more space is usually better than less space. But don't think that you'll have to chase Oscar all around. If you are doing OSCAR correctly, the learning brain will be seeking you out instead of fleeing your area. In fact, it is a well-known aspect of OSCAR therapy that no matter how large the arena, and no matter how large the species, the OSCAR brain will quite often seek out walls, especially corners of walls, on which to lean. Animals choose to lean on these walls in order to balance themselves in unfamiliar, and newfound cognitive space. Even flighty species will bring me to the corner of any room.

In all cases of all species, beware of their huge footfalls and ultra wide sidesteps. For animals who have never reached into these new spaces before, they don't know how to do it and they don't know their own size toward that vector until they learn from trial and error. Until I learned to jump out of the way like a jackrabbit, I couldn't quite believe that even though the animal was way over there they were still stepping on my feet way over here. This knowledge makes me happy that I don't work with large, winged birds. I can imagine being knocked over a lot in an Oscar session with a swan.

Lastly, we have to talk about the sun. Overcast drizzly days are my favorite kind of weather because brainwork goes measurably faster on days like this. In weather where everything has the same brightness with less contrast, animals worry just a little bit less about spatial dimensions. It's just you and the animal, and you get to work.

But when the sun is bright and when eyeballs and irises have to adjust to sun patches and shade, shadow and light, the brain has to do even more work. Back in the day, I didn't know why yet, but it felt like OSCAR cases were somewhat more unpredictable when we worked in the bright sunlight. It was like there was some third-party ghost hanging around who was giving the animal a whole other set of questions, cues, and rules. I couldn't figure out why I seemed to be playing second fiddle when no one else was even there.

I finally got frustrated enough to start tracking why and how animals were erring. It turns out that the third party players in the OSCAR sessions were sunbeams. When an animal learns a new spatial interface, for the first few times they practice it, animals will insist that they be allowed to rotate into the same position *in relation to the sun* that they were in when they learned it a few minutes back. It's like their eye/foot coordination has a light meter on it, which gets locked into short-term memory. If the sun isn't in the same spot it was when they had the good idea, they get lost in space, and their good idea suddenly seems "wrong" to them.

Sun today has nothing to do with behavior tomorrow; it only means that today, you have to "watch the boom." Just like tacking into the wind on a sailboat, when the mainsail boom (beam) flips over, you need to duck or you'll get knocked overboard. Just like this, animals will flip to match the sun memory from a minute ago, and if you don't see it coming, you could get inadvertently hip checked. On sunny days, try to keep rotation to a minimum or be very ready to jump out of the way.

4.6.e Extra Safety Measures With Horses

1. At all times, provide access to close-at-hand drinking water.
2. Weather: guard against mud and wind; both are hazards.
3. OSCAR work must always be done with the HORSE AT LIBERTY.
4. Have a pal horse nearby if possible, for company, if horse is anxious.
5. List ALL known risks / hazards ahead of time.
6. Does s/he strike?
7. Does s/he barrel kick? Does s/he cow kick?
8. Does s/he mow you down or plow through you?
9. Does s/he bite? Adding spikey surfaces on what they bite at does help them learn that biting is the least good option.

4.6.f Extra Safety Measures With Dogs

1. At all times, provide access to close-at-hand drinking water.
2. OSCAR work is done with DOG AT LIBERTY, in home or in large outside enclosure.
3. Dogs must be free to move around.
4. Have NO other dogs nearby or within sight during session
5. List ALL known risks / hazards ahead of time
6. Does s/he mow you down or plow through you?
7. Does s/he bite you? Bite others?
8. Muzzled dogs must be able to eat and drink and pant while wearing the "teeth restraint."
9. Very thin threaded metal rod target poles work better with biters than muzzles. When dog bites on safe but noxious metallic threads with own lips, s/he learns faster that biting is the least good option.

4.6.g Where Can I OSCAR? Any Safe Area Can Be an OSCAR Session Location

Many clients are very happy to hear that having "facilities" is just not a prerequisite to the OSCAR Therapy session. Any practical standing or sitting area works just fine. The only real environmental need is that the ground you are on be relatively flat and relatively free of tripping hazards.** OSCAR is a little like slow dancing at arms length; you will be moving around as the animal moves but neither of you will be looking at your feet, so it's better when you both don't trip on something and fall down.

Personally, I prefer areas that are shaded from direct sun so that I can see Oscar without the influence of shadow lines, but the animals never seem to care about shade. Also, whenever possible, turn any nearby electric fences off, because sometimes in OSCAR sessions, you both might just have to mildly lean up against that fence.

And speaking of fence lines, any OSCAR session may collect a peanut gallery of on-looking, mesmerized, and jealous neighboring animals. According to many of my clients, the most heart-breaking part of OSCAR Therapy is watching the on-looking animals out of the corners of their eyes. These are the animals who belong to other people but wish they belonged to you as soon as they see how engaging and fun and rewarding this game is to play.

Horse Case OSCAR Session Locations:
1. Stall guard across open stall door with horse inside, person outside
2. Small paddock or indoor: flat, no mud, remove all HUMAN trip hazards
3. In stall: well lit, flat, no trip hazards, all bedding must be pushed over to the wall so ground is as flat as possible
4. Portion of empty aisle way (I often clip cross ties together to act as a mild visual barrier)
5. Work across split rail fence if horse is a hazard.
6. Work through TALL round pen fence at first if horse is vicious.

Dog Case OSCAR Session Locations:
1. Sit on floor or ground with dog
2. Sit on hassock next to dog
3. Sit on couch with dog also on couch
4. Use baby gate if biting is a hazard
5. Work across chain link fence at first if dog is vicious

Note: ALL animals (you too!) must always have free-choice WATER available INSIDE the animal's OSCAR Therapy session area. Hydration is what keeps all brains in the learning mode.

4.7 The OSCAR Game

In any sort of relationship, it's a pretty *good* idea to approve of someone right from the get go and for almost no good reason at all. That's an initial pearl of wisdom about how kindness works. But, just as true, it's also a pretty *bad* idea to bring enough of your own presence to bear so that you can *touch* someone who hasn't been allowed to touch you first.

That's the second pearl of wisdom about the inner workings of kindness. A teacher can add approval or gifts to any situation for no good reason at all, just to get a communication ball rolling, but presence is NOT to be added like this. Any presence that *is not first invited* is usually, and rightly, considered to be an intrusion.

The OSCAR Therapy game is all about encouraging Oscars to come up with their own unique path toward developing *that initial invitation*. And since most of the "work" in the game is done by Oscar himself or herself, anyone and everyone from A to Z can learn how to play the role of the receiver (or the practitioner) in the OSCAR game. Below, I'll use the shorthand descriptions, but if you don't understand parts of this list yet, don't worry.

All ages, all genders, all income levels, all disciplines, all education levels, all backgrounds from prisoner to CEO, all languages, all species, all of these individuals learn OSCAR just fine. And OSCAR can even be done by those with most medical limitations. With a digital interface, people could even do it from a hospital bed.

Here's the cut-to-the-chase, quick and dirty, short-list, recipe description of how to initiate an OSCAR Therapy session/conversation.

1. Choose your Oscar. Choose safer Oscars first, harder Oscars later.
2. Get ready to pay Oscar for working hard to understand you.
3. Protect everyone's safety.
4. THOU SHALT NOT TOUCH Oscar!
5. Use Operant Conditioning to teach Oscar to push your button.
6. Reward Oscar for reaching out to touch you with all points on body.
7. Discover who Oscar actually IS, for the first time; reward exhales.
8. Try some game-coupled-to-goal scenarios.
9. Discover what Oscar CAN ACTUALLY accomplish, for the first time.
10. Understand.

Now here is how I give those same quick and dirty instructions to other professional behaviorists who will be working starter cases or difficult cases:

> *OSCAR is a contact-based OC game. But it uses the exact opposite dynamic of every other modality you can name. With OSCAR, don't reward for letting <u>you</u> touch them; the rewards come only from <u>them</u> touching you (your hand is the target)... with every single part of their body, bit by bit. And when you find a hot spot, a spot they won't touch with, then build every single angle of contact from there, up, down, sideways, inwards, 360 degrees.*
>
> *At the outset, and then again if a zone is too hot/toxic/dangerous /inaccessible, please put a buffer in between you and that zone, like a fence, and use an extender pole to represent your hand. Concave rubber bell drain plungers work best for the starting phase. Once it's safe to get in there, build it up, and don't forget to build your interior angles, muscles that pull body parts inward, tucking toward the core/midline because when those are missing, behavior gets nutty and too large.*
>
> *Allow for rest, flashbacks, and crazy reactions at first, and jackpot the exhales. Allow a minimum of 48 hrs recovery time whenever possible. Avoid sugar, fats, or aromatic oils; use staple foods. For Oscar it's not about the commodity; their reward comes from the empowerment of self-control, and finally understanding how to relate to others. When Oscar gains this language, their guessing games are over, thought is engaged, PTSD is recovered, and safety skyrockets.*

OSCAR Therapy can very easily (and fairly) be described as a game. Except that in *this* game, both sides win. OSCAR is never about asking permission for you to touch them; it's always about inviting them to touch you.

The game is thus: "Oscar, I dare you to use this here bit of your body to reach out and touch this here button (and also untouch it) in a rational manner. And the first rule of the game, regardless of whether it's Oscar the Horse, Oscar the Dog, Oscar the Human, or whatever species you want to talk to, **the main rule of the OSCAR Game is this:**

Thou SHALT NOT touch Oscar...

...until Oscar reaches out and touches you.

The concept of the "OSCAR button" touch, the touch we are looking for, involves the *idea* of a Tymbal button. You might know this kind of button as the totally addictive pop-o-matic bubble button in the middle of the kid's table game *Trouble*, or the shrewdly addictive "Easy" button from *Staples*, the office supply superstores. But the Tymbal "button" you probably experience every day is the one on the end of any ballpoint clicky pen.

A Tymbal button not only acknowledges you audibly, but also physically, because of the pop-o-matic, two-beat d-donk you feel and hear when... first you press it, and then *it presses you*. But in OSCAR Therapy we do the opposite –first it's them, then it's you. They touch you causing you to then match their amount of press with one of your own, just like two "fingers" pushing on each other, each giving the other something it can feel.

It does not matter what portion of your hand you use as your button. In the beginning, some people find it easier to use a closed fist or back of the hand as the button because it helps them remember to never pat or touch Oscar first. Later, I encourage OSCAR therapists to flip the hand around and use the butt of the hand or even the whole palmar surface as their button. We have many more sensory nerves there and our sensitivity (our ability to tell the different between more and less) is at its highest through that particular surface. So it helps the work move along faster.

Oscar's body is to lean in and touch you (your button), making the first beat from your imaginary Tymbal button, and then you match it with your own press-in at nearly the very same time, just with your own microsecond delay because it takes just a splash of time for your nervous system to register that Oscar initiated a contact. And when you push on each other (sometimes with only the weight of a butterfly wing) you do *not* touch them after they touch you, you touch them <u>because</u> they are touching you.

The result is that Oscar is pressing the button at basically the same moment that you are. You are *touching* each other at the same point in space, at the same time, much like touching one's own reflection in a mirror. But the very important additional point is that just like that ballpoint pen, the button also makes a sound come out of your mouth, so that the button is not only something Oscar can feel but it's also something that Oscar can *hear*. When Oscar touches you, it makes a "Good" come out of your mouth, maybe even followed by a gift of payment.

And that's the game; that's all it is. Basically, what we've created here is an animal version of an all-body-points fist bump. And it's the most effective communication tool I've ever seen in all my many decades working with the brains of other species. (High fives are obnoxious; fist bumps are encouraging.)

Your second session will make much more sense to all involved. Everyone's participation will be much more voluntary after all brains have slept on the game for a night or two. Freaked out animals need just one overnight to catch up to the game, but relatively normal animals will master the game inside one session. Freaked out or not, all animals catch on to the above-stated *rules* of the game within five minutes.

If you "do OSCAR wrong," if you attempt to play the OSCAR game while breaking its very few rules, it literally will not work because when you break the rules of OSCAR, you are breaking the laws of social, biological nature. Luckily though, when you break the rules of social nature, you will know it right away, because any animal will leave the session outright. When you do them wrong, animals won't even bother to mug you for your treats; they'll just walk away.

Since the animals in OSCAR sessions are usually at liberty, they are always free to leave the session. When animals are at liberty that's how you know that they are participating by choice, and not for any other reason. It's also how we know when an animal's brains are full; when they are spent, they begin to meander. To keep Oscar interested in playing this game at an efficient rate of speed (even as we are learning to play it ourselves) we pay Oscar for playing. (See Payment, Chapter 6) And you can even use increasing values of poker chips, as brains work harder and harder.

Humans by and large find OSCAR to be a hilarious game, and animals seem to love OSCAR more than anything else they do with us. But that doesn't mean that OSCAR is all about fun and games. It's hard-core rehab. When brains are allowed to reach out and be "the toucher," maybe for the first time in a very long time, if ever, it's an *extremely new* if not unprecedented experience for them.

The novel experience is often seen to hit animals even on an electrical level at the beginning. New Oscars can act like a bag of bees... just nervous energy looking for a conduit. Why, even two days ago I got smacked in the head by a nervous horse in session #1.

Upon Oscar's first ever considered contact, you may even see an Oscar experiencing an obvious electric jolt that looks like anything from a mild localized zap to a strong, whole-body, jarring lightning bolt of some kind. There are no actual sparks like the ones you see in low humidity winter weather, but internally, Oscar feels those sparks nonetheless. And with every passing try, what the body part is obviously feeling abates and softens in a progression of lessening, from shock to "stinging" to mild irritation to normalcy.

In OSCAR Therapy, you allow others to (safely) bounce off of you, in order to find out about you both. And just like a tree, you can hold out any of your limbs in varied ways that change your fixed-in-place shape, in order to alter Oscar's experience of what touching a human is like. You can even make your "branches" be any shape you can muster. Be that tree; you can be a transplantable tree that can roll around on your own two feet, but trees never reach out and touch or grab Oscar.

Suffice it to say; when you have good Presence yourself and then you allow Oscar to collide with you, you'll have close access to Oscar's trouble spots. And you'll also have an Oscar who will be able to use you, like a tree branch or like a toothpick to help him/her expose what s/he needs to let out into the light of day. So your Presence has to be mild enough for you to be used as someone else's tool. Allowing your Presence to be used in OSCAR Therapy will make it possible for you to diagnose and fix a ton of what's wrong with Oscar, close up and personal.

The final important point before launching into the "how to's" is this: **PLEASE READ THIS ENTIRE BOOK BEFORE YOUR FIRST ATTEMPT AT USING OSCAR Therapy**. Many of the safety considerations and clear communication instructions that are critical to already know about *at the very beginning* of <u>many</u> OSCAR cases are only discussed later on in this book. And since every brain is different, you'll be the best one to know which of those instructions might apply to the Oscars you'll be working with. That said; let's get to it...

4.7.a Where on Oscar's Body Is Button #1?

Any location at all on Oscar's body is a fine place to begin an OSCAR Therapy conversation. But unless it's unsafe to do so, the quickest and most *efficient* place to start is on one side of the face, or on one side of the neck. Unless a large phobia or a danger to either participant is a factor, the front part of the body is the easiest (and least frustrating) part from which any animal can quickly learn the game. Mainly this is because everything you need to start the game is close at hand: Oscar's eyes and mouth. When Oscar successfully hits a button or two, s/he has earned one reward.

After all, the chewing part of the animal is right there within a short distance from the action. The farther the mouth gets from your button, the more running back and forth a person needs to do to hand over earned rewards, and/or the more spinning or bending the animal would have to do in order to be able to reach your reward. Basically, the straighter the animal is, the better. Remember this rhyme: a straight dog is a great dog; a straight horse is a great horse, etc.

When animals can see your button hand without the need for a rear view mirror, it's easier for them to learn the game. Additionally, when Oscars are touching you a little too hard with their denser parts, the straighter animal often learns quickly that softer touches (on their part) are best for everyone involved.

But, often enough, when animals are understandably phobic of using any part of their front end to make contact with humans, you may not have access to any of the front end at all. Sometimes the only body part an animal can imagine touching you with is a butt cheek, sometimes only a shin, and sometimes only a chin is what you get, as it clonks you on top of your head. The animal is trying to muster up any way s/he can to touch you, and in the beginning you have to take anything (any part) you can get.

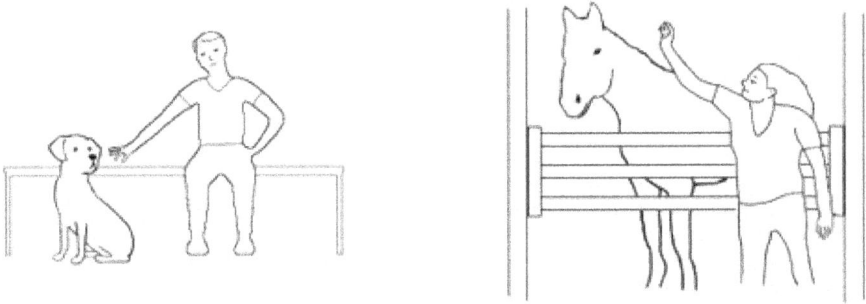

Figure 15: Easiest way to begin the OSCAR game in the majority of cases

If Oscar will allow it, the OSCAR diagnostic process calls for running an all systems quick check on the entire brain-body map. We check the front head and neck, followed by a quick lateral line along the *widest* part of the animal. I call this interface zone the "wide line" or the "waterline," and it is marked with blue dots (w) in the diagram below.

If you were to float Oscar's body shape in water as if it were a toy boat, think about to what depth in the water it would float. This waterline does NOT follow the spine or any skeletal structures. This is the "social interface" map, remember. Just like a cue ball does not touch all the other balls on the pool table with its top or its lower regions, bodies touch each other most often on their widest parts.

If Oscar will allow it, the green dots (t) below show that we also run a "tilted dorsal plane" line which is about 30 degrees off midline. The red dots below (b) show that we then run a "belly/ventral/interior line," which is about 15 degrees off midline. Usually one of those two non-horizontal lines will be worse than the other... scarier for Oscar. We run the easier line first and the harder one last.

After both sides are quick checked this way, it will be obvious to all observers present just which 3-D quadrants of front to back, side to side, and top to bottom, roughly, Oscar is missing in the brain-body map. Digging into the specifics of the missing zones is where the Therapy comes in. Any ultra-specific diagnostic testing and then the actual therapy itself will then involve what I call "slicing the bread loaf." We follow the upper arrow below to check the animal with buttons that are moving away from the wide waterline toward the ceiling. Then we follow the lower arrow, checking all that is below the waterline toward the floor.

We test all the way up to just shy of the dorsal spine, and all the way down to the midline on the belly (ventral) side, or as far as we can reach with an arm or an extension tool. The arrows show that we are checking transverse slices of the whole height of the animal. Basically, that means that we are checking everything related to one vertebra at a time. Once we know all about that slice (*on that side only*), we move over one bread slice and check the one next.

Note that this is the time, during the bread slicing, that we also check the associated limb. In the diagram below, the red button dots that would travel down the inside of the left hind leg (which would be not visible on the drawing) are shown instead on the inside of the right leg. Even though they are within reach, try not to check the locations on the other side of the body from the one you're working on. Especially in the beginning of an OSCAR exam, when an Oscar is still anxious, engaging both sides of the animal usually causes a feeling of over stimulated and/or trapped claustrophobia. Oscar might feel the need to flee in an outburst.

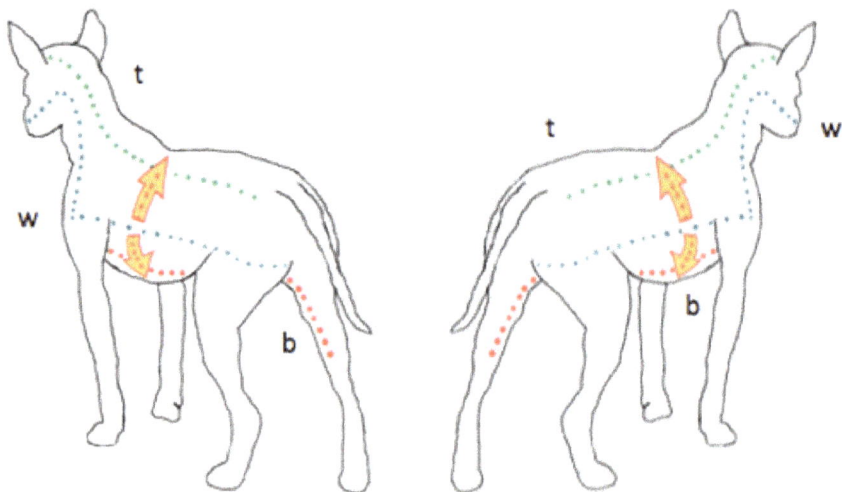

Figure 16: Typical OSCAR Exam Guidelines for Seeking Ruleouts

It makes no difference whether you start your diagnostics or your therapy on Oscar's right or left side, but on one of those sides Oscar will find the game easier; so that's where you should begin. And once you have spent some time on the first side, try not to switch sides during the same session unless you are doing specific work about the midline. When you have lit up the Christmas tree of nerve endings on one side, it's unnecessarily difficult for the brain to *not* keep lighting up those new-today pathways even though you've moved to a brand new side of the body. For example, if you switch sides to now ask for a left foot, OSCAR will keep giving you the right foot that you already asked for many times already in today's session.

Teaching Oscar to discriminate which side an invisible button is on comes later in Oscar's therapy. (An example might be when you are in a saddle, asking a horse to reach UP with the alternating front legs that are required in some Olympic level dressage moves or in other fancy movement skills like the Spanish Walk.) Any time Oscar is very confused by the location of your request of a contact point, be patient, it will come pretty soon. But any time

Oscar's *unwanted behavior escalates* because of a request that you made for a contact point, it means that you have likely hit upon an OSCAR-troubled body part.

Note that if any individual (humans included) is missing three or four different zones, like someone who is missing 10, 2, 3 and 5 o'clock, then this individual has likely elevated to a different level of trouble in life because of new survival mechanisms that have kicked in. The brain is no dummy. Such a brain will have accurately *generalized* that all interaction is risky and it has learned to avoid or refuse all engagement. This brain's *totally rational* answers for most questions would either be to evade or to preemptively attack in self-defense.

With a brain like this, it would be appropriate to forego any assessment diagnostics and launch right into building the OSCAR map. And if you were to start in with this specific brain from the previous paragraph, take a guess as to which body part of this particular Oscar (10,2,3,5) is most likely to come and push your button first... If you guessed 6:30 or 7:00 on Oscar's clock face, or Oscar's left butt cheek, you're right on the money.

Regarding cases that are mostly missing *interior* OSCAR angles (discussed later), we still have to do all of the exterior "clock work" first. So the approach described here in this section is usually the best way to start.

Warning:

Do NOT reward Oscar by using *ANY FORM OF TOUCH OR PHYSICAL CONTACT* <u>during</u> any and every OSCAR Therapy session. No petting, no patting, no hugging, no kissing, no reaching out and touching of any kind!

(On a break, it's ok to make contact with a small OFF-STAGE body part only, and only if necessary.)

The overarching rule is that you are not allowed to touch Oscar at all during session time. Oscar and Oscar's muscles must be the ones doing *all* of the reaching out and touching. Be the tree branch, the stanchion, the solid beam that Oscar bumps into but be only that. Breaking this rule will set the case back a bit because it usually corroborates/justifies Oscar's phobia that "the world is always touching me before I can touch it."

4.7.b Mimic the Exhale (and Give Three)

You know of the coffee break, you know of the cigarette break, but you should also know about the much smarter idea called the "exhaling break." This is what those other two kinds of breaks are really for anyway. It could be a great boon to the "break the habit" industry if cigarette smokers could find something to exhale that didn't first have to be inhaled, because the exhale is the money piece. The exhale is a very powerful tool indeed.

If I ask you to push a button and I give you money every time you push it, normally, you would opt to push that button more and more. If I ask you to push a button and I give you money every time you push it, *but you opt to flee the scene instead*, we say that this is an abnormal choice. We deduce that there must be / is something *significant* getting in the way of your clear opportunity for obvious gain. And since excavating the buried reasons for these significant barriers is heavy-lift work for any brain to do, when Oscar seems *worn-out* from all of the re-processing during OSCAR sessions, it's because s/he *is* worn-out.

Every single brain that learns via OSCAR Therapy will be observed to and heard to exhale and exhale deeply. When any of us learn something challenging, at certain times that our brains designate, we let out a big sigh. Sometimes these sighs express pent-up worry that can finally dissipate. Sometimes these sighs express brain drain that comes from thinking hard. And sometimes these sighs express a resignation to (or a new awareness of...) a new reality. What I tell clients is that each exhale is like the mainframe of a computer rebooting itself, re-starting on fresh, new circuitry.

Just as these big, passive, full exhales (which sound like a fully deflating bag)

are true for us, they are also equally true for all animals with lungs. An exhale is an exhale, across the board. The record for OSCAR session #1 in my cases to date is 13 real (not mimicked) deep sigh exhales over the course of 1.5 hours. Now that is a lot of pent up anxiety pouring out, wouldn't you say?

It is true that most of us "teachers" are often unconscious yet determined breath holders; humans hope with bated breath. But it is also true that *anyone* who does not breathe, especially while they are waiting for someone else to change, has a much-reduced prognosis for survival. It's one thing to save yourself before you can save someone else; it's quite another thing to wait for someone else to save themselves before you can save yourself. You could be waiting there a long time. If you stop eating or sleeping or moving or *breathing* in lieu of "something happening," then the only one who's going to suffer is you.

So this is a rare time when teaching via mimicry is not only helpful but also necessary. But in *this* application, you are the one that needs to be the mimic. When I have a human client who is routinely forgetting to breathe, I remind that person of a very clear directive about dealing with Oscar. It is a solid rule that is always true, without exception, and no matter the circumstance. And here it is: Whenever you hear Oscar let out a deep exhale, you must immediately follow suit.

Every time Oscar exhales deeply, you must do the same, right away. (You should also hand Oscar a reward and then another and then another. Exhales should earn 3 separate rewards in a row, every time; that's how very valuable exhales are. And that's how to also make sure that you are giving Oscar the few moments of break that s/he has created and earned.)

When you exhale deeply, at a socio-biological level, you are not projecting frustration or weakness. When you exhale deeply you are expressing, "I have just learned something," and the learning ought to be allowed a moment or two to sink in. When *you* mirror an exhale, you are indicating that you just learned about Oscar too. And you are opting to "second the motion," literally.

Even if you have no breath in you, snap one up and get rid of it. It's that important. This is not an option. This is mandatory. Even with an Oscar who has a ton of authority over you, if you do this, s/he will unconsciously calm down a bit, but more importantly, so will you. In Yoga, you can exhale for no good reason at all. But in OSCAR Therapy, you must exhale on command, as a knee jerk response, without thinking, every time you hear the sound of deflating lungs.

Rewards to Use in OSCAR Therapy

Since a physical contact interface is the one we're building, touching them during session is out. Try very hard to not use touch-based praise: no pats, no scratching, nada. Never forget the first rule of OSCAR Therapy: Thou Shalt Not Touch Oscar.

If you're using food(s) as rewards, use clean whole foods. Use no or low sugar and salt, and avoid processed food, because you're going to be using quite a bit of it. The tinier the food bits, the better, within reason.

For the toughest cases of picky eaters, you'll need five or more food varieties, all in separate containers. Variety is a very strong motivator; when Oscar is maxed out on one food item, switch to another. Keep the most tasty food items for last; when Oscar is too tired to go on, just like James Brown, Oscar will keep throwing off the cape and coming back to do more of the hard work for the good stuff.

Wet or mashed foods are too sloppy and slippery. Drier or diced, firm fresh foods are better; crunchy foods are great. The more the jaw has to work to chew, the more blood gets passively pumped up to the brain. Crunch is especially important for the "paralyzed with fear" stone statue dangerous cases. Crunchy food and jaw work is what increases the blood flow to the brain, which is what keeps Oscar down here on Planet Earth instead of drifting away to other planets and into the scary memories from other times.

For biters, or uncivilized biter-snatchers, use something like a plastic spaghetti strainer on a long handle; put food in there for Oscar to get. But the better way forward is to teach Oscar to not bite. Lips cause a closed hand "money purse" to open up, but teeth do not.

Teeth should make your food rewards drop out of sight. *Sorry, Oscar... If you only had better lip control, the monies might actually make it into your mouth!* Use blocking barriers for the nasty biters, and use "birds spikes" for the hunter/biters. (Any spikey object you can add to a wearable surface works well; we use Shakti acupressure spikes from Yoga matts as they are just horrible to touch but are so short in height that they are largely safe near eyeballs/eye sockets.) In short order, Oscar always learns that biting is a waste of time and money. Reward the evolving choices to use self-expressions other than biting or clawing.

Note that when you're working in cold weather, moisture from food, saliva, and breath will keep your feeding hands wet. Your wet hands will start to freeze, and you'll loose finger dexterity. The best solution for this situation is nitrile gloves. They offer just a touch of heat retention while maintaining your dry yet flexible finger dexterity. Some are textured for grip, and some are even biodegradable.

Toys can also be used as rewards. Oscar loves pushing buttons that make toys appear, however, when a toy is difficult to win access to, the value of that toy may drop. Retractable toys are obviously best at not wasting session time.

4.8 How to Co-Create Every Point of Interface

Even though you may not expect to hear it put this way, OSCAR Therapy is really never about talking to or building bodies; it's really only about talking to and building the brains that/who are controlling those bodies. Even when a brain cannot yet reach out and touch you with its body, its intention to do so is usually visible. And that intention is the first, second, and third thing to be rewarding. Say YES to intention always. But when the intention is the thing that's *missing*, there are many ways to coax the right ideas, guesses, tries, and attempts out of Oscar's brain.

4.8.a First, Get Parallel

For those who have never experienced the benefit of a geometry class, the word parallel means something like this... two long straight lines pointing in the same direction and that never cross each other, never ever. If one line is pointed "north", then the other line must also be pointed exactly north, but just one block over. Effectively, these are like two "intentions" pointing in the very same direction, both basically "doing" the exact same thing.

Here is another way to think about intentions that are pointing the same way, in tandem. Line dancers at the bar, birds in flight in a migrating flock, schooling fish traveling in groups, they are all giving us the right hints. The orientation we strive for in OSCAR Therapy is this kind of "same direction" orientation, just like we and the animals are all Rockettes, dancing in the same lineup.

When you are in doubt of what the heck an Oscar is up to, when you don't know what Oscar is focused on, freaked out by, or anxious about, your best bet is to find a way to line right up next to Oscar and see if you can't see (from Oscar's perspective now) what the heck s/he's looking at! Embedded international spies exist to gain this parallel perspective, to see things as the subject sees them. But really, the idea is no different from the dogs under the kitchen table; they're not really asleep under there, they're aligning themselves with the people who might drop food.

In the movies, the proverbial scene that captures the "sway-capability" of this idea is when the desperate person is about to jump off a window ledge, and then the "savior" goes up there to be right in the thick of it with the would-be jumper. Not that I'd do that exactly. But getting as close as you can and putting yourself in Oscar's exact physical situation (not necessarily in his circumstance), is always the best thing to do when you don't know how to get hold of what's coming next. If Oscar turns to the left, you need to turn to the left. If Oscar gets down on the ground, then you get down on the ground. If Oscar is stuck in an Apollo 13 capsule, then put yourself in one too. Only from his/her vantage point can you be most observant, most influential, and of most help.

The other reasons for first getting parallel are to quickly convince any Oscar of any species that a) you are not the one causing Oscar's immediate problem, that b) you are kinda in the same boat Oscar is in, and that c) when you place yourself in Oscar's "place and time," when you yourself try out a solution for yourself there, Oscar is much more apt to follow you down your path to that solution. If Oscar can't decide what to do, it's a ton easier to just follow along with what "the crowd" is doing. And yes, you qualify as "the crowd" according to any stressed and keyed up brain.

Begin by quickly attempting to match Oscar's intention. Get parallel to Oscar and once you're there, do what's needed to STAY parallel with Oscar. If Oscar shifts in the wind, you shift right along with the same wind. Match him at all times. Match her at all times. If s/he swivels counter clockwise, do so too. If s/he backs up, you back up. Keep your person and your OSCAR button right next to the spot you've chosen; don't let Oscar ooze away from you. Stay on him like glue, *which never ever touches him.*

The point is... if you don't know where Oscar *is*, then you have no capacity to even comment on where Oscar is *going*. And if you can't comment on where Oscar is going, then you certainly cannot *change where Oscar is* or cause him to bring himself to a new place.

Basically, until you're exactly parallel, don't assume that you know where Oscar is. I guarantee you right now that you don't. You may have "been *there* before" but you have not experienced what Oscar is experiencing right now in THIS day and age. His/her exact background experiences are not what yours were. Having that age-old problem, but in the weather and conditions of TODAY, is something you have not experienced. You have NOT been where Oscar is. So get parallel. In real time. It's the only way to even have a shot at an accurate assessment of what Oscar can and can't yet imagine.

What's more, getting parallel in OSCAR Therapy also has very real *electrical wiring* implications. One of the strangest things about building the hindquarters OSCAR maps in any species is that the *physical wiring* of parallel-ness is even more important than the button itself. To steal, paraphrase, and morph the ancient saying that's attributed to so many famous men (*there's something about the outside of a horse that's good for the inside of a man*), there's something about the right side of a human that is good for the left side of a phobic animal, *no matter where that human is standing*.

For instance, say a large animal has a very deep OSCAR hole in the left hip. You will have to go back there in order to request that it come into existence; and yet, no one is allowed to be standing there in that hip's phobic zone. Still, you must request, so you'll have to be standing near there someplace. And remember, this is all happening in the rear view mirror of the animal who is looking straight ahead. No matter what you're doing, Oscar is watching it; all they're doing is *feeling* it.

After a zillion times needing to do this, I can acurately state that as long as you are talking to the left side of their body with the right side of yours, *that contact-to-contact wiring of "parallel interface" is all you need to achieve.* Your actual therapist's arm can be standing over your actual therapist's feet that are standing on *any* patch of ground. I call this the "Oscar ventriloquist" trick; it's like a virtual alley-oop. Your body can be standing as far away as possible at Oscar's RIGHT SIDE body, but as long as your *Right* arm can reach Oscar's *Left* butt, the button will work and the zone will build like normal.

Figure 17. This horse is about to take a CLOCKWISE step with the front, swinging his Left Hind end to the LEFT, in order to learn how to hit the OSCAR button presented by my right hand.

This alley-oop trick is a little hard to describe without a visual demonstration, but to describe an example, the practitioner stands directly behind or to the right of the animal and uses their right arm to reach over to the animals left side, *in order to achieve the same relationship you would have AS IF you were allowed into that parallel location.* Using your closer left arm WILL NOT WORK.

I'm guessing this is for reasons of mirror-neuron wiring, or some such ancient schooling fish neural physiology we mammals have maintained through the ages, and yet still have no clue about. But the difference between the result you get when using the wrong arm versus using the correct "would be parallel" arm is like night and day. It's yet another weird and unexpected thing about the inner workings of social neurology and OSCAR Therapy.

4.8.b Starting an OSCAR Conversation (*OSCAR for Dummies* and Non-Dummies)

We beg (not just urge) you to read this entire book from beginning to end *before* you go trying OSCAR Therapy on your own. We also beg you to watch a bunch of the videos on our OSCAR Therapy Channel on YouTube before you go trying OSCAR Therapy on your own. That said, too many of my editors also begged me to add this super simplified "for dummies" section into this book someplace, and this is the only location it logically fit. However, each step is going to refer you out to other sections that will provide more detail on that step.

Here we go...

Step Pre-1: Let's get your button working right:
    a.   Honk your imaginary red, rubber clown nose and honk loud.
    b.   Now pretend that your fist is a clown nose and honk that.
    c.   Now pretend that your palm is a clown nose and honk that.
    d.   The hand that you are honking/squeezing with is pretending to be Oscar.
    e.   Your other fist/palm is your button.
    f.   The HONK/Good/Gd is always coming out of YOUR mouth.
    g.   It's Oscar's job to HONK ("good") your button.

Step 1: Have a pile of TINY rewards AND WATER ready(see section 6.2)

Step 2: Assure safety; consider fences (see section 4.4)

Step 3: Pick an easy zone to begin asking Oscar about. (see section 4.6.1)

Step 4: Face the exact same way your Oscar is facing. (see section 4.6.4)

Step 5: Hold up your arm that is CLOSEST to Oscar (see section 4.6.1)

Step 6: DO NOT TOUCH Oscar

Step 7: Put your own "button" (your own hand or forearm or target object) so close (1/2-inch) to Oscar that s/he will end up hitting/honking that button by accident. (There's no need to overthink this part.)

Step 8: Reminder: Every time Oscars *touch-untouch* your button in ANY way (ex: a human fist bump), their touch needs to make a short sound come out of your mouth, like a click or a clown nose honk or a "good." Their touch "makes the sound." (see OSCAR Therapy Channel on YouTube)

Step 9: Reward each purposeful button they push. The more careful and rational their attempt, the more rewards they earn. Give all rewards one at a time, as Oscar mistakes a handful for 1 reward. Don't bother re-rewarding the buttons they have already learned well. (see section 6.3)

Step10: Since some buttons will be harder for Oscar to touch in a rational way, score each try somewhere between OS-0 to OS-10. OS-5 is the goal. (see section 4.5) Reward Oscar for trying; more improvements earn more reward. Triple reward all exhales/sighs. (see previous section)

Step 11 thru Step 99: Use this same language to work out all of the specific troubles/beliefs/fears in the animal's day-to-day life or job: "Oscar, can you experience x, while touching this nearby button? *Example: Can you button this equipment?"*

For instance, can the dog touch the button during thunderstorms? After thunder claps? Fireworks? City noises? On the other side of a fence from a scary dog? For instance, can the horse touch your button hand while it's holding a halter? Bridle? Saddle? Spray bottle? In a trailer? Can you touch halter with your nose? Can you touch me with your hip even when in a small space?

There are literally hundreds or thousands of examples that could be listed here. It's all dictated by whatever specific troubles your own Oscar is having. But in all of them, your role is to say, "Oscar, please prove to me that you know that *you exist and you still function*, even in the presence of Frankenstein."

The button game is meant to bring the animal's rational brain back into the driver's seat, even in the presence of a phobic trigger, thereby converting the trigger from "a tiger" into a "friendly kitty cat" and an invitation to play the game. "When you are lucky enough to hear thunder, Oscar, that means that our fun button game has turned on." When the thunder is no longer a trigger, just stop accepting your animal's invitation to play. The phobia will NOT return, and Oscar will learn to just ignore the *no-longer-game-promising* thunder.

4.8.c The "Easier" Button to Hit: Sometimes It's Closer but Sometimes It's *Farther Away*

Breaking down a skill into its smaller parts, *as many times as it takes,* is the standard bread and butter teaching mode of all operant conditioners. Dolphin trainers, good dog trainers, and psychology 101 students are all taught that this break-it-down role will be the basic foundation of their work in behavior development. And indeed it is; it's a terrific skill that everyone needs, even though the majority of adult humans have not been exposed to it since Kindergarten class.

When you keep making the current question only half as difficult as the previous question, you are giving Oscar the best chance to actually connect the dots, learn the task, and meet the goal. I think of this teacher's role as aligning the dominos close enough together that Oscar can't help but knock down the whole line when s/he makes the first move. And the initial assist is to make the first bit so easy that Oscar will end up stumbling into the first right move all by him/herself, even by mistake.

In OSCAR Therapy, though, the trick to making each *button* easy is that you have to know *which* kind of question makes something easier *for this particular Oscar* and which kind makes something harder. You should not assume that what would be the easier parts to you are also the easy parts to Oscar. Likewise, you shouldn't assume that the more difficult parts to you are the hard parts for Oscar; s/he might sail right through the parts you'd experience as more difficult.

Bisecting any task always means chopping it in half, into two smaller / easier *tasks*, but in OSCAR Therapy, we also know that this does not necessarily refer to two smaller, easier DISTANCES. Depending on Oscar's comfort level, spanning a whole two feet might be easier for him to do than starting closer and spanning just 2 inches, in order to touch something scary.

Frequently, Oscars need to take "a running start" and use some physical momentum to actually muster a contact. When your shorter distances to the button are not working, you might not be seeing this particular forest for the trees. One of your distances, either closer or further away, will be the easier for Oscar to touch or even to just get a bit closer to (if they can't touch it yet). If one is not working, just try the other.

Sometimes animals will crane their necks around to look directly at the button to assess where it is in relation to their body. Actually, this happens a lot. You should interpret that as an "intention to know" where the button is, so you should reward it as if it were an actual touch. In the OSCAR game, Oscar's *intentions* are everything.

But when in doubt, when you can't possibly make the dominos any simpler to knock down, when there is nothing left to dissect, then zoom back out, way way out, and set the difficulty bar "very far or extremely close" if Oscar still can't hit it. Show him/her the whole challenge and the purpose of what s/he needs to muster, and s/he may just get it right away, "saying", "Thank you for giving me a lot of room to try it *my way*."

4.8.d The "Over-Present" Oscar: How to Be a Porcupine

Some brains have had to acquire unfortunate beliefs, including behaviors-for-survival. When the Oscar we are dealing with is using OS scores (OSCAR Scores) of 7, 8, 9, 10... we have to teach him or her to dial it down into the civilized ranges of contact. And obviously, the sooner the better.

The OSCAR Therapy game is usually talking about buttons and targets and points of co-contact. But regarding the OS7-to-OS10 cases, your button is about to be smashed to smithereens and your arm bones along with it. In these cases, I tweak the terminology we use. In these dangerous cases, we talk about using our "Point of Presence" to mean anything that we can safely urge Oscar to attempt to touch, knowing full well that we have to avoid injury both to Oscar and to ourselves.

One time, when I was 9, I punched my father. Who knows what I was mad about but I WAS mad, and I felt like I wasn't being heard. I hauled off and nailed Dad in the leg as he was sitting on my bed doling out some sort of information I couldn't get behind.

Not one quarter of a second after I punched him, OWWWWWWW!!!!!!! ...He hit me right back. Right in my leg. He said he hit me with equal force to the force I hit *him* with, but by my calculations, his punch was quite a bit harder. He didn't flinch when I hit him, and yet I doubled over in pain from my now throbbing leg. And still, through all the yelling, I remember clearly... that I immediately started to laugh. I couldn't help it. I had been stunned.

I was angry and horrified at him and yet also bemused all at the same time. What I was laughing at was myself because it was so clear, even to my 9-year-old brain, that I had brought his punch upon myself. It was like I had punched myself out in a mirror. It was like I punched the mirror and in doing so, I punched myself. I was pissed at him, and I had been crying. And yet now, I also couldn't stop laughing. Even though I was still very upset.

"Whadidya do that for !!!???" I moaned through my tears.

"That's what you did to me," he said.

Even though it's not a popular approach in the operant conditioning and positive reinforcement circles, I always give my clients some important advice. These are the clients that are owners of noxious, bitey, nippy, jumpy, or otherwise "overly-present" animals. I tell them to let their Oscar dog or Oscar horse or whatever species it is... let that brain "impale itself on you."

To help ANY SINGLE "point of contact" between you and Oscar turn into something that is totally safe and functional, you don't need a big instruction manual or any expensive equipment. All you need to know is how to create a "Porcupine Point of Presence" (PPP). I further tell them that in order to follow this advice, they have only 3 jobs, supporting the three rules of the PPP:

a.   It's your job to keep yourself safe. Distance may be necessary.

b.   It's your job to help Oscar experience the futility of the actions s/he's investing in (whether consciously or unconsciously) *without* getting hurt.

c.   It's your job to make sure you *don't generate <u>any</u> consequence beyond embarrassment, because to a brain, embarrassment is the most effective consequence there is.*

Also, do what you can to invite Oscar's whole sensory system into the conversation. Whenever possible, make sure that the consequences can be seen by Oscar's eyes, if she were to choose to see with them. Make sure that the consequences have an aspect that can be heard by Oscar's ears, if he were to choose to hear with them. Make sure that the consequences are accessible to any channel you think Oscar might notice. Buttons that are wet or cold are also easy to sense.

The consequence MUST be *caused* entirely BY Oscar in order for Oscar to have a shot at recognizing it as something they directly brought upon themselves. Only then might they realize that if they stop creating the thing that is happening to them, then it will stop happening TO THEM. By employing the PPP, Oscar is the only one who is doing anything to Oscar; you are not. For example...

If an attacker is lunging at me, I'd rather s/he run himself into the end of a long thin stick. Never ever create an actual impaling situation, but Oscar's self-impaling is the *idea* to shoot for. So in keeping with the first rule of creating a PPP, the more force Oscar throws at you, the farther away from you the point of contact ought to be, and that's pretty obvious: a point of contact that's farther away from you keeps you safely away from Oscar's force, mass, and leverage.

But the *less obvious* second rule of creating a PPP is that the farther away from you the point of contact is, the *less* sharp that PPP needs to be. The closer-to-you that you have to put your PPP, the "sharper" your PPP needs to be, especially so that Oscar doesn't have a lot of surface area there to push on (leverage for Oscar). A sharper PPP is also going to hurt Oscar more, should s/he push into it. So *only* use sharpness when you need to discuss the topic of Oscar attacking you at very close range.

Lastly, the third rule about creating your PPP is the most important: it has to be *really* embarrassing. The PPP's capacity to create an *embarrassed* Oscar is achieved by using the Element of Surprise. Since Oscar doesn't want to hurt AND EMBARRASS himself/herself, by inadvertently bonking into something they didn't know was there, Oscar will learn fairly quickly to slow down and start assessing the situation. From your "let him bounce off of an *unexpected* me" type of Presence, Oscar learns to stop allowing his body and/or brain to have knee-jerk reflexes. Oscar learns to start using his intention instead.

For instance, if a horse is trying to knock people (and me) around with his wrecking ball of a head, all I have to do is sneak my hand slightly closer to Oscar than he's aware of, stand firm like a tree, and he'll bounce off me like a running kid bounces off a clear glass candy store window. The horse meant to knock me over, but instead, he made himself lose his own balance, and now he feels like a dumbass. And since attackers and other dominating wills HATE feeling embarrassed more than they hate ANY of us, they quickly learn to stop attacking.

Whenever Oscar is infringing on your personal space, pulling your hair, yanking your chain, swinging punches or generally being obnoxious, all you have to do (as soon as you see Oscar coming) is put up an unexpected "Point of Presence" somewhere between you and the part of Oscar that is coming at you. *Be* that unexpected wall for Oscar to bonk into. As soon as he hits his fist or shoulder or nose up against an unexpected barricade (even if it doesn't hurt), he will take an embarrassed step backward and diffuse somewhat. That slight pause begins to build the essential "mental space" in which you can start approving of his new choice of *backing away*, and from there, he can finally start learning.

Note also that the same Presence Point that keeps Oscar off of you is also equally good at stopping Oscar from *dragging* you. Whether you're using a leash, a lead, a lunge line, reins, or whatever, perfect use of a line of presence (a rope connecting you to Oscar) has nothing to do with the actual line. It has only to do with the two Presence Points at both ends of the line.

So logically, it really only has to do with how you use your own Presence Point at your end of the line. It has only to do with whether or not you are letting Oscar *bounce off* of an *unexpected* point in space (put there by you), which is exactly the same game as with the PPP, it's just in the opposite direction. In the first scenario, Oscar is coming at you, and in the second scenario, Oscar is fleeing even though you are attached. Oscar needs to find out that there will be "self-inflicted" consequences to both. Unexpected walls *are* that consequence.

I can't ever think about consequences without thinking about Ema. Ema was a horse I met when she was 9 years old. That's about 30 years old in human years. Ema was not only a biter, but a stealthy attacker too. She was a lot more like an angry parrot than a horse; she also had a very unusual brain.

Ema would purposefully create a mattress every night out of her hay, so that she would not have to sleep on the ground; horses don't usually do that. She loved making music with loud, clanky objects. She hated being touched by raindrops. She did not have a history of abuse, but she suffered a life changing injury when she was just a few months old. Ema is one of the most interesting animals I have ever met. It took much more than a month of Sundays to get to the bottom of Ema.

At some midway part along Ema's recovery path, and there were many, it was time to rebuild Ema's Right front neck and face. For if Ema saw you standing there, she'd ignore you once. But if she saw you standing there two times in a row (even 30 seconds apart), she'd lash out to bite you hard with her giant horse teeth.

So I put Ema on her own side of a string fence. I encouraged her to hang her neck and head over the fence. I stood on her right front quarter. And in my hands I held a long white PVC plastic pole with a broken off pointy point at one end, not sharp enough to break skin, but sharp enough to get your attention if you were to run into it by mistake.

I held the point of the pole out near Ema's lower jaw. I told her that if she looked at the pole or acknowledged that the pole was there, I'd give her a cookie. She would always look once, but on that second look, she'd always slam her head to the Right in order to take an "underhanded" bite out of whatever was there. The biting I wasn't going to be able to get a handle on, but the head whip that preceded it was something we COULD talk about.

So I braced myself and held firm on that jagged PVC pipe, aimed straight at her jawbone. It would be her own "choice" to slam her jawbone into that sharp stick as much as she needed to. And I swear on a stack of taxonomy books, with Heidi as my witness, this horse impaled herself on that stick for 35 minutes straight before she slowed down enough (was tired enough) to be able to even notice it and begin to take stock of what she was doing to herself by tuning out of reality in this "bite reflex" way.

Ema was hurting herself reflexively and unnecessarily a zillion times in a row because her reflex would not let her brain play an active role in her "knee jerk" reaction to *any* thing in that scary zone near her body. No part of Ema was cut or bled during this phase of work, but she did come away with some self-induced welts on her cheek.

My PVC javelin was not a weapon; it was Ema's self-impaling opportunity, merely held in the right spot by me. You shouldn't EVER be using weapons of any kind to teach with, and you shouldn't be using your own body as a weapon either. Bodies are great weapons when you want a weapon, but weapons just don't teach.

When you attack Oscar, Oscar will start looking for your weaknesses; he'll look for holes in your armor. He will be looking to find out how *small* you are. But when you let Oscar be the one who is attacking, who is attacking you, that's when Oscar is allowed to learn. That's the time when s/he'll find out just how *big* you can be, and just how irrational, *and then embarrassing*, s/he is being.

If it's safe, you can indeed use your own body as the prickly porcupine point of Presence. Just don't use it wrong; use it like a teacher. Oscar wants to know about where he stops and about where you begin, spatially, mentally, and emotionally, but mostly spatially. You need to let Oscar discover where your own edges are. First, use a wall, and if they don't notice your wall, use a Point of Presence, and if they don't notice that, sharpen it. They'll notice.

So that was an introduction to the part of OSCAR Therapy I don't recommend trying at home, unless you are very good at protecting both you and Oscar from further harm during this learning process. And until you are ready to reward an Ema with a cookie for every time she exhales, slows herself down a tad or actually uses her eyeballs to actually examine the thing she believes she needs to kill. Unless you are ready to reward all of the "less bad" progress with all of the rewards it deserves, from moment to icky moment, do NOT play these games with a dangerous Oscar.

But if you ARE ready to use your approval, your bubble, your porcupine spikes, and your muscles to hold your spear steady, then you will never see greater reward than helping Oscar understand that THEY are in charge of themselves, and that the consequences belong to them and them alone. They are both the creator of the consequence AND the solution.

After much OSCAR Therapy, Ema became a very rational and well-loved member of her household. She even was good at teaching and helping other horses to overcome their own baggage. I kid you not.

4.8.e The "Under-Present" Oscar: Using the Social Vacuum Vectors (Leveraging Your "Leaving" in Freeze-Frame)

Just like any under-present individual is more likely to fly under the radar, the under present Oscars are harder to point to in a crowd. Sometimes, you might even call them mild-mannered, and yet this half of the population is a little bit harder to treat than the loud half. Reversing the issues with these animals is about building something that probably hasn't ever been there before. But if it was there originally, it has definitely learned not to be.

By and large, this half of the population has more going on in the brain. The OS-0-5 zone has more thinking, consideration, extrapolation, learning at play, and they logically deduce that they better not get involved in things that are overwhelming and complex. And yet, every brain is still beholden to the laws of social nature. So even with these less-is-more individuals, there are ways to amplify their efforts, so that they can be present in the social realm and have a vote at the table.

Draw an OSCAR clock with a human volunteer (you) at the center. Put an imaginary puppy dog at all angles off of your clock's center. If you were at the center of the clock, and if the puppy were *facing you* from any point on the outside ring of the clock map, then you might wonder if that puppy is going to come pounce on you.

But instead, let's imagine that same puppy facing away from you. Playful puppy is trying (and usually succeeding) to pull your location *around*, like you were a balloon at the end of a "nonexistent" string. Puppy bounds after a butterfly and you go after him, maybe to stop him from bounding into the street.

Figure 18. These puppies are showing us potential social-vacuum vectors.

So imagine that you are standing in the middle of the circle above; your job is just to stand there in the center. Your nose points to the location of 12 o'clock. Now imagine that a puppy is trotting away from your location at the center. (When I'm teaching this in the class setting, I assign someone to play the part of the puppy.) Don't move at all, don't move your feet at all; just stand there." Now, when puppy gets to about 15-20 feet away from you, ask yourself this question: "How do I feel right now?"

When puppy is at your 3:00 or 9:00, at a location parallel to you, maybe you feel curious, like maybe puppy found something on the ground. When you're parallel like this, people in the center usually report feeling nothing special; they say it feels neutral. (We are not discussing any OSCAR-positive brains at the moment.)

A puppy going away from your 12 o'clock also seems to have not much effect. Most people feel curious about where puppy is marching off to, but watching where puppy is going is all most people want to do.

But then, a most interesting thing begins to happen when we watch puppy go away from us off of our fronts toward our 11:00 or 1:00, and it's even more pronounced at our 10 and 2. Something happens that even the "herding experts" and the horse whisperer ilk have not as yet described (to my knowledge.)

And there seems to be at least three intensities of the response from the humans in the middle; but all responses yield exactly the same answer. The answer from 99 percent of people is the same. (I have only met one person who gave a different answer and his answer still made sense after I asked him about himself.) Here's what happens with the vast majority of people *and animals* when I ask them how this angle of "puppy leaving" makes them feel:

They all say that they better follow the puppy because he's going someplace too far away. "But following the puppy is not a feeling," I begin to pry. "How does puppy there make you feel?" The answer I always get:

"Anxious. Nervous. Not ok. Don't know why, but not ok. Unsettled. Unsecure. Needy. Alone. Lonely. But I don't know why."

"Does it feel neutral to you?" I always check to make sure.

"No."

"What's happening here?" I ask this very non-leading question that could be answered in a million different ways.

"Maybe I'm being left. Maybe there's a predator or a fire or some other danger behind me. Or maybe puppy doesn't care about me. Or maybe I'm not valuable to puppy. Whatever the reason, I feel like I'm being.... *left behind.*"

"Yep, that's what everyone says. Now I want you to look down at your feet."

To a person, I have never seen a single individual not express the same automatic "spatial reflex" to this mild feeling of abandonment. People display different degrees of the reflex, but everyone does it: every person's body mass has shifted toward the abandoner. If "puppy" is leaving off to the North West corner, the person's weight will have shifted to their left front. If "puppy" is leaving off to the North East corner, their weight will have shifted onto their right front.

Most people actually take a fully unconscious full step or even two steps in the puppy's direction. Presence-light people actually cannot stop themselves from flat out walking in puppy's direction to be where puppy is. I ask them why they are doing that when their only job was to stand still at the center of the circle, and they say, "I have no idea why..."

Now, there was that sole solitary person who had absolutely no emotional reaction when I asked for the verbal description. No matter what puppy did, it was all neutral to this person. You may have already guessed that this person was an adult male. I was curious to root around inside the mind of someone who seemed to be missing a normal animal reflex. So I probed with some non-leading questions, and here's what this man told me:

"I'm a Marine. I mean I was a Marine. Once a Marine, always a Marine. I went into the military because I had a real bad relationship with my abusive father. He was no role model, you wouldn't want to follow in his footsteps if you know what I mean... so now I'm one of the few, the proud, the unswayable..."

And yet, as I looked down at the ground, I silently noticed that although this man's feet hadn't moved off his wide-stance position an inch... the center of gravity of this arms-folded, brawny Marine had *shifted*, and he was leaning, hard, like a wind-blown fence post, in my direction. I didn't mention it.

There is a subconscious, primal instinct to close the gap between you and another individual, presumably so that you can effectively avoid being abandoned by the group. This instinct is so ancient that I actually have no idea how far back it goes. But it shows up like a beckoning neon sign at your (and Oscar's) 10 and 2 o'clocks.

In my experience as a behavior and motivation analyst, this reflex seems to be a much older reflex than any of the other social reflexes. In my work, the pull of this "social vacuum" feels much older than our cravings for approval. It even feels older than our anger, if such a thing can be imagined. Because even an angry and savvy opponent will still follow you right into any trap you set, IF you Disengage from them at their 10 and 2 o'clock angles.

I do wonder if the mammalian propensity for following (along their 10 o'clock and 2 o'clock angle vectors) goes all the way back in our evolution to our fishy (swimming in schools) days. Birds and marine mammals are known to migrate in the familiar V shape formation, thought to be caused by the beneficial boost the second animal gets from the turbulent back eddies from the leaders' wings... fins... etc.... And I wonder if we mammals also follow that vector setting simply because there was no time in our past history when we didn't.

In mammals, we certainly know about the immeasurably strong social-pull dynamics that are unmatchable by competing forces: the herding wildebeest, the mob behavior, the church mentalities, and the teenager trends. We go because we must. And if we don't know that we must, we go because the others are going, and because staying behind forfeits our "safety in numbers" survival policy.

Not only does this "social flow" dynamic work to bring us "warm blooded" animals toward you, it also attracts at least some of the "cold blooded" animals that find themselves in our midst. I tried out this social vacuum on one small coral reef barracuda when I was snorkeling on the coral reefs of Belize. Juvenile Barracuda are known to be some of the most curious fishes in reef ecosystems, but they don't chase you. This fish was not following me around when I got in the water, but he *was* following me around after only 3 minutes into my experiment of applying the social vacuum to him.

And this kind of "follow reflex" may even hearken back to the original pre-neural chemistry of the collective network, the chemical ooze that kept mats of single cells from blowing apart. If the smell of the collective us is creeping up toward the light in the morning, then who am I to choose to stay in the darker depths alone? This tendency in living beings may be so old that it might even predate the wiring of the "hard wired" stuff we call choice. To follow follow follow is not something we choose. It's something we just do, without knowing why, and without even realizing that we're doing it.

Going further, I think that this social vacuum is "animal-ese" for the word TRY, in parental species, anyway. Most mammals are parental to a high degree but so are most birds, many reptiles, many fishes, many amphibians, and even some invertebrates. If mother wants baby to try to do as she does, she uses this social vacuum. Instead of using some food as bait, a parent can use its own body in relational space, as very effective, well-placed bait, that no baby wants to be left without.

If you're wondering what all of this jazz about ancient reflexes has to do with OSCAR Therapy, here it is. When we practitioners set our own bodies along these specific vector angles to Oscar's brain-body map, from there is where we have the most amount of "pull/influence" to actually suck a non-existent part of Oscar _into existence._ This statement is both amazing and hard to believe, but it's true.

These social vacuum angles are both the safest and the most effective/efficient angles in which to play the OSCAR game. Through these angles is where Oscar's brain gets the most help and momentum from the natural world and from his/her own ancestry and genes. When you place yourself and your button at these angles, Oscar is much more likely to see you as a mirror, as a partner, and as a helper, instead of seeing you as an opponent, a threat, or a danger.

By leveraging the natural momentum that is built into these social angles (no matter the locations of the holes Oscar has), you can bring an under-present, _shutdown Will_, back to life.

Note of Caution:

Here's the one thing to watch out for in this "front pull zone." If you are trying to teach Oscar to leave a scary thing behind (something that is terrifying and or mentally paralyzing to him) then you must NEVER position your self at 11-12-1 o'clock, which would be 180° opposite (directly opposite) of the scary thing.

The reason is obvious: if this scary thing lashes out at Oscar, then Oscar might leap DIRECTLY out of it's way and land on top of you by mistake. Oscar might run right over or through you, because you have positioned yourself exactly in Oscar's best exit path. Don't do that. But if you are at Oscar's 10 or 2, Oscar can safely escape the dragon and run away WITH you, not run away OVER you.

4.9 The OSCAR Findings: Recording Progress Notes

When both a well-meaning attempt and a full-on attack are two ends on the very same continuum, it's easy to feel lost in your assessment. All we know for certain is that Oscar is somewhere on the spectrum between bad and good. And yet, Oscar's brain experiences both of those "extremes" as essentially the same thing: guarded intention. So that overall intention can be measured.

Since keeping track of changes over time is important to every case, OSCAR Therapy had to develop a system of accurately noting where Oscar's brain is on the spatial learning continuum. Unsurprisingly, the most practical way to measure both Oscar's problems and Oscar's recovery (from one session to the next session and/or from one brain to another brain), is with a scoring system.

When measuring animals, the idea of "normalcy" is an idea we should all probably just toss out the window, since we each have a different idea of (and expectation about) what is normal or what *should* be normal. The only thing that really matters to us humans is where an animal's behavior actually *is* compared to what we *want* it to be. When animal behavior spans the entire range from the very problematic to the not exactly problematic to the not exactly constructive to the very constructive, those arbitrary designations merely reflect the arbitrary expectations of their humans.

And yet, for any given point on the body, there are two critical skills any brain needs in order to meet any and every expectation we have: its ability to come up to meet a stressor and also its ability to withdraw away from a stressor. In fact, we humans all use these skills every day, but we just don't think about them; they are automatic. But *automatic* comes in a range of available options, and so, so does any Oscar. And in OSCAR Therapy class, it's here that I always find myself talking about the tarantulas, or at least, *our reactions* to them.

A tarantula is any one of a thousand unique species of your typical gigantic, hairy spider, with leg spans of between 3 inches and 1 foot wide. And if I were to hold a live one on my hand in front of you and ask you to come over and pet her, you'd probably do one of three things. You would:

a) Jump/run back and away

b) Gingerly approach with outstretched hand that would become more reserved, slower to reach out, and faster to recoil the closer you got

c) Run to me and smack it out of my hand and then you might also proceed to stomp the innocent animal to death, even though it had done nothing to you

None of these reactions is any more or any less normal as responses go, but each stems from a different kind and a different *amount* of previous experience with big hairy spiders. If you have never ever been exposed to such a thing, not even a plastic version on Halloween, your brain might quickly choose a), to not interact at all.

If you love animals and see them for who each individual is, just another being on this Earth trying to make a living, and if you've had no very bad previous experience with arachnids to date, your brain *might* choose to interact in fashion b).

If you grew up with an older brother who woke you up by dropping innocuous daddy long legs on your sleeping face, then your brain might quickly choose c). If you chose c, the a-type people screaming behind you might even call you a hero, even though you are still just a victim, a PTSD victim of your brother, and you are passing on his vile ways to yet another innocent victim: the spider. [If you are a c-type person, trust me when I tell you that you are *no hero*; you have acquired a learned pathology and OSCAR Therapy can help you to get rid of it. But I digress.]

All of these three impulsive reactions are within the normal range of "average" responses in a world where so many of us come with vastly different and widely varied social interface histories. And yet, only one of the three responses above gets you anywhere good. Because... the *next* time it happens:

Person a) has learned nothing, and will be still afraid to learn something new.

Person c) has merely perpetuated the same old senseless and pointless battle, they probably apply to all aspects of life.

But Person b)...

Person b) has learned to learn, has learned a little more about the world of other perspectives, has learned about courage, failure, grit, and trying... and has gone into science, gotten a job that uses her brain and is on African Safari as we speak, finding a wild tarantula on her shoe as they chat around the camp fire. She has to get a stick to help the spider climb to a safer perch 'cus you know... those relatively puny spiders could get scared or even hurt if she were to jump up with a startled response.

Person b) is whom we ought to strive to actively teach all of our working animals and companion animals to be. Because we, the relatively puny humans, could get scared or even hurt if our animals were to jump up in a startled response. Whether that startle comes through Oscar's feet or through Oscar's teeth or even through Oscar's electrically shocked verebrae that are bending and twitching in unexpected and lightning fast ways, it all happens too quickly for us to safely avoid.

It's much better to know that the animal you're with has evaluated, understood, rebalanced, and prepared, just like the Boy Scout motto says everyone should. The safest animal to be around is the one that has learned to strive to be the most rational "person b)" they can possibly muster, by using that powerful planning and intention organ between their ears. We don't want them to be runaways, and we don't want them to be attackers either. What we ought to want is a brain that is smack dab in the middle, capable of both options, but mostly, able to absorb and diffuse the chaos of an unpredictable world.

The remainder of this chapter will introduce our shorthand for record keeping and documentation. The kinds of case recording and reporting we have developed to keep track of, and educate owners about, our findings, our treatments, and the progressing results of a case are a critical and necessary part of the OSCAR Therapist's job.

4.9.a OSCAR Score

In OSCAR Therapy, the challenge presented to the learning brain is simple:

Can you try and will you try to reach "here," with the part of your body that is closest to here, in order to touch "this thing?" But any given animal's answer to this simple question will be only one of a wide range of possibilities, and their answer will even evolve every time they try.

So the wise OSCAR practitioner will keep accurate records, not unlike a doctor's medical chart. We will be filling them out after each session's work. What you are scoring is how much "Presence" (acknowledgement of self) is showing up to a social interface at each particular location on the body.

The experienced evaluator will thereby compile a map of the animal's OSCAR clock. If an animal can *purposefully* touch your hand button immediately adjacent to (but not touching) that body location *even one time*, then that spot passes the test and that body location is called "OSCAR negative." When an animal uses a given area like a fist bump exactly zero percent of the time, this area qualifies as "an OSCAR positive hole." It is a missing part of the animal's own brain-body correlation, or social interface capability. The OSCAR hole cannot reach out toward someone else's space, and thus it is an abnormal finding; you've found a zone that is abnormal.

The OSCAR scoring system has only two aspects to it: Score and Vector. And yet these are two very different kinds of measurements. We will discuss Score first here, and then we'll discuss Vector in a later section.

So, the OSCAR Score is the number on a 0 to 10 scale (where 5 = normal) that measures the "amount of animal that shows up" at every spot. On the OSCAR scale, there are two ranges, stretching out from a midpoint at 5, kind of like the pH scale in chemistry. And also like with pH, OS is sort of a logarithmic scale (which is a nonlinear scale) meaning that the next number on the scale is a full ten times (10x) bigger or smaller than its neighbor, not just one bigger or smaller.

For super simplicity, our OSCAR scale runs from zero to 10, with 5 being the "normal," the level we seek to build towad with OSCAR Therapy. The "type a" runner above would score somewhere between a 0 and a 3. Five is the midpoint (person b). The person c) victim/attacker above would score somewhere in the 6 to 10 part of the range. So instead of just these three a, b, and c types of intentions, OSCAR Therapy slices and dices them into a total of eleven. So the OSCAR grading system goes: 0-to-4, 5, and 6-to-10.

In the table below, each of the 11 OSCAR Scores is described in two different ways. The Description column describes Oscar's emotional and physical state; you might call it the "presentation of behavior." But, OSCAR scores also refer to a whole bunch more than just behavior. More accurately, the Description column is describing the brain's point of view, the state of Oscar's own intention/Will. But the Your Sensation column describes what the OSCAR *practitioner* will perceive, with all of their own senses.

Oscar's Contact Ability *The Amount of Oscar's "Socially Available" Presence*	OSCAR SCORE is a number from 0 to 10	Your SENSATION *What Therapist Feels at Points Having This Score*
no ability to reach out to touch OSCAR button- "stone statue" animal buries part on the ground or part is held way up in the ceiling	OS-0	extremely fast but silent vibration. A stone statue about to explode
whisper of an idea, but no physical reaching	OS-1	very fast contact, brush of a whisker
extreme tentativeness	OS-2	weight of a butterfly wing
cautious, very hesitant	OS-3	pressure of one finger
receptive presence	OS-4	pressure of a normal handshake
neutral presence	OS-5	exactly equal to pressure coming from the button
tad over-present. louder than necessary.	OS-6	pressure of a firm handshake
inappropriately over-present	OS-7	rude, pushy, slap hand
shoves, slams, throws self into you	OS-8	single burst attack, weight of a full potato sack
attack response	OS-9	'provoked,' but then repeating attacks until stopped by external force
preemptively hunts you like prey, plans the attack	OS-10	stalking, slowest approach

Table 4: How to use the OSCAR Scoring system

Now, there is a major difference between OS-zero and OS-10 cases. While the OSCAR game is exactly the same for cases on both ends of the spectrum, the practitioner will need an opposite set of skills to handle each extreme. At one end, we are teaching Oscar to dial it back into the civilized realm; and at the other end we are successfully teaching Oscar how to light their first fire. And even when Oscar only has "wet sticks" to rub together, it still works.

At the OS-5-to-10 range, the work is obviously more physically dangerous to all involved, but an OS-5 to OS-10 Oscar can at least always be relied on to provide the necessary energy and momentum to power all of the forward progress. So in that regard, this is the *easier* end of the spectrum. (Wind power generators work best in a storm.)

If what you're looking for is an OS-4 or an OS-5, and Oscar is giving you an OS-6, just ask Oscar to try again. Only reward the answers that are going in a better direction. When Oscar is sure that "smaller can't be right" and answers your next request with a OS-7 or a head-slamming OS-8, just say, "Ooo sorry, but thanks for playin,'" and just ask them to try again.

Remember that an over-present Oscar has been operating their whole lives from this "bull in a china shop" approach; they don't know about anything gentler until you help them find it. And yet, I guarantee that smaller expressions are in there. If you're not seeing them, watch more *frequently* and more *quickly*. That's not a typo. Watch quicker; observe faster. Smaller tries fly by fast.

All you have to do is protect yourself, re-route Oscar's scary energy and stay positive by always rewarding progress. You may get knocked around a little bit, and you may even drip some blood, on a bad day. But still, for all of these *in-your-face* reasons, this is the side of the OSCAR Score range that represents the easier work. [If you or Oscar is at risk of physical injury during session, then the practitioner/therapist has skipped a safety measure someplace. If physical harm to anyone is a possibility, go back to the drawing board and add failsafes to your plan.]

On the OS-Zero to OS-5 end of the spectrum, though, the work is (*NOT obviously*) more dangerous to Oscar (and *not* the practitioner). This is because it is more *emotionally* dangerous. The difference on this end of the spectrum is that the activation energy (the momentum) will have to come from you, the practitioner, until Oscar can muster enough self-esteem to drive his/her own momentum.

This end of the range will require more imagination on the practitioner's part, to be able to imagine what Oscar is feeling. It will also require more therapist support of Oscar's own choices, as Oscar's will-based brain learns to flicker on. Note: If any practitioner or owner is *also* experiencing some unexpected emotional reaction during the under-present session work, then what is likely happening is that their own human brain is also needing/getting some help and rebalancing from the OSCAR Therapy. (See the last section of Chapter 5)

For all of these reasons, this end of the range is the tougher work, the less obvious work, and the less "showy" work, even as it is the more rewarding work. While you're merely dialing back an OS-8 into a more civilized OS-5, on the OS-1 end you are helping a mere seed grow exponentially into a fruit tree.

The great fun of it all, though, is that *both* of these ranges will likely be present in almost every single individual brain. When a brain has a missing shoulder, for instance, they often have a wrecking ball of a neck (maybe OS-7), to compensate for what the shoulder just won't try (maybe OS-1).

Regarding ultimate goals and what to shoot for, in my opinion, the best score for an animal who is interacting with other non-human animals is an OS-5. But the best score for an animal who is interacting with the *human* animal is an OS-4. Since animals are usually bigger and/or stronger than we are, pound for pound, they need to learn how to handle us gingerly. Even many of the tiny animals could stand to learn how to play nicer with their humans (*and we with them.*)

But in truth, whatever the animal's job is in the world, that is what will dictate the best OSCAR number to build toward. Some rodeo bulls make a zillion dollars because they are taught to have OSCAR numbers up in the OS-8's. Some police dogs are taught to use an OS-9 on the job. But if an airport security sniffer dog doesn't bring an extra reserved OS-3 to all of their own body parts when sniffing around the general public, dog-fearing people may get scared of and avoid them, making their jobs harder.

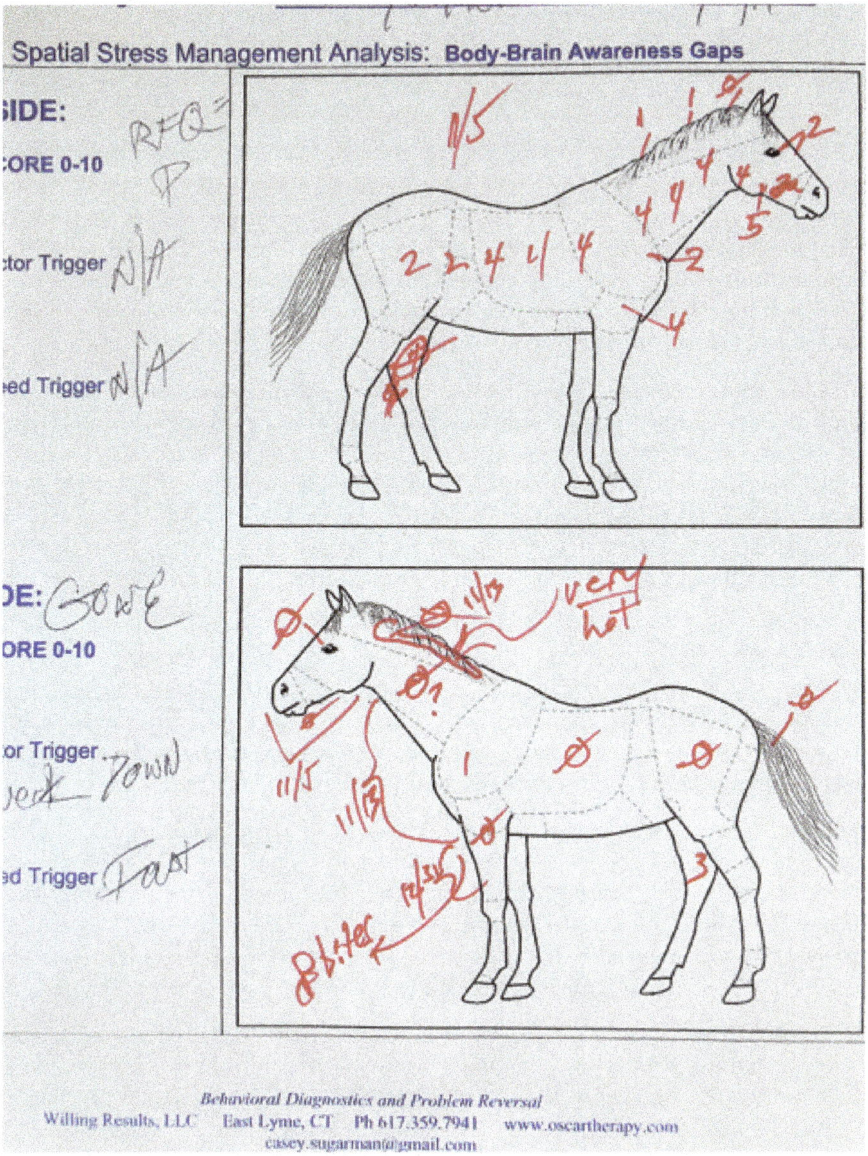

Figure 19. First page of OSCAR Exam Form at Willing Results, LLC

4.9.b OSCAR's Vitals: Exhales, Water Intake, and the Worms

The total time of any single OSCAR session is always at the discretion of the animal first, the owner second, and the practitioner third. The smart OSCAR Therapist does not cut off a conversation midstream because of upcoming appointment times.

To use Oscar's brain at top efficiency, plan longer time windows than sessions will need. A single OSCAR sessions can last anywhere from one to three hours depending mostly on OSCAR's age; younger brains usually tire a bit sooner. In an emergency case, though, as many as three session, with long breaks in between, can be packed into a single day. OSCAR animals work hard!

Sometimes animals need short breaks mid session (30 min max) because the experience is intense and the learning is thorough; but mostly they don't. When Oscars do need to exit the session, don't chase or follow or try to retrieve them. They will come back soon enough to work the puzzles some more because the OSCAR game is so positively empowering that it's almost addictive to Oscar. For them, it's just like looking for burried treasure.

For all of these reasons, OSCAR sessions are so intense that the other way to monitor Oscar's hard work, dedication, and level of investment in any given OSCAR session is to monitor some simple vital signs. And yet, we can't monitor the vital signs you're used to getting in the medical world. We can't monitor heart rate because we are not allowed to touch OSCAR's body or hook him up to anything electrical. And respiration rate is always too small to see in nervous animals who are often breath-holding.

Luckily though, the sign we love to measure most is also ultra-obvious; it exists to make itself known. The first and most important sign that we monitor, count, and record is Oscar's *deep exhalations*. These are like deep release sighs. They are very obvious (after you've trained your ear to notice them), and they look and sound identical no matter the species or taxa of vertebrate animal (even humans) that you're working with.

Not only are these deep exhales signposts and windows into Oscar's experience, but they are also extremely therapeutic and assistive self-relaxers to Oscar's brain. We also call this exhale the "brain reboot." Practically, deep exhales are like the brain resetting itself on a new starting place. If a fragmented and overloaded computer could unplug itself from the wall and plug itself back in, that's what an exhale is and does.

We want to encourage more of these deep exhales, so we pause to reward each one we hear with three consecutive rewards. And because we reward them so heavily, most animals and humans will occasionally learn to "fake an exhale" during the more mentally challenging puzzles. Be on the lookout for the fake exhales, like when Oscar is merely mimicking a deep sigh. Although there is still some benefit to even a fake exhale/sigh, we try not to reward the fake ones.

How do you tell the difference between real and fake? You'll know. The fake sighs have more of a cough/snort sound to them. Once it's obvious that fake exhales don't win any reward, Oscar will stop faking them and go back to expressing only the real thing.

Second, an equally important vital sign to monitor in every session is *Oscar's level of thirst*. I have no idea why this is, but animals in session often need to drink inordinate amounts of water, usually more in one sitting than the owner has ever seen them drink before. We don't reward drinking, so this is 100 percent caused by the animal's need to rehydrate. This behavior could possibly have to do with the dryness factor of dried food reward items, but there's never a salt factor, as the food rewards we use are always regular whole foods, not processed foods nor special treat items that have added salt and sugar.

And yet the timing of when the animals choose to bring on water is telling. Usually they drink the most right before or during a major leap forward in courage or in re-experiencing something that used to be quite fear inducing. As it is for us, water may be soothing to the emotional brain. The thing that's hard to figure, though, is where all of this water is going! Horses chugalug gallons of extra water and yet there's never any sweating or excessive urination. Dogs can go through a small bucket, and I have rarely seen a dog ask to take a pee break mid session, although we frequently offer.

Whatever the reason, and no matter the species, every brain undergoing OSCAR Therapy should have free choice water available at every session from beginning to end. If this is not an option, take a water break where water is temporarily brought in, or bring Oscar to a water source during a few mid-session breaks.

Lastly, in OSCAR Therapy, you are not just dealing with Oscar's intent, you are also dealing with the actual electro-chemical wiring inside Oscar's body. So the final sign we monitor is not as obvious as drinking or sighing. Nerve twitching, reflexive muscle jerking, muscle surface "crawling" and muscle twitching, to us, are all basically the same thing. Like a neon sign that is flickering back on, it's amazing how *never even touching* an Oscar can elicit such involuntary effects in the musculature.

Bringing a localized, blocked zone back on line after years of non-use often causes miniscule but noticeable "involuntary" muscle tremors and random neural firings inside the tissues and muscles you are discussing. You will likely see the evidence just under the skin. (Under fluffy fur, it's sometimes harder to see.)

It will look like a small lightning storm of unorganized electric signal, making the muscle twitch involuntarily, as if the *muscle tissue itself* is "reaching out to touch" the OSCAR button or the phobia item, even when the nearby limb or body isn't able to cognitively reach out yet. This is a normal part of phobia reversal, and it is evidence that Oscar is on a good learning path. It feels to me like the "muscle memory" hard drive is getting overwritten right before our very eyes.

A client once told me about her own personal experience with trauma-triggered neuromuscular pathology (while I was working with her dog). She said that the day her muscle beds came back on line (using Alexander Technique), it felt like ants were crawling around in the muscles on her back, which is exactly what it looks like in our Willing Results, LLC phobia cases as well.

The reason why these "worms" of crawling nerves are so important to record is that they are literally the noticeable road signs that *light up the way* toward Oscar's recovery. When you are building a brain's intentional use of a body part, the muscle that you are near will show these worms for about two whole minutes, and then they will subside in the next moment and be gone forever.

But if you then ask all zones right adjacent to that repaired area, only one of those trajectories will grow worms. For a minute or two. You are being shown that this is the direction that goes deeper into the source of the *original* problem, the originating impact zone, during the phobia-inducing event(s) in Oscar's past. It points you toward the original locus of attack, which is the area that will need the most rebuilding of the deepest holes.

If you just follow these worms, they will show you where to go next. They will tell you whether you should track up or down or right or left to find the next most curious body part, the one that is next in line to "reach out and feel/understand/assess" the memory of the attacker or the originating incident(s) *for the first time ever*. (Remember that during the original traumatic events, the already overloaded brains simply refused most of the experience.) Oscar's brain will play back each memory in slow motion, in freeze-frame or in slow pictures, moment by moment.

By exposing Oscar to a mild experience of needing precise intentional control, you will be re-wiring the part of the brain/muscle feedback loop responsible for that entire "old but real" well-earned fear. It's like a whole new neural "experience" gets created just by "hearing from" and attempting to use these previously abandoned channels to Oscar's major muscle groups, in the face of social impact.

It's no wonder that Oscars need extra oxygen (exhaling) and water to both feed and cool the furnace of the brain. In session, it is doing a tremendous amount of heavy-lift, hard work "math" even though the body hasn't done any physical exercise at all. By feeding Oscar information (with your "Goods," your own exhales, and your rewards) as s/he reaches out to touch your button, you help Oscar re-grow his or her own brain-to-body garden, piece-by-piece and context-by-context. And often, it feels like the growth happens almost overnight.

Warning:

But whatever you do, do NOT reward Oscar *WITH ANY FORM OF TOUCH OR PHYSICAL CONTACT* during OSCAR sessions. The overarching rule is that you are not allowed to touch Oscar at all. Oscar and Oscar's muscles must be the ones doing *all* of the reaching out and touching. Be the tree branch, the stanchion, the solid beam that Oscar bumps into, but be only that.

If you touch a phobic Oscar with the scary thing *before Oscar touches it himself/herself*, then you'll be no better that the scary thing itself. In fact you'll be worse because you'll have made an inanimate monster *animate*. You will have brought the Vampire back to life. Oscar will simply extrapolate out his fear of the scary thing and learn to also fear *you* as well.

4.9.c OSCAR Angle Vectors: Any Point Has Its Own Clock

Thinking back, let's remember what the name O.S.C.A.R. stands for: Operant Social-Spatial Cognitive ANGLE Reach and Recoil. This topic of social interface is so important that it's right there in the name. Notes about OSCAR angles look menacing on paper (which is why I'm not including them here), but what they are describing is really quite straightforward and intuitive. They make sense when you think about it.

With a normal, functioning brain-body map, any individual can push or pull any body part toward a wide range of angles. For example, you yourself can push your own elbow up, out, down, in, and toward all the finer angles in between. However, if that elbow had at one time been speared by an arrow, maybe in an unfortunate summer camp incident, that elbow might now be afraid to reach out toward the angle the assaulting arrow came from.

So these missing angles that Oscar *has forgotten how to* "push a button toward" are sometimes described in our case records, especially when they are starkly apparant. We descibe the missing angles as a vector, symbolized by an "arrow" with a number at the end. Each arrow's number represents the amount of Oscar Score (or Presence) that shows up from Oscar at that spot *but especially through that exact angle*, as they are attempting to push on your button.

Once you can teach a specific body part to come touch you, you can then teach that part to regain its full 360° use in all directions, and in all (x,y,z) planes, very quickly. All you have to do is wait for the right guess and say yes to it. After many anxiety-releasing exhales from Oscar, they will have regained a fully operational, cognitively directed, body part.

If you'd like an example you can probably relate to, here's one that's straight from the Hoss's mouth. If you remember the character of Hoss Cartwright (played by Dan Blocker) from the old Western television series, *Bonanza*, then you'll already know this friend of mine from the backwoods of Connecticut. His was a case of a missing OSCAR angle, and here is his account...

4.9.d Son of a Banjo Picker !

I'm a big ole' mountain man, a homesteader you might say. And there I was on a hot summer day in New England, getting ready to can pickles. Everything was going great until my finger decided to slide into the knife edge of the slicer. Instantly, I jerked my finger back and looked at it and said, "oh no." A good chunk of finger and half the nail was missing.

Every time I thought about that bandage and my finger underneath it for the next few days, and every time I thought about that slice, I was squeamish. I couldn't get it out of my head; i just couldn't get that action to stop playing... It was playing over and over in my head for a week.

I happened to bump into Casey who asked about the bandage on my finger, so I was telling the story of the pickle incident. I was miming what I had done, the action of my arm, and the slicer.

Like any friend would do, Casey listened; she was grossed out like everyone else I had told. I was too. I told her how I just couldn't get the image out of my head either, and how it was giving me the heebie jeebies many times a day.

Casey said, "Hang on a second, show me again the slicing action with your arm..." I sliced down.

"Ok good, now take your finger AWAY, show me what taking your finger AWAY from the slicer would look like. I yanked my hand back. She said, "Now repeat that, but slower." I did. She said, "Ok, now repeat that removal motion, but exhale while you do it.

I COULDN'T DO IT!!!! "Oh my God, I can't! I can't exhale as I take my hand off an *imaginary* slicing blade!"

Casey explained to me how OSCAR Therapy works. I thought to myself, "this woman is nuts." But WHY couldn't I exhale?!!

That's when she gave me homework: "Ok, here's your homework. Your brain needs to regain its control over that incident AND BUILD THE FUTURE from the point where it lost control. Mimic the removal action but in ratcheting portions. Exhale after every ratchet. When you get that down, add different angles to your elbow. Up, down, in, out, AND EXHALE THROUGH THOSE.

"Why again do you want me to do homework?"

"...so that your brain can let go of this incident, so you can get your hand back from creepy town," she said.

I'm an open minded individual, and I *was* shocked that I couldn't exhale. So when I went home I did what she said... *and son of a banjo picker!!!!!*

I couldn't believe that my brain couldn't grasp the thought of control, just like Casey was saying. I tried it several times over the next couple days, and I could not believe the thoughts flooding into my mind of the day I cut my finger. I did the homework for a couple hours total.

I'm amazed. The experience was mind blowing. I thought back to years before when other farm incidents had happened, and if I would've had the knowledge back then that I have now I could have overcome a lot of issues that have happened to me. I could've corrected them myself.

For the days after the pickle incident, I had to wrap my hand in a towel at night because the thought of hitting the injury up against something in my sleep was such an overwhelming thought. But after the OSCAR homework THAT I DID ON MYSELF, all of that stopped. No more gritting my teeth. I'm past it totally. I can use my finger now and tap on it and I'm back to normal. And my finger is finally healing too!"

4.9.e Assault Forensics

Just like in the game *Clue*, if forensics (who or what done it and with what weapons) are germane to the case, we can also evaluate the "hottest speed" of the angle of attack, as sometimes a slow approaching button is much scarier to a brain than a fast approaching button. That information does tell you a bunch about the details of what exactly was experienced here at this anatomical location on the animal.

But over the years, as I have become less interested in the origins of the Oscar holes, I don't put the brain through the unnecessary stress of going back to excavating the exact memories of a precise crime scene. We just dive right into the hole, rebuild it to normal, and move on.

It is important to know that OSCAR Therapy does provide all sorts of "forensic evidence" snapshots of precisely what Oscar experienced at a visceral level in the distant or recent past, i.e. what a brain is specifically *but subconsciously* afraid of happening again. Whatever is plain to see is plain to see.

However, it is equally important to not let creativity leak into your observations, thus making them less accurate. It's all too easy for our story-telling-oriented species to surmise about who and when and where *it all* took place. How easy is it, exactly? So easy that I just laid a trap for you and you probably fell in. The non-invested observer must ask: "...who and when and where WHAT all took place?" The fact is that unless you are Oscar him/herself, you were not there, and you do not know for sure what IT *really was* that caused that brain "hole" (the walling off or sequestering a portion of body awareness in certain contexts).

I've met a horse with a full-blown phobia of snapping turtles and lawn mowers. I also met a horse with a full-blown phobia of plastic bottles and Portuguese Man-o-War jellyfish; he was a for-hire horse working on the Galveston, Texas beaches. I met a dog with a full-blown fear of snakes and coconuts. Turns out he was feral on a beach on a tropical island before being rescued after a hurricane. I have met dogs whose electric shock collars have gone on the fritz and shocked them at totally random intervals that were also weather dependent. Not fun!

And how would we have guessed that our animals had come from those backgrounds had we not had first hand evidence or seen the events with our own eyes? Phobia doesn't always mean that some jerk abused our animal at one time, with a plastic bottle. Always remember that to Oscar's brain, the backstory doesn't matter as much as the tremors it leaves behind, as they still impact her or his *rational-to-her*, *rational-to-him* assessments of risk. It is only the surviving brain-body's glitches and ripples from the past that dictate their strange reactions to "normal things" in the present day.

4.9.f Remember to Build the Interior OSCAR Angles: OSCAR Tucking Cures Oscar's Claustrophobia and Other Phobias

Out West, (where I'm *not* from) the animal trailers that you see going down the highway are called "stock trailers." All they are is one big empty box on wheels. There are some slits in the side for airflow. Whatever animals you've got just "pig pile" in there. Animals step up into the box and you shut the door and y'all go on down the road. Even if your horses are expensive show ponies, they can basically just cram all in there and be perfectly happy and safe. In fact, I hear that horses that are used to each other don't mind it at all. And horses in general give me no reason to doubt that claim.

But back East, where nervous Nellie and well-heeled horse owners hold the purse strings, our horse trailers have gotten a little nutty with the bells and whistles. First, we put in dividers. Clanky metal walls keep horses straight and parallel with each other, like pieces of toast in a SMALL bread toaster. Now, because what walks in must BACK OUT, we needed to add front escape doors for the people.

And also, because of the interior walls, we needed to add quick release latches. But when they learn about the quick release latches, scared animals start pushing on the walls and bars. Because of the pushing, horses start trying to *run* backward to get out of there instead of walking. Because of the running backward, we added ramps, not only back door ramps, but side door ramps. Because of the bells and whistles, we add a price tag and an ego to boot. And "animal handler ego" causes even more trouble than these psychologically unsavory tin cans do in the first place.

Long story short, horses back East often get nervous about being in these NOT empty boxes. When a horse refuses to go for rides anymore, and who can blame them, some of those horses meet me. And the more horse trailer cases I work on, with their various phobias of what all scary things are inside horse trailers (I have a list of 73 known triggers of trailer experience-induced phobia), I've noticed that these complex cases more often than not have one unifying thread that runs through them. So much so that I *also* found out that this thing that most vehicle-phobic animals truly suffer from can create phobias of even the big empty stock trailers.

The thing most of these animals have in common (and I always laugh when I say this...) is that these animals are "just plain screwed," because I mean that *literally.* We humans just don't realize how *accurate* that exasperated description actually is.

Ok. So... the "screwed" problem is not dissimilar to the human experience of driving into a parking space in a crowded parking lot. When going into a slot, what drives in must also be able to back out. Now, when you back out, do you back out always to the left? Or do you back out always to the right? Obviously, you need to be able to do both.

Horses are big. Even if you can add one of them into a breadbox, they are going to have to be sensible about exiting or they could get hurt. Horses aren't so afraid of what happens inside the trailer as they are afraid of not being able to get back OUT of the trailer, once in. And, lest we forget, only after rational and comfortable exiting will your horse be able to volunteer for that 2nd and 3rd trip down the road to the *next* event.

And the *reason* most of the horses I meet seem to feel so trapped in horse trailers is *not* a phobia of small spaces, but it's a fear of their OWN bodies' capabilities 24/7. This body-fear problem merely gets AMPLIFIED when standing in that small space. And because of that, their *experience* of being in there is actually a 2-dimensional experience, not a 3-D experience.

To many of the horses in straight load trailers, they feel like the prisoners in the Superman comics' jail called Krypton's Phantom Zone. When all you can do is put yourself in and out of a slot... when you cannot swivel or rotate yourself at all to the right and you cannot swivel or rotate yourself at all to the left, that's when you feel the most trapped of all. And without those transitional 3D brain-map-building experiences of "being fully in charge of your own body" inside that space that you've packed yourself into, then you will not feel fully comfortable (in control of yourself) in that space.

Proof: If you are able, escort any claustrophobic or vehicle-phobic animal into any empty tiny space (even just a shed, stall, or crate). Once there, ask them if they are cognitively and physically able to rotate *themselves* (by themselves) to follow yummy food or a beloved toy clockwise *and* counter clockwise in that very small space, you will most likely find that one of those two directions is missing from that animal's brain.

It turns out that claustrophobics just have not yet learned or re-learned the concept of folding in on themselves in one of those directions in order to tightly rotate. And the reason is probably that they have had a history of even mild knee or hip or shoulder or eye trouble. Even if the trouble has already been healed and resolved back to full physical function, Oscar thinks s/he can't swivel on/with it.

Actually this kind of phobic presentation is not only diagnostic, but it's also very obvious, even to the point of being pretty funny. I call it the "bath cat." In one direction, Oscar rotates no problem. But in the other direction... if you know what a cat looks like as you slowly lower them down into a tub of water, that's it exactly. Suddenly the cat takes up as much space as physically possible with legs outstretched in every direction, trying to get braced against ANY and EVERY wall. All of a sudden, your wrong-rotating Oscar will take on the behavior of plywood.

Any human with any amount of personal experience with hip joint or knee joint issues will tell you that doing stairs is hard. It's not the weight bearing (we weight bear every time we walk); it's the swiveling-to-compensate part that's weird. And it's no different for any animal in any small box. Even small dogs are often claustrophobic in large cars or huge crates for the very same reason.

The solution is to teach or re-teach these Oscars how to tightly turn themselves (doing whatever maneuvers they need to do to accommodate their tricky knee or hip). In order to pack themselves in *on themselves* and rotate themselves about an imaginary center pole in the center of the space, the gravitationally shifting space as the car moves and turns and dips. They have to re-learn 3-D balance. For instance, they might have to try to learn to swivel their outer hip and knee out in order to give the inside hind leg more room to do its full interior swivel.

[When you need to teach Oscar how to pull/tuck a limb interiorly, toward his/her body's own center, use Velcro. Not actual Velcro, just the idea of Velcro. Teach Oscar to suck up into the inside core of his/her body by merely a) placing your hand on their exterior and then b) using OC to reward them for "pulling away from my hand," which feels like teaching them to pull their own Velcro patch off of your "Velcro hand." The more vacuum suck, or draw-in they can muster for their "tuck in," the more you should approve. It's the same language as OSCAR but instead of reaching out *to* us, we are rewarding them for recoiling inward, away *from* us.]

Once Oscar has learned that s/he can indeed "tuck in, suck in, and turn that way," the way they never knew they could turn before, their brain's cognitive visual map will *almost instantaneously* immediately widen up like a pop up children's book, and they will FINALLY be able to see this small interior space as a 3D space, a place where they are still in full intentional control of their own bodies, even when inside it.

Once Oscar feels like s/he can turn this way *and* that way inside the breadbox, suddenly, s/he doesn't need to get out of there anymore. I've had "claustrophobic" horses absolutely demand that I *let them back on* the trailer in mere *minutes* of their discovery of their interior/tucking OSCAR angles. Claustrophobic dogs start demanding car rides and even crate access! Once they can imagine themselves both exiting right and exiting left, via both hip joints swiveling inward and outward, (sometimes ribs and armpits need to learn to pull in too) then there's no more problem.

What's more, after that, these very same animals also have very little problem with the additions of divider walls, butt bars, padding pillows, and the clanky metal sounds of the door and wall locks. If they can IMAGINE the freedom they have in there, then they don't need to ACTUALLY HAVE the freedom in there. Even with all the East Coast contraptions, these previously un-trailer-able animals are in there and goin' down the road as snug as a bug in a rug, instead of as flat as a cat suspended over a vat.

CHAPTER 5: THE OSCAR THERAPIST'S ROLE

As OSCAR Therapists, it is our aim to teach animal brains and human brains to physically reach out to touch us and then to touch the scary parts of life as well, with all parts of their bodies. This means that (in addition to needing to be good teachers) our real prime directive must be to only provide *less than half* of the total presence of the entire physical transaction. While we facilitate brain learning, we shall not do their learning for them. We are not leaders; we are guides.

In order to be successful guides for any Oscar in any situation, we must be able to stand firm like a tree, and also to receive gently like a butterfly wing, depending on what Oscar needs us to be at that very moment. We must have a *flexible* Presence. Hence, we need to employ many different "versions" of ourselves in order to show Oscar the next safe rock in the stream on which they can safely stand.

Also, it's our job to see beyond the obvious. For example, if Oscar is aggressive, it's the therapist's job to recognize that the cause is nothing more than a missing brain hole + PTSD. It is all-important that we see aggression for what it is; it's merely a smoke screen an animal throws up in front of a missing piece of information. An aggressive Oscar is experiencing a vacuum (of missing information) where clear information ought to be. Our job is to help Oscar fill in the gaps while rerouting any of Oscar's exploding shrapnel, so it helps if we can make the process safe enough so that we don't get killed or even hurt in the process.

Because of all of the deep-seated emotional damage that needs repair, OSCAR Therapy cases can be hot potatoes. But remember, just like with any Disney film monster, just because Oscar has sharp teeth, that doesn't mean that s/he doesn't know how to also use those teeth to gingerly pick up babies. Even when Oscar is a huge animal, that doesn't mean that s/he can't learn that the humans need to be handled with kid gloves. It's our job to teach them that.

So this chapter, Chapter 5, is all about how to apply this OSCAR language in useful ways to tackle both of these: reversing real problems and meeting tall-order challenges. Although OSCAR is a fun game, an absorbing game, and even an addictive game to play, OSCAR Therapy is not meant to be a destination in and of itself. It's a therapy; it's an avenue to get from an idea you have to a real live skill. Crossing your fingers and hoping that the next encounter between Oscar and whomever will now go well (just because the animal has been made OSCAR-round) is exactly the WRONG way to use OSCAR Therapy.

OSCAR is not a hope; it's a language. If you are just sitting back and observing while your dog is surrounded by Yo-yo's, then you're not using OSCAR as the lever that it is. You must get right in there and help Oscar to practice his own new shape in a *will-try* way, even in the presence of that Yo-yo. OSCAR Therapy helps you be the best kind of mediator, bringing both Oscar and the scary Yo-yo to the same table, to realize that they are actually friends.

And as with any kind of brain building, there are little tricks (and even huge shortcuts, timesavers, and interpretation hints) that make the job go faster, smoother, and with more bang for the buck in time spent. Basically, this chapter provides solutions to many unique kinds of snafus you will run into when you adopt OSCAR Therapy as a daily working language, whether you are using it on the job or just around the home. In short, if you were to spend a few weeks on the job *with us*, Chapter 5 is about the work-a-day skills you would pick up.

5.1 "Lion Attack" : An Induced Separation Anxiety

Account of CJ S., East Randolph VT and Florida

People have often commented on how well behaved my horses have been. However my two previously independent competition horses had been jointly attacked one night while in South Florida by an unknown assailant (to this day we don't know whether it was animal or human) who left them covered with blood with long, curved cuts from withers to hindquarters. One horse also had three extremely painful punctures on the abdomen. My horses emerged from the experience neurotically bonded together, and with one aggressively protective of the other.

Although their physical wounds had healed, four years later I still could not leave one horse alone, and they could not travel alone as before. It was more than a standard case of bonded horses. For example, one time on the way off the farm, while solo in the trailer, one of the horses jumped the breast bar of our gooseneck when the other called to him, becoming trapped upside down in the headspace area. His hind legs hung over the breast bar.

Another time I was paged at a competition when one repeatedly tried to jump the temporary stabling (8 ft) and, failing that, was almost 3 feet down in what was apparently to be a dug-out escape under the stall wall. I had already consulted various trainers to no avail.

Casey's approach methodically resolved the trauma inside maybe 6 sessions. She is professional, timely, kind, extremely intelligent, and remarkably effective, which is important because her approach is decidedly unusual. I still can't put into words what she does, even after watching it carefully, but it actively engages the horses, and she carefully manages their mental stress level so that they can learn whatever specific answers they need.

First, Casey evaluated each horse separately to make sure it was aware of all its own body parts (which I was dubious about, until it worked). When she reacquainted them with their "missing" areas (she calls it "learned paralysis"), I noticed they both began to seek out separate fields without anxious concern for where the other one was. We trailered each horse around the arena with the other loose to observe their concerns, progressing to separate road trips.

Casey is an extremely keen perceiver of animal emotions, and knowing that she was making sure each horse wasn't pushed too far was psychologically critical to me. (I was horribly nervous about those first solo trailer rides.)

In my opinion, Casey, leveraging her years with other species, has pioneered an incredibly effective new approach to horse training (and behavioral problems) that is a leap forward. I have had horses for 34 years, and I have seen everything from the old "show 'em who's boss" methods, to traditional training techniques, to various new natural horsemanship approaches, and I think Casey's approach is different and more effective because she has the horse actively engage, understand and participate.

Casey's addendum:

These two horses seemed to be stuck together with "mental Velcro" both hiding their damaged parts inside the functioning parts of the other. They acted sort of like a pair of people in a potato sack race, where the middle leg (the abnormal leg) was shared by both brains. One animal had been attacked on the upper left and the other had been attacked on the lower left. If they both kept their right sides facing out, they could survive ok as "one unit." After OSCAR had fixed the first animal, their co-orientation persisted. After OSCAR had fixed the second animal, they immediately got un-stuck and in the next half hour, their separation anxiety switched off like a light switch.

5.2 OSCAR's Repair Progressions

The larger mammal babies usually need a few years to learn how to use their bodies. But in a flash, body part use can also be unlearned through traumatic events.

In cutting edge human brain therapy research, Dr. Vilayanur Ramachandran PhD has discovered a nearly immediate curative therapy that is totally effective for phantom limb pain, a condition that has been considered untreatable for centuries. It is a "visual-cognitive treatment" that uses nothing but a bathroom mirror and a tennis ball.

If the brain can see the correct "image" (a reflection of the remaining arm in a mirror) of it's own arm as it is unclenching an object (the ball), then the brain can finally experience what it needs to see in order to release the "action" of the death grip clench that the arm was performing at the time the arm was lost. Without being able to experience the signal to switch off, such a wiring circuit will remain *on.*

Dr. Ramachandran has shown that neural feedback loops can become misaligned during trauma, as when the brain perceives a limb that is still "electrically" present, merely because it never received the cue to turn off the circuit of the original trauma. When the pain-looping circuit can finally be switched off by the brain, the real pain goes away like magic.

So in the reversed direction, I posit, a brain can refuse to be aware of a limb that IS there because the brain never received a cue to turn the circuit back on! OSCAR Therapy locates the circuits that have been switched off during trauma (mild or severe) and then helps the brain realize that it's safe to switch those circuits back on.

5.2.a Stages of Recovery: Recognized by Their Speeds

For the patient (the learner), OSCAR recovery is not like recovering from surgery, where incisions and cut bones need weeks or months to heal. Each phase of recovery (that I will delve into below) is fairly independent of our notion of Time, like on the clock or the calendar. Sometimes it takes time on the order of hours or days for a missing zone to get through all recovery phases to the end, but sometimes all phases are completed in a matter of minutes.

It's not important to the case to know about the amount of time that has passed (other than its possible affect on a client's checkbook). What is important to know, however, is what *phase* of recovery Oscar is in, because that is how you know where Oscar's brain is in the process; it's also what predicts the phase that will be coming up next.

Knowing what to expect next is helpful so that the different phases don't catch you by surprise when they suddenly appear. And yet, it's important to let Oscars advance through the stages at their own rate of speed. Sometimes, a given phase can be a real slog, especially if we have somehow missed a step in helping Oscar to connect the dots. What happens more often, though, is that the brain will jump into the new phase faster than we are ready for.

During the relatively short process of treatment to a missing zone, Oscar's recovery pattern always hits at least three predictable phases: fast use, slow use, and super slow-motion use. After the brain goes through these phases, the practitioner can then help Oscar ramp her or his speed of use back up to a normal speed of interaction (or better-than-normal). Oscar's new everyday use of the previously missing zone now becomes what you'd call normal (or approaching normal) at all speeds, gaits, actions, skills, or what have you.

5.2.a.i Fast Tries: "Fast Tries" and "No Tries" Are The Same Thing

The *first phase* of recovery is the phase that is the hardest one of all to be able to observe/see, which is why this first phase is also the most dangerous. These two unavoidable truths about the first step in the recovery process are likely the main "co-reason" why the "OSCAR problem" all together has taken so long to become known. If we can't even see our way to and through the first step, how will we ever know what happens next, let alone get to the end product?

The first hints of recovery are like an elusive creature in the wilderness; they are always around, lurking in the shadows, but they blend in so well that they are never seen. And when we caretakers are of no help in getting a process started, then not only does the problem never get solved, but we aren't even aware enough of the cause to make a diagnosis.

In the first phase (Phase 1) of contact from a long-time-missing area, the animal's usage of the body part goes by in a flash. Actions may appear random and hard to see to the untrained eye, but the animal's intentions *and actions* are not actually random at all; they're just very, very fast. An animal touching you for the first few times will appear as a quick swipe, or a flick, or a flash of contact.

Of significant note, the most dangerous brains are the ones that are vibrating so fast that you can't delineate their choices. These are the brains who are imagining different exits at such a rate of speed that their physical body cannot possibly keep up. The brain disconnects from the body altogether; Oscar will stand frozen like an internally vibrating stone statue, until, in a minute, the brain comes shooting back into the body like an asteroid, and sets it alight with a firestorm of flailing, ramming, and gnashing of teeth. Those are the animals I physically drag the nearby humans away from, because they can't see the immediate danger they are in.

In Phase 1, both the safety and the high alert awareness on the part of the practitioner are paramount because most Oscar brains will avoid use of this particular slice of their "personal space" at all cost. Onlookers will immediately observe an animal's quick pivots (whipping around), shooting away at straight angles, and/or "skipped over" angles. If the Oscar brain is that of a human, Oscar will even start offering up *verbal* smoke and mirrors by saying and doing anything to change the subject away from the evidence of their "hole."

In Phase 1 of any type of hole (OS-zero to OS-10), sometimes animals will indeed jump OVER empty space when they can't make a move in that direction, as if jumping over imaginary hot coals. These animals are the ones that are usually labeled as "unpredictable rearers, lungers, buckers, and biters." These actions are not active choices made by the brain; they are more like peripheral nerve auto-feedback loops which bypass the thinking brain entirely. Many horrid "behaviors" are not choices; they are really more like knee-jerk automatic reflexes.

It is ALWAYS the practitioner's job to preemptively move all nearby observers to safe locations, to prevent them from being hit by any of the predictable, fast shrapnel storm that happens in Phase 1. That said; everyone in the area *should watch the process* from his or her safe distance or from behind thick walls. Phase 1 provides extremely important but short-lived learning opportunities for all OSCAR Therapy students and all rehabbers from any other kind of therapy modality, alike.

For the practitioner-in-training, learning the why and the how (and believing it) behind all of the spooky jazz (like biting, striking, slashing, bolting, rearing, or spinning) that is *likely to soon be coming your way* is invaluable experience that is also of paramount importance. It's what convinces all witnesses-in-training to take no chances and to figure out a divider wall setup <u>ahead of time</u>, so that they can *safely* begin work with any new case of a dangerous animal.

5.2.a.ii Slow Tries

In Phase 2 of recovery, the quick movements of the previous phase slow remarkably. Body part use begins to present like physical pathology. Often observed in Phase 2 is a true loss of balance, joints that seem out of joint, tripping, and/or seemingly constricted or restricted muscles and ligaments. And yet, not surprisingly, all of these "physical issues" that crop up are usually confined to the OSCAR treatment sessions. They are not usually observed at home in between sessions; nor do they appear even immediately before or after the session.

Animals can begin limping, on legs that hang heavy. Legs can look "left behind," or like they are being held in ridiculous shapes. Owners often begin now to accuse their animal of faking injury and "lying" to avoid doing the difficult brainwork. This assessment, however, could not be farther from the truth. In actuality, Oscar's body is experimenting with every possible solution to the challenge of "purposeful reach to touch," and the brain is working overtime to build a new map to support that new intention.

This rehabilitative work can be so mentally exhausting (even while standing still) that the animal often falls into a deep sleep right after *or even during* the session. When a brain does this, do not disturb it; it needs to switch off for a time. Take a 5 or 10 or 15 minute break and watch in awe as the animal dreams or even shows evidence of deep REM sleep (rapid eye movement). The animal will wake *themselves* up and come right back to the session in short order, as if nothing had happened.

5.2.a.iii Super Slow-Motion Use

Phase 3 is marked by attempts in super slow motion. The practitioner does not create any of these slow motion movements; the animal creates them all. During this phase, the animal is appearing to be *consciously* confronting a fear or specific memory. In this stage, individuals are now mentally and emotionally ready takes "shorter time than you think it will take" once you identify OSCAR as the cause. With owners who are supportive of and take part in the treatment process, fully rational and normal animals are typically the result. (Read *typically* as always.)

5.2.b Typical OSCAR Repair Progressions: An OS-9 Hole and an OS-1 Hole

The following two progressions (that are 25-or-so-steps each) show the action-pathway that Oscar generally follows when s/he consciously rebuilds a PTSD-traumatized part of his/her body. Again, these are rough outlines of the average progression. Do not expect Oscar to follow these mini-phases to the letter.

OS-9 type "aggressive" holes are easier and faster to fix because the brain is quite engaged. And yet you have to take things slower than the brain needs you to in order to make sure you're not going to get commensurately attacked or hurt by deeply rooted, knee-jerk reflexes.

OS-1 type "no one's home here" type holes require more skill to fix, are more gratifying, and take longer on the calendar because Oscar's brain will need more days to sleep in between sessions. Comparatively though, when all is said and done, the OS-9 takes a little more session time, just because "better safe than sorry" is always the best way forward.

In animals, a typical rebuild of a missing "slice of their pie" in an OS-9 proceeds like so:

Let's say a right shoulder's 2 o'clock is missing and also has a Score of 9; this animal is a ramrod. In this case, any recovering, learning brain will follow, generally, this learning process:

a. Leap above/over Oscar's 2 o'clock (presents as a jump, rear or leap toward 2)

b. Bolt thru or ram thru Oscar's 2 o'clock

c. Run thru Oscar's 2 o'clock

d. Stand still like a stone statue

e. Other ideas (pivoting and or causing distractions)

f. Sleep**

g. Whole body leverage. Use all body parts to "block" for shoulder at 2.

h. Whole body will "wrap around" 2 shoulder

i. Dead weight. Shoulder will not move by itself.

j. Nerve crawling; nerves that serve those muscles begin to crawl like worms

k. Muscle shaking; tremors in the muscles that serve and support that shoulder

l. Panic breathing; rapid, deep breathing with many exhales

m. Shaky lift of right front (RF) leg; shoulder is "lifted" as if for the first time as would a baby

n. Sleep

o.   Flail. Shoulder does not aim well. Its movements are too big and wide.
p.   RF has unsteady association with ground/gravity/weight bearing as if new
q.   Super slow motion lifting
r.   Exaggerated slow movement as if a "marionette"
s.   All angles are attempted. Full range of reach/motion is explored.
t.   Sleep
u.   Over use of this shoulder as if to lead with, for about 4 days.
v.   Reliance on this shoulder to "take the brunt" of all novel interactions
w.   Automatic rebalancing with all other limbs
x.   Normalize

In animals, a typical rebuild of a missing "slice of their pie" in an OS-1 proceeds like so:

Let's say a Left hip's 10:00 is missing with a Score of 1. In this case, any recovering, learning brain will follow, generally, this learning process:

a)   Oscar spins away, counter clockwise rotation
b)   Stand still like a stone statue
c)   Lift left hind (LH) leg
d)   Step to 3 o'clock
e)   Step Back
f)   Step to 4 o'clock (indicative of a 10 o'clock avoidance)
g)   Exhales begin
h)   Sleep
i)   Dead weight. Leg will not move
j)   Hung weight. Leg hangs like meat on a hook, ankle bent
k)   Toe bounces off ground
l)   Three other legs dance around to see if they can solve/compensate
m)   LH Leg moves one inch toward 8 o'clock, lose balance somewhat
n)   Sleep
o)   Front Left Leg goes to 10 o'clock to "pull on back legs"
p)   Right Hind Leg goes to 10 o'clock to "pull on" Left Hind
q)   Body rocking, looks like " a running start" to fling leg toward 8 (not 10)
r)   Fling a "dead LH leg" into 8 o'clock, tripping
s)   Drag leg 1 inch toward 9 o'clock

t)   Step 12 inches toward 9 o'clock

u)   Gingerly step one inch toward 9:30 o'clock

v)   Gingerly step 1/2 inch toward 10 o'clock (deepest hole requires hardest try)

w)   Sleep

x)   Step 4 inches toward 10 o'clock, then 48 inches

y)   10 o'clock works fine

z)   11 o'clock works fine

aa) 12 and 1 o'clock work fine

bb) Normalize**

**Anyone, me included, would swear that there is a physical problem with a ligament or muscle in the above progression, but there almost never ends up being one. Either that, or all animals are "magically cured" from their "injuries" overnight. And since magic isn't reality, that can't be the explanation.

In real time the above two lists are "learned through" at a rate of about 5-7 bullets per session. So on average, the above lists would each need roughly 3 separate sessions (of about 2 hours each). Even if a few days of rest are encouraged between sessions, then the whole repair is complete inside a week. In an emergency situation, such a repair can be forced into one or two full days, but it's a little too stressful on the learning brain to do that much work that fast. Nerve chemistry needs some rest time to catch up and recover, so rushed fix may be incomplete.

OSCAR practitioners aim to fill in the deepest, most crippling (most danger-inducing) OSCAR holes first, just like in any medical triage situation. And danger to the practitioner counts as dangerous on the triage list. If an animal might injure *anyone* before the next session, then that offensive part is the part that needs to be repaired first. The other smaller OSCAR holes can go to the end of the line. Animals who understand the game and trust that they are safe will build the lesser-deep holes in body parts quickly, usually requiring only one session, with a test/reminder/re-check on the next visit.

To gain more in-depth, real-time exposure to instruction on the use of motivating, OSCAR coaxing, OSCAR building, OSCAR angles, OSCAR timing, and OSCAR contact points, contact Willing Results.com for opportunities that may be available to you. Whether you learn best by doing, seeing, or reading, we can help you get the experience you need in order to feel comfortable incorporating OSCAR Therapy into your life or work with animals, even if it's with the human animal.

5.2.c The Peculiar Behavior of the OSCAR-Positive Limb Quadrants

Most OSCAR-positive animals of all ages and all states of health seem to have some limb involvement; a leg or even a few of them seem to be out to lunch. At least, I personally have never seen a case without some amount of under- or over-present limbs. Even in the cases of head- and neck-shy, or the cases involving extreme head behavior like the "wrecking-ball head," they all have legs that create an offensive or defensive stance. The job of holding the body up against a storm of scary head interactions is hard work; just ask any young kid at boxing camp.

There's just no predicting which quarters are going to be the ones that are out because other quarters have become so good at compensating. Like the little round ball that is easily hidden in a carnival table shell game, at the beginning, it's hard to pinpoint just which limb has the biggest trouble. With a quick rotation of Oscar's body, two or three other legs become readily available to defend the weird one(s). These others may be better able to absorb whatever social trouble was facing the leg(s) with the biggest OSCAR hole(s).

The OSCAR Therapy practitioner needs to be skilled at thoroughly checking every leg. The limbs with OS 5-to-9 holes harbor your familiar and more obvious "boundary over-stepping" leg presentations like clawing, pushing, kicking, jumping on you, and the like. But more often, when a case makes it way to us, what we see more of is limbs with holes in the OS-0-to-5 OSCAR range.

The following categories I've delineated stand as evidence that we do limb-rebuilding work frequently. And if you think that the presentations below sound cookey, you ain't seen nothin' yet! Because we find these same limb holes in many of the *humans* we work with as well. Human legs and arms are not immune from being *subconsciously* "withheld from" the social world. Some human limbs have a "punch first and ask questions later" approach to survival, and others have a "recoil and forget the question altogether" approach.

The following categories are common presentations in limbs; these are what a whole limb quarter of an Oscar animal or human will often *behave* like:

The NO-SHOW Limb:

Animals often leave whole limbs behind, on purpose. These are, for example, like the hind limbs that get left outside of a vehicle or left on the outside of a door. These animals are reminiscent of the Stretch Armstrong toy of my youth. The body will stretch longer than you ever thought possible, in order to leave "that leg" off stage. It's happy where it is, thank you very much. It prefers to be like the guy who is way behind the other guy who is facing the tarantula. If that hind leg could saw itself off from the rest of the body and run away from the scene, it would. And front legs can be tossed aside as well, with just a simple rotation of the core of the body.

When you are dealing with a "no show" limb on a stretched-out animal, there is a point at which they have stretched as far as they can. Oscar's body feels like it just cannot reach any farther to get to your button. And when the brain is feeling inadequate in this way, it often feels like it *also* can't reach your food reward either. These No-Show animals, no matter the species, sometimes revert to *grabbing at* food offered freely from your hand in a snappy manner, as if it's hard to reach. You may suddenly feel unexpected teeth, right out of the blue.

If you ever feel teeth inside an OSCAR session, "no show" is usually the reason. But try to see the glass as half full. In truth, these grabby mouths are evidence of a very good thing; it's a sign that you have hit upon a very important locus of phobia that is being repaired. As my apprentice likes to joke, "If your own blood starts flowin' you know you're doing good OSCAR repair." But also, don't forget what moms say: "It's only funny 'til someone loses an eye." So make sure that your button is something Oscar can reach without too much trouble. Try not to take any food snappiness personally. Oscar is doing very difficult work.

The SAIL-AWAY Limb (Horizontal Angle Widening)

Just like it sounds, when we hold a button up anywhere within a foot or two of that limb, that whole end of Oscar's body just slowly drifts away like a beach ball on the lake. The brain rotates that leg away from you, creating a wider-angle gap between you both, thus achieving for Oscar's leg a larger and safer distance from you.

For instance, the repelled part will often magnify in degree. If you approach with only ten degrees, the body part will sail away 70 or 130 degrees of rotation or distance from the animal's initial stance. The body part is literally sailing away from potential contact.

The REBAR Limb (Elevation Refusers)

This is a stunning display when you see it, and we see it literally every day on the job. This leg is just plain stuck in thick, imaginary mud. It truly appears as if the leg has a metal armature inside it that is locking it deep into the ground, just like the rebar that is often buried into a cement block to give it rigidity. This "limb rebar" will even learn its way into becoming something more like *bendable* rebar, but the leg will still be firmly stuck to the ground. The foot will not leave the ground without going through familiar recovery stages, like panic breathing, rapid heart rate, and loss of balance. These bodies literally trip while standing in one spot.

Although it looks like there must be a physical injury somewhere in that limb (or in the alternate hip/shoulder), there is not. For many reasons, Oscar *thinks* s/he cannot maintain balance on the other three legs; maybe one was injured at one time. But for whatever reason, Oscar has been too afraid to lift this leg in social scenarios in the past. When we finally talk them into trying it with us now, they find out that they can lift it just fine.

It's just like when you're treading water for dear life and then you hear someone say, "Hey, just put your feet down." When you attempt to stand, it turns out that the water is only four feet deep. That's the best metaphor. When animals learn that they are more capable than they knew, they are instantly so happy (if exhausted) to find this out. Dogs start licking your face, and horses start high-fiving you with their knees.

ENTANGLEMENT Phobia (Specific Angle Refusers)

For limbs with documented or undocumented entanglement histories, Oscar's touching of anything weird with that limb frequently brings back memories of that leg being trapped or feeling out of Oscar's control. These legs can actually act as though they are (caught on) your butt hand. This kind of limb must learn to push away your button (the memory of the thing.)

For instance, let's think about a leg that was caught up in some barbed wire that is still nailed to a fallen fence post. This scene can be gross to think about but this kind of accident is quite commonplace in the life of the farm animal, especially one that has been moved to a new property that used to be old, abandoned farmland.

Remember, getting untangled from an offender sometimes requires pushing out, but sometimes, it requires pulling/sucking in toward you. On the day of the original entanglement, if pushing on the leg made some metal cut deeper, then Oscar must now learn to PULL through to an imaginary solution now. If pulling made the attack worse, then Oscar must now learn to PUSH the leg away to safety.

Whatever direction of freedom-seeking was failing and shut itself off at the site of the incident, that switch must now be turned back on in order to repair the OSCAR hole in that leg to make it work like normal again. After Oscar Therapy, it's as if the entanglement had never actually happened.

Joint Instability

If a joint is physically injured, even subtly, it usually cannot push back on an OSCAR button with *any* amount of physical strength or stability. It can only "get pushed around" by an outside force. (We don't see this issue very often, because remember, the animals that find us have already been cleared or treated by veterinarians.)

And yet, we sometimes catch things the vets can't find on palpation exam, on flexion exam, or even by imaging. When OSCAR find a specific balance that the animal can create on one side of the body but cannot create on the other side (that we cant cause to strengthen within the same session) that's when we are likely to blame an actual physical limitation. An OSCAR hole will get better and better as guarding muscles begin to relax. A physical hole will get worse and worse, as compensating muscles become exhausted.

OSCAR in Ankles (Any Limb's Distal Joint Crevices)

The very distal ends of limbs, meaning the parts farthest from the main body, like the toes and the bones of the hands or feet, these can certainly be victims of bad things happening to them. When something bad does happen to a finger or a toe, the Oscar hole tends to be found not so much there but up in the shoulder or the hip that controls that limb's reflexive recoil, just like when you jerk back after touching a hot stove element by mistake. However, I certainly have seen plenty of Oscar holes buried in the flexing joints of the "ankles and wrists" of any species.

I include this section, about what an animal *sees* behind them, into this Peculiar Limbs essay because the eyes of animals are often found at the end of a "long limb of a neck." Animals use the leverage of a long neck to act sort of like a limb. A long neck can be useful for reaching, for leverage, for balancing, and for craning the eyes around so they can see very different vantage points. But that's ONLY true if the animal's brain is *willing* to see what's there.

The reality, though, is that plenty of perfectly good necks go wasted and unused because animals have learned (from us humans) not to use their necks as nature intended. If a brain is too afraid to see what it might catch a glimpse of back there, then the brain will often tell the neck, "Please don't help my eyes to look that way."

Quite often, an Oscar will even *absolutely refuse* to look at what's back there until they go through the rebuilding of those OSCAR holes in their visual field. Where the eyes want to newly go, the neck can then be freed up to go as well. Where the eyes won't go, the neck won't go, and the spine won't go. So all of the legs will be no-show legs in the animal won't get anywhere near you!

5.2.d The Caboose on the OSCAR Train: The Strange "Savior Leg" Builds Last

This is where I am going to attempt to write the very last (because it is the hardest to write) essay of this entire book. Even though it belongs here in Chapter 5, I'm writing it last because (and I admit this wholeheartedly) I really don't understand this very well yet. It's a hard essay to write because I don't have a good feel for what's going on here. I can only describe it to the degree of my current understanding.

This essay is about what I call "the Savior Leg." Basically, this is the leg on any OSCAR positive animal that initially seems to have the *least* amount of OSCAR trouble. It's the leg/quarter that seems to hold up the entire animal, when the other parts don't quite know what to do. Where this leg's "courage" or "normalcy" comes from, I have no idea. Maybe it was just never involved in scary experiences. Maybe it was the one that pulled an animal to safety.

The first step of any build is about learning the game; this usually happens on Oscar's strongest front quarter. The missing holes are the parts that build at the fastest rate (on the calendar), because the animal is merely lacking some critical information. Next, the phobic zones (which build at the fastest *speed*, minute to minute) take a longer time to build (on the calendar), because there can be a substantial amount of layered emotion to get through.

But the zone that always seems to be the caboose on the OSCAR train (the zone that always seems to get built last) that honor goes to the Savior Leg. This is the part that has always done the major share of the steering toward survival. It is the part that is the most unwilling to change or learn or let go of the responsibility to be the central tent pole in the Big Top of that animal's nervous system.

Lately, as OSCAR Therapy has been gaining fans, I have been seeing a bigger number of large puppies who live with older people. A large puppy's bounding and jumping obviously causes trouble for this more fragile owner population. These wise owners are trying to get out ahead of growing problems before somebody gets hurt. So to prevent having to give the animals up, they are getting their animal's social body skills built early on in age with OSCAR Therapy.

These young dogs are physically fit and rambunctious. But they are also truly too young and bendy to have acquired any history of even mild physical injury. These dogs are roughly six months old and healthy, but most have also been failing puppy school. As my intern and I are building up these young dogs, we're surprised to find that almost every one of these young animals seems to have a Savior Leg.

This seems to be the first *sacrificial* leg, in that it's the one that goes into physical collapse first. Thinking as a biologist in a veterinary department, I used to assume that there was an original physical insult in the leg there that then develops layers of behavioral protection around it (like the irritating sand at the center of an oyster's pearl), but I've come to find that it's actually more like this analogue... The rest of the animal is crazy all around it, as if the Savior Leg is the eye of the hurricane.

So, I had to ask, "Which comes first, the chicken or the egg? "Which comes first, the injury or the Savior habit? Does injury to a leg cause it to be the dominantly used leg? Or does the dominantly used leg and its overuse *cause* its own injury? And yet, only one of those stories makes sense.

Evolutionarily, as animals go, limbs are pretty cool inventions, and in mammals, there are usually four of them. Not only are they used for locomotion and doing jobs (like digging holes or tearing at food) but they also serve as spare parts. Just like we mammals have two kidneys and two lungs for redundancy in case one limb gets trashed, you always have a spare leg at the ready, at least temporarily.

And yet even in this convenient scheme, any one limb is not meant to be the singular center of gravity for the life of the animal. When one leg is being shut down by a phobic brain, then the leg next to it has to try to play the part of both legs, especially by doing a lot of extra "interior angles" work of reaching under the body more than it should normally have to. And yet these right-handed and left-handed structures are just not built to play both roles in that way. So when they *do* get used that way, more like a pogo stick than a limb, that's probably a big factor in why they are the ones that give out early.

When only one leg has been doing most of the emotional/physical absorbance work for all of the other quarters, then that one leg is doing the lion's share of the living; it's also getting most of the wear and tear. And as they say in used cars, it's not the age; it's the mileage. If early damage is going to be anywhere in the physical scaffolding of the animal, it's wise to look for that early physical damage (and less mental damage), here in the Savior Leg. Chronic overuse, over-stretch, over-torque, over weight bearing, misaligned joint stacking, and lack of "lift" etc., all seem to collect here. If you are looking for any undiagnosed injury, or maybe even a history of past injury, aim your diagnostic efforts into the Savior Leg.

If your animal is still a young sprout, and a balancing-out would afford them a life that doesn't have to rely solely on their Savior Leg, then definitely do OSCAR Therapy to build a well-rounded body-brain. But on the typical timeline of building of a whole body OSCAR map, you can expect that the Savior Leg will end up being the last one to build.

You can blame the owner and trainer for creating an animal that needs to be saved by his own sacrificial body parts, but try not to blame Oscar. If s/he has a body part that is the first to fail, or the first to get ground down and break, try not to blame Oscar for that either. S/he's earned the battle scars.

5.2.e The Walking Dead: OSCAR Therapy Can Revive a Crushed Spirit

"Do You Exist?"-Therapy Uses Initiation Transfer

Zombies are hard to identify in amongst the throngs of people you meet on a daily basis. You'd think they'd be easy to spot, what with their rotted out eyeballs, their arms hanging by tendons, and their knees all out of joint... But they somehow hide all of their partial death under navy blue business suits and dark sunglasses, so they blend right in.

The walking dead are usually mild-mannered types who never even make a blip on the radar until the day they go postal. But before that, the reason that the walking dead make little effect on the world is because they don't believe they can. Their will is bottled up deep inside, so deep that it's even foreign to them.

I am sometimes asked to help awaken the walking dead, the animal versions. These are the animals that have crushed spirits for whatever reason, usually after years of abuse, neglect, or illness have been imposed on or endured by a "sensitive soul." These individuals need us to focus on both safety and motivation. These souls are not only the most tear-jerking cases but also the most rewarding cases you'll ever work with, because you can provide the road that brings a "gone zombie" truly back to life.

I find that many adult shelter dogs (and other species) I meet have a gigantic *fear* of their own *Will, which is a sad state to be in, indeed.* They give you the feeling that they have been passed from person to person so many times and from such an early age, that they've become someone who constantly walks on egg shells, trying to make sure they don't ruffle any of the feathers that would make their pack abandon them yet again.

When I meet these dogs, I dig around a little into who they are. No matter who they pretend to be on the outside, no matter how jumpy, barky, whiney, and tail-wagging, all of that seems to be a cover for the fact that they actually perceive that they have absolutely no influence on their world at all. And they believe it deep, deep down.

Now these dogs are lovable dogs, which is why they were lucky enough to survive the shelter system. These dogs clearly love to be touched, petted, rubbed, and fluffed. They seem to like paling around with human family members, but often, these dogs also show extreme separation anxiety; they often stick to one person in a house of many people. They seem to get along with other dogs well enough too, but they have this weird inability to play. They don't play with sticks, balls, or other toys.

Some zombie animals are even so far gone that they are afraid to move, and they freeze up. With an Oscar who has opted to be dead weight in the world, you may think you have the advantage. With no will present to work against you, Oscar is psychologically and "physically" absent, meaning that you can handle him or her like a rag doll.

But a Zombie Oscar's dead weight can turn dangerous. If you pick such an Oscar up like the sac of potatoes that s/he is, and then plunk him or her down in the middle of something s/he's been avoiding. If you then wait for Oscar to come alive enough to get out of that "pit," s/he will somehow get the body to safety but s/he won't be learning much of anything at all about the experience.

Remember that saying, "Aw, that wasn't so bad, was it?" *never* works. Oscar is terrified by his predicament and his inability to solve it, and it's your job to provide a ton of support and approval just for his breathing in and out while he's anywhere near the pit. Throwing him into the hole may wake him up in body, but you're corroborating that his original terror was totally valid. And now he's afraid not only of the pit but of you, too.

You can take over the responsibility for Zombie Oscar's physical being in space, and you can even change the environment under his feet. But if you do that, that means that you have to do his whole job for him. So no, your job is not to throw Oscar into the "deep end of a pool," metaphorically to make him "instinctually swim." Your job is to coax Oscar back into her/his body so that he can re-own all of his/her faculties and come into existence.

To find out if a dog is actually a zombie in a dog suit, we begin the usual way, with OSCAR button number one. But in the zombies, what happens next is mind blowing. Many (not all) adult x-shelter dogs *cannot* bridge the 1-inch gap from their body to my button. When I remind them of the *Good/clicking noise = treat* part, they are happy and tail wagging. They expect the treat, and they eat it.

But then, when I again wait for them to *think of* crossing the one-inch spatial gap, to be the one to reach out to touch me, ...nothing. These dogs wait forever, desperately hoping that I will "happen to them." And if I don't, the dogs whine (some bark) at me, get a little agitated, sigh deeply, and walk away to curl up on the living room rug in utter defeat.

Even though they understood the game, these dogs have no confidence in their ability to "happen to me." The capacity to impose themselves on an outside world, which is not happening to them first, is simply not there. I often call this kind of session "existence therapy" because I feel like I am teaching their *wills* to come back to life.

These animals who will eat out of my hand if I offer it first, will walk away hungry before they will cross an inch of airspace to *initiate* contact. They will not / cannot even "bop me into being" to remind me to hold up my end of the game. Is it because they don't believe they can be as important as a human? They definitely believe they can't be the prime to my pump. It's like they believe that compared to someone else, they are *always* smaller; they believe they cannot *do unto others*. They act like they believe that they themselves don't exist. But they can learn to.

Any normal animal, and even most of the OSCAR-positive ones (the ones with holes in their maps) will invent pressing my button in two minutes or less. And yet, it has taken up to one hour to create that single first inch in some of the adult, formerly traumatized animals. And this one-inch of intention is the whole ballgame.

Just yesterday, my apprentice who has been building OSCAR dogs for a year told me about a dog that she couldn't crack into even after a whole hour of doing everything right and using every tool in her toolbox. There were no buttons to be had with this dog, no first inch of space. This old, lovable dog is a zombie in a dog suit. Next week, I'll help her tackle that one inch using the following approach.

With any zombie animal, back the button way off, so that it's much farther away. Your sheer existence is too much for them to handle right now, so your job is to recede. Place your button hand even many feet away from the body. Offer your butt no more than half way across the distance. That way, you are only in charge of less than half of the conversation.

The context is still the same, but now in order to get the fun and treat, the animal has got to muster up some courage and even maybe "take a running start" to bridge the gap of space between us, to meet me half way, literally. If s/he wants us to touch, this animal has to make the *initiation* part happen, because I refuse to do their showing up work *for* them. Oscar usually tries to pick up some momentum by moving through 2 or more feet of space, so as to "hurl" themselves through that toughest, final one-inch.

When Oscars finally find that one inch, it adds a new belief, a belief that it is ok for them to *initiate* the interaction with someone or something outside of themselves. And once that idea comes back on line (they presumably had it before, until it was forced out of them), these animals begin to explore their worlds and experiment. And not only is that the definition of play (remember their inability with the toys), but these individuals can now experience trial and error in ways they couldn't before and thus finally be able to *rationalize* (draw conclusions) that they are safe.

They instantly become more at peace with their own environments, and then their overall systemic anxiety subsides on its own. Owners often tell me that after a single "who's touching who" session, "s/he became a different dog, more calm and self assured... what in the world did you put in that food that I gave you?!"

Never fear a case of an OSCAR zombie. Invite Oscar to overcome fear at a quick pace, but ultimately, at the pace they choose. The most scared animal will take a little longer to believe that they can actually be in control of their own bodies and selves. But once that switch is flipped, the animal who originally seemed like a half-dead ragdoll will actually drink up social interaction like it was water in the desert.

5.3 Pauses, Waiting, and Sleep All Create "Forward Slide"

Speaking of time, learning brains benefit enormously from what many of us would call the "empty times" in between the times of focused work, even if those empty times are only just a few moments long. The smart practitioner of OSCAR Therapy and of any intense re-orientation program will learn to *leverage the benefits* of sleep, of Oscar's pauses and breaks, of your own hesitations, and of your own ability to Wait.

Using these downtime spaces strategically is what creates a forward momentum in the case, which feels like skipping rocks over the surface of a very still pond. The momentum seems to go on forever, maintaining a strong forward progress no matter what barriers are in the way. In such a system, "backslide" never (if rarely) happens. Actually, the opposite thing happens. I call it "forward slide." When you come back to the next session with Oscar, s/he is always a little ahead of wherever you left off. Your job as practitioner then becomes to spring yourself ahead so that you can catch up to where Oscar is now.

5.3.a How Long Should You Wait for a Button? The Two-Thought Pause

For many perfectly good reasons, Oscar will get distracted sometimes during your conversation. But it's not just sounds in the distance that distract Oscar. Oscar often gets distracted by past memories of previous experiences s/he's had. And it's important to let these memories wash through, while still not wasting time in your session. Oscar sometimes would rather talk about anything else, and yet the topic at hand is the topic at hand.

As you are waiting for Oscar to let go of her/his unfortunate beliefs or reflexes, your own ability to pause is of monumental importance. It's very important to let Oscar fumble around without inordinate input from you. Even third party distractions are assistive; they give Oscar a chance to *remember* to re-focus.

So when can you say you have waited *long enough* for Oscar to come back to the conversation with you? How do you know it's time to ask Oscar your same question again? At what time is it safe to remind Oscar of what you're still curious about or what you're looking for? How can you be sure you won't squash Oscar's related explorations? How do you know you won't make it worse by re-imposing yourself, uninvited, into his/her meandering cogitations or fear-riddled memories?

Luckily, this dilemma is an easy one to answer. I have found that there is an extremely helpful and impressively accurate rule to follow that helps you decide that you have waited long enough. If you follow this rule of thumb you can't hurt or hinder Oscar, and you also won't be wasting session time.

The answer is 2, the number two. Ahh, but remember, there are no *time-telling* clocks in OSCAR Therapy. Don't wait for two seconds, or two minutes, or two hours, or two days to go by. The two that you should be waiting for is two thoughts. Whenever Oscar veers off task, or is having trouble coming back for the next attempt to hit your button, just wait for two of Oscar's thoughts to go by, like the waves that lap up onto the edge of the water. If you can count waves in the water, you can count Oscar's thoughts.

A thought is a thought. It's not a neuron, it's a thought, like "what can I eat for dinner" is a thought. I won't even mention another example of what Oscar's thoughts should be about because it doesn't matter what they are about; there just have to have been two of them, and every thought under the sun counts.

They don't have to be new original thoughts; they just have to be two "distinct from each other" thoughts. In typical real time, Oscar will have two distracted thoughts before s/he either comes back to the topic at hand or forgets it entirely. Wait for two thoughts to go by before you remind Oscar of the topic at hand. So I call this the "two-thought pause."

Most of the time, your average Oscar will have two new thoughts in maybe 8 seconds. But for many, two thoughts happen in 1 second. For some, having two thoughts takes a few minutes. For some, it may even take hours before they are calm enough to think up two different things or to have any new perception at all about the rut they're deeply stuck in. Sometimes, it seems like our ruts are the only things keeping us going forward in life and that's no small thing to try to put aside. I try hard to help Oscar find a new thought, but I am not in charge of Oscar's brain.

Sometimes I wait five thoughts and sometimes I don't even let Oscar think at all before I launch in with a reminder from me. But waiting for the two thoughts from Oscar (maybe 80 percent of the time) keeps everything going along smoothly, no matter what gear you're in, no matter what skill you're practicing, no matter how wide the band width, and no matter how fast the cross talk. Watch the respected leaders you know in your community. When it comes to keeping everyone on topic, they will gravitate toward the number "2" as the number of distractions they allow before they put the main topic front and center again.

5.3.b Quittin' Time: End on a Striving Note

Myth: Sessions have to be short to be effective.

Myth: It's best to end on a FUN/GOOD note.

Conversation sessions do not have to be short to be effective; on the contrary, most animals that are focused on the OSCAR game will outlast most of the humans involved in any session. No matter how long we've been at it, animals always get upset when we leave, unless they are emotionally exhausted from treating their own fear, at which point they then crash into a zonked-out sleep. Even if never having moved a muscle or sweated a drop that day, their brains have been working very hard.

If Oscar is driving, let him decide how long he wants to be behind the wheel. My experience of the graphed pattern of Oscar's learning progress in any single session goes like this... The learning curve curves upwards, then a level out, then a ramp upwards, then a level out, then crash #1, then one giant leap forward, then crash #2 and then no more progress can be made in this session. This is when Oscars should take a few hours off.

Better yet, come back another day. The sweet spot that preserves the most forward momentum is 48 hours later, giving a hard-working brain two days off to rest and recover. But you can also come back at any later date, weeks, months, or years later and pick up the game right where you left off. Oscar *will* remember it.

But there are only so many hours in any given day, and there are only so many moments in an hour. Everyone has other things to do today. So when you have to quit for the day, you have to quit. But pay attention to what's happening right at the end so that you can jump out of "this game of Double Dutch" without getting you or Oscar all tangled up in the ropes, and so that you can set yourselves up for the best jumping in place "tomorrow."

Quitting on a good note (as most of the experts recommend to do) is not only unnecessary, but it can even work against you in relaying to Oscar a false change of priority. Instead, aim to quit on a *striving* note, always *only* on a striving note. A "striving note" is when Oscar has decided to try and has a toe hold on the really good idea. Even when he's trying and bombing, that's a fine place to quit with congratulations. When they've almost got it but not quite, that's a powerful place to quit.

Imagine going on a game show and you're doing well at staying in the game, and then just before the final one million dollar question, you're told, "I'm sorry, we're out of time. You'll have to come back again next week to finish the game!" After the applause, what's the likelihood that you'll find a way to come back next week with your A game? It's guaranteed.

Don't wait for Oscar to do something do you want in order for you to call it a day. Holding out on anyone who is already very tired is a risky thing to do. If you decide to quit on a good note, you have to go searching for one, and you may never find it because Oscar is exhausted; so then, you may never quit. Or you may settle for something that's *not so good* and call it good just to get to the end. Your settling is confusing to Oscar because it may seem contradictory to what Oscar has learned so far.

If you do decide that you both have to end on a "good" note, remember too that your "good" has no meaning to Oscar. Since they are not "in the know" yet, they have no idea why some arbitrary thing along the way is "good," and why other arbitrary things are not. Quitting on a good or easy or winning or simple or positive note is a) an insult to Oscar, b) a stroking of your own success-oriented ego, c) non-instructive to Oscar, and d) a waste of everyone's time.

Oscar doesn't need to be "happy with you" at the end of any particular conversation; what Oscar needs to be is happy with his/her own efforts. If you have been mean to or dismissive of her in this conversation, then she won't want to talk to you next time anyway, no matter how much s/he's won in your game show today. But if s/he's playing to win, you can safely put that game on pause for as long as you need to, no matter whether Oscar is up or down in the game at the moment.

The length of "a session" should not be measured with a clock or a calendar. A session should only be measured by belief changes. One obviously permanent change today, not in action, but in *belief*, now *that's* a lesson. As soon as one or two beliefs have changed, it's ok to quit. If zero beliefs have changed so far, it is a little risky to quit.

The risk you run by quitting too soon is that Oscar is learning that interactions with you have comparably little value. A useful session is not 20%, 40%, or 60% better than before. A learned *piece* of a skill is a choice that was 10% when we started and grew to 95% by the end of the session. Even though you may study algebra for a whole year, you don't "get" algebra until the *day* you *get it*. On *that* day, you learned what algebra was *for*.

Here are some tips for allowing the appropriate "drying time" that helps Oscar learn new things with the most efficient use of quitting times, time off, and sleep.

- ✓ If it was or is (or needs to be)* a big leap forward, do not touch that topic again for a while, maybe even a week or more, so that Oscar can build up reserves for the next launch. *(Some challenges cannot be made easier.)

- ✓ If it was or is or needs to be** a small leap forward, keep loading Oscar up with more teaching, and sooner than later, so that you don't waste time on the way to the next plateau. **(Some challenges must be micromanaged by you.)

- ✓ If it was or is or needs to be a risky, dangerous, or questionable leap forward (like if you have to come clean after a manipulating lie you had to temporarily tell Oscar), or if you have made no progress or have slid backward away from your goal due to a mishap, then you really need to pound it out right now. Even if you have to keep Oscar up past his/her bedtime, do not stop communicating until you get somewhere/anywhere that is relatively *emotionally* safe.

This last category is why most teachers and trainers are addicted to "ending on a good note." It's because their teaching methods are (inadvertently yet sufficiently) questionable, risky, and/or emotionally dangerous. The "good note" is sought because it's the only *safe* buoy in what is otherwise a sea of tension. And that tension is going both ways; it's being corroborated every time the student is slipping through their fingers. This makes teachers uncomfortable.

But I can't even count how many times in OSCAR sessions that Oscar has crashed into an emotional or even a physical wall at the very end of our session only to come back much stronger the very next time. This is due to the fact that his or her Will had been maintained fully intact during the previous session, *even* if it was challenged to the smoke point. These will-driven, huge forward lurches in progress are not the exception in Oscar sessions; they're the norm.

And it is very important to know that, because this truth is what will dictate the best way to begin each new session. Always begin every next new session with the big "finish-line end-goal" question. Give them a chance to show you if they have surmised it and learned it all by themselves in their sleep. If they still can't do it yet, that will become obvious very quickly after your first or second ask, and then you'll just pick up where you left off. But if you *assume* that Oscar still can't do it, then you will never know what they have already created all on their own, possibly in *a better way* than you could have taught it *to* them.

5.3.c How to Tell Oscars They're Done for Right Now

Oscars are usually nervous in the first few minutes of the initial two or three therapy/treatment sessions and conversations with me, because after meeting me once or twice, they are now under no false impressions about what I am there for. Half of their brain wants to participate in the fun and empowering game, but the other half realizes that this is the real deal. This is serious business, and it's not merely a game; it's about their deep dark monsters in the closet.

So they just start out a little keyed up. Oscar's mind starts revving even before I ask the first question. They bring a little too much energy to the table, and it takes about 10 minutes for them to calm their minds. But later on in the session, after working so hard for a long while, brains do get tired. Their "brain glucose" (the available gas in their tank) gets all used up.

Whether you are working with animals or children or adults or even business partners, it is very important to implement the following. When a conversation is temporarily over or must go on pause, or if you have to be done for the time being or done for the day, you must really try to send this message to Oscar clearly. Don't ever just walk away unannounced. To Oscar that can feel scary, and it's also disrespectful.

With animals, give them a verbal and visual cue that means, "Oscar, your work here is done." We use what the Marine Mammals often use, a two-handed "no more" mild wave, just like you'd use to tell the waiter who wants to know when they've grated enough cheese on your entre. We call this our Release cue or Exit cue. It tells Oscar that they can now stop thinking hard about us, because our "store is closing" for the day. When you use such a cue, teach what that cue means by NOT engaging or responding to Oscar for at least 15 minutes after you have given the cue.

And regarding Oscar's comings and goings at the END of a session, do NOT reward Oscar for sauntering off and do NOT reward Oscar for coming back. Done means done. (Getting compensation for coming back just teaches Oscar to bait you by leaving again, in order to come back again, in order to get paid again.)

But there's one more important note regarding the topic of when to quit for the day. In the event that you and Oscar failed to meet your goal today, sleeping on it and coming back with a new plan tomorrow is actually NOT the most efficient, respectful, or even sensible way to get your message across. If you plan to try an alternate approach to today's goal, or even if you want to change to a different goal, it's best to make that switch *inside* a single session.

Changing plan or changing topic in between sessions is actually the best way to cause Oscar to be suspicious of you on that subsequent day. To them, you dropped the last conversation mid-thought for some unknown reason, *and maybe it was a scary reason.* To them, you are also ignoring their very current memories of what you both recently talked about; Oscar has every reason to feel ghosted when you come back later acting like a different person. Instead, it is most efficient and usually works best to make any shift of approach or shift of topic INSIDE your current session:

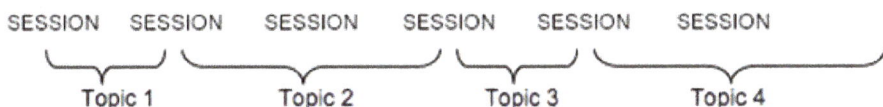

Figure 20. Introduce new topics DURING session.

And not only for Oscar's benefit but for your own benefit too, you should note that if you try two different approaches in the same session (on the same day, and under the same conditions) only then will you really be able to compare apples to apples regarding which approach works better for Oscar's current brain. For more reasons than I can name, try hard to not make any switch in tactic or goal in-between Oscar's sessions.

5.3.d Currently Experiencing Technical Difficulties: Sleep Causes Forward Slide

New clients always ask me some form of this question... "Since you won't see Buster for the week/month/season while we're away, how much review will s/he have to do in order to get back to where we are now? How much backslide will we have to deal with?"

And here's the answer I give to every client: "None. There is no back slide; but there is forward slide. You could come back next week, next month, or next year, and he won't do any worse than he did today because no brain forgets what it actually learns on its own terms. In fact, Buster is much more likely to do *better*. There is no back slide, but there IS *forward slide*."

Forward slide is my name for a progression where Oscar comes back farther along the learning path than s/he was when you left him/her last time, and forward slide comes from sleep. In the learning process, sleep is mandatory; and *for* sleep, you must wait. Sleep is not only a muscle rejuvenator; it's also an imperative neural learning phase. Sleep helps to sweep away extraneous, unimportant information so it is an inherently fundamental part of the learning process.

When you give a "learning animal" a break or a vacation, during that time off the clock, she always goes farther down the path she was on, following her current vector, all by herself. If you put a size-8 hurt on an animal today, she'll come back with a size-12 anger tomorrow because overnight, s/he learned. If you put a size-5 dare to him today, he'll come back with a size-9 determination tomorrow. And within reasonable time frames, the longer the "time off," the further down that path Oscar will go.

If I want an animal to learn a complex concept that he is having a hard time picking up, I make sure to give him two weeks off in between sessions. By that time, he has already crunched all the numbers in his head, purged the information that was unhelpful, and has been dying to show off the results for a while. By the time I come back, he is tearing the place down in his eagerness to play the game, which is exactly the drive we'll need to make that big leap forward.

Why does the time off have such a big effect? Dreams. That's my best explanation. Of course, I have no direct proof (except for my own experience with dreams, where I find lost keys– where I solve emotional quagmires– where I create new tools), but there is no way to argue with time-stamped case records. Animals do better after a few days off than they do if they have to work a marathon weekend with me. And they *always* do better the next morning after a marathon day with me.

Have you ever watched your dog chase rabbits in his sleep, or your cat hunt mice in his sleep? Those activities are pretty much the most engaging things that our dogs and cats do when they're awake, right? Well, facing fear, phobia and being out of control is as engaging an activity as you can get. If you were afraid of flying, and you were in a "face your fears" program that was curing your phobia, don't you think you'd be dreaming about airplanes a little more than usual?

Maybe you crash in your dreams, or maybe you learn to pilot the plane in your dreams, or maybe you crawl out the window and fly around the outside of the plane in your dreams. But regardless of the storyline, your subconscious is working the same problem over and over, experiencing the emotions elicited by this problem as well as also experiencing the *alternative* emotions associated with all of the possible outcomes and solutions.

Dreaming is one of the only activities that can really solidify the ownership of what is learned. Why? Because during sleep all of the threats, all of the demons, all of the ideas, and all of the solutions, are coming from *inside* Oscar's very own brain.

In Oscar's dreams, "I am there" to challenge them, but they are the ones who are actually writing the script and "playing my part" opposite their own part in the play. So in effect, they are challenging themselves, but only to the exact degree that is *imaginable* by their own brains. A body in sleep mode is not actually trapped; yet the brain is going over and over, in great detail, what it feels like to be maybe trapped and *maybe not trapped*. In dreams, Oscar is simulating not only the problem but also *all possible solutions*.

Trainers and veterinary professionals have a favorite approach for getting an animal to behave in a certain way on an urgent basis at a critical time:

"Spring it on 'em—but don't give 'em time to think because we'll only get one shot."

And yet, in OSCAR Therapy, the best way to elicit that MUST DO PERFORMANCE is the exact opposite.

First, we refresh the buttons on the body parts that will be needed. Whenever possible, we do a brush up or even a dress rehearsal a day or two before the event. The more Oscar gets to think about and dream about using the skill you're going to need them to perform, the better Oscar's ultimate performance will be during crunch time.

Sleep is the brain state where anxious, scared, phobic, challenged, or creative individuals all resemble each other. Their brains are all using sleep time to "work on" what is most engaging to them at this time in their lives. And the smart animal owner will leverage this predictable "free work." Because for the concepts that weren't quite there yesterday, no matter how hard we tried to help Oscar create them, concept mastery will often show up right out of the gate in the very next session after sleep, just like someone turned on a light bulb. Sleep is what enables that growth, and we practitioners can't take the credit for what it grows.

5.3.e The Finish Line Is an Executive Decision

With Oscar Therapy, you've learned how to start and create an incredible conversation; now, it's time to learn how to END that incredible conversation! At the end of every single topic or goal, you are the only one who can decide whether Oscar has met that goal. Give Oscar a "Tada!" However you can relay the, "You've done it!" information to Oscar, that's what you'll need to do. You started this conversation, so you must be the one to finish it.

Some people jump up out of their chairs. Some people do a touchdown dance. Some people run up and hug Oscar (which you should not do in an Oscar session: *Thou shalt Not Touch Oscar.*) Some people use the high-pitched and loud voice of applause. Whatever works to relay the idea of the finished goal, it's your job and ONLY *your* job to say it. No one else can say it for you. *"That'll do, Oscar, that'll do..."*

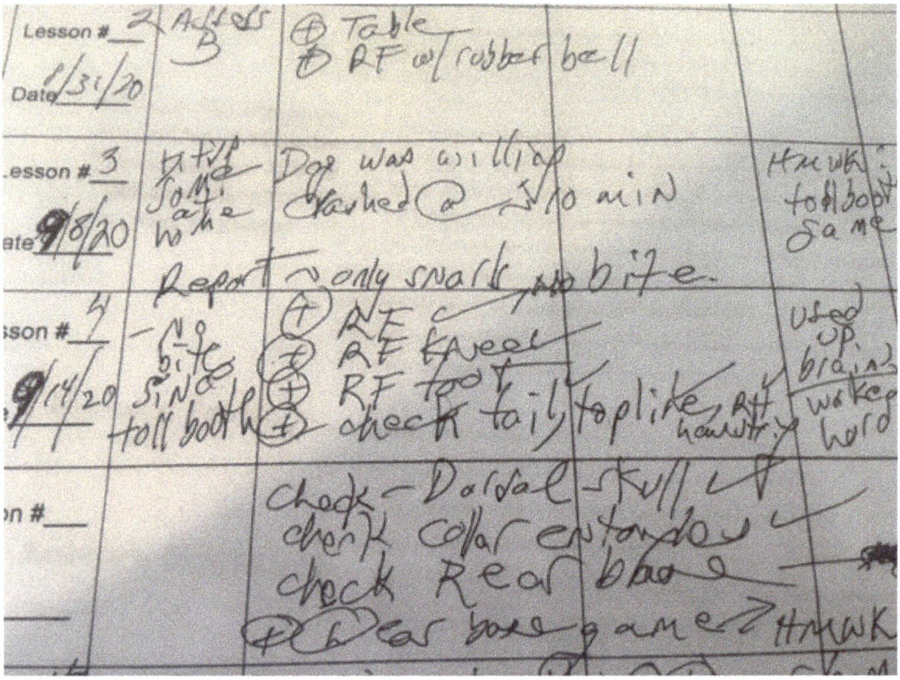

Figure 21. However you record your session notes, make sure to log them in after EVERY session.

5.4 Superhero Goals – Apprentice Level

If rainbows and butterflies and superhero powers are what you wish for in Oscar, then, whatever you do, do NOT throw out the can of worms that you see right now. It is usually true that what looks just like a can of worms is actually a can of butterflies in the making. Take advantage of the potential that Oscar represents. If a superhero partner is what you are wishing for, then all you have to do is build one in Oscar. Keep neither butterflies nor Oscars in a can; it's always best to help them out of there, so that they can be all they can be.

Here are some of the remarkable yet humbling outcomes that can be achieved using OSCAR Therapy.

5.4.a Oscar, Please Present Thyself: Tractor Beam Buttons

At a client's farm, it was time to collect up an Arabian mare for her session number three or four. The owner said, "I have to go over to the far end of the herd to get her, so I'll be back in 5 minutes." I said, "Don't bother; I'll get her."

I walked only about 15 feet sideways to put myself at the best angle to the mare who was a whole big field away. I made a few loud banging sounds to get the herd's attention, and then I took a couple steps along that vector to put a social vacuum on only that one mare at the far end. The mare immediately weaved her way around and through the rest of the herd of horses, who were none the wiser. She got over to us in about two minutes.

The owner said, "I don't know what you just did to make that happen, but before I even get into that, I have a question first. Do you do *that*, do you have her come to you, I mean instead of going all the way over there to get her, do you do that in order to establish dominance roles? By asking her to come all the way over here by herself, are you trying to tell her that you are the leader, the one in charge?"

I laughed as I said… "What's a leader? No, it's because I'm too lazy to walk all the way over there. She's gonna have to walk all the way over here anyway to talk to me, so if I have to go fetch her, then I have to make two trips while she also makes that trip, so between us that's three trips including two trips worth of wasted energy. Why do I do that? It's just easier if she decides to bring herself over here, right?"

The reason that my correctly angled hip button (using the animal's 10 or 2 o'clock vectors) works so well *even at distance* is a little more subtle. It works because the reward it holds is of even greater value to Oscar than Oscar's own freedom. The Button works as a tractor beam on Oscar because you are giving yourself over in trade. This is a big, big deal. You are underscoring Oscar's influence over you. "If you follow me, Oscar, I'll soon be following your lead and the OSCAR game." But this manipulative tractor-beam strategy is so advanced that humans are the only animal species to have you figured out this social tractor beam capability. Right?

Wrong. Arf Arf! What Lassie? What's up, girl? [Lassie runs 20 feet away and stops, looking back…. *A pre-emptive, baiting disengage causing a tractor beam pull on you.*] What's up girl?? [Lassie runs another 30 feet and stops, looking back at you again.] You say Jimmy's stuck under a tree and the water's rising in the creek?! Lassie, go back and help Jimmy! I'll get the Sheriff! [Lassie tears off down to the creek.]

This is not fiction. Many of us know that most dogs, especially the older herding breeds, will make exactly these choices when they perceive a crisis. The point to be made though is *not* that the dog is acting like a human. The point to be made is that we humans can act like the dogs and like all of the other social *animals* we are all related to, way back towards the trunk of the evolutionary tree. This disengaged OSCAR button tractor-beam is a well-conserved *social animal* grouping skill, and it is not merely the domain of the savvy corporate merger lawyer. The savvy corporate merger lawyer just tapped this old well. If he gets over zealous and greedy and falls into that well, Lassie will bring the Sheriff to fish him out.

If you prefer science over the old boob tube (though neither fact nor fiction is any less real than the other because the reality is that *you are the one seeking the information*) then just replace the idea of Lassie with some other animal who disengages in order to draw Oscar toward participation. Herding Gazelles split off from the herd to draw the lions' attention away from the newborns. Why? Because they can. Today's newborns are tomorrow's precious gene pool, and you don't really have to think ahead too far or have a brain too big for that behavior to be reinforced. Plus it's fun to taunt the lions on a nice day. It's what gazelle legs were made to do.

The disengaging OSCAR button is not rocket science. Children, puppies, prey species, and hunters-in-the making of all social species disengage from each other all day long, in play. They bop their sister in the nose and take off, baiting for a chase. Whether in play mode or in crisis mode, social animals know how to draw a crowd and steer it too. But I would bet that the "following" behavior is instinct, and the tractor-beam behavior is a learned skill that gets passed down.

So once you have any body location basically built or "buttoned up," you can then use that button to suction that body part toward anywhere you need it to go. By moving the button and causing the animal to reach farther out *toward* it, or even farther out *away* from it, depending on which direction you reward Oscar for going, you'll get pretty good control. We practitioners regularly drag animals around through empty space just this way– voluntarily.

Lead lines and ropes become antiquated tools, stuff that's no longer needed, as it only gets in the way. A stand of trees or a pile of other animals in the vicinity no longer gets in your way; you can work with your animal right inside them. But the coolest part of using buttons like tractor beams or vacuum suctions is that they work that way *at any distance*, provided that you are lined up somewhere near Oscar's 10 and 2 o'clocks and are calling attention to your own button.

Sociologically, the power of the "authority" did not originate from its power to punish you; nor did it originate from its power to banish you to the desert when you did wrong. The power of any authority truly comes from its option to leave you behind, far behind, when the family begins to move, like when they are traveling toward better resources, like *when they are on migration.*

The primal power of "the family" or group is endowed with is its power to leave you behind when the whole group, in it's entirety, goes on the move. The train leaves the station only once, and if you are not on it, you will find yourself alone, to fend for yourself. And when you are at a greater distance from Oscar, you are tapping into that original emotional state of that original stream, the flowing river of movement.

So when Oscar's first job is to show up, and to come to you ready for any kind of work, OSCAR Therapy makes "the impossible volunteer" commonplace.

Coupling the attention getting, the addictive game, and the social mandate together is a draw that no animal, not even a human animal, can resist.

5.4.b There's Too Much of Oscar on Me! : Button Clamps

Many people learning OSCAR Therapy seem to get flummoxed by this one, but for the life of me, I'm not exactly sure why. To me, whether an Oscar can touch a button or untouch a button, those seem like the very same idea. But I guess for some people, they seem like two very separate ideas.

So for clarification, I'll now describe what OSCAR Therapy often means for many of the non-extreme cases, like the cases that barely need a behaviorist, a "trainer," or a teacher of any kind. (Although, their owners may need some basic tools.) What I'll be talking about here are the over-bearing animals.

To begin, let's note that in the basics of OSCAR *Theory* (which is less a theory and more of an approach), a brain has to learn how to *push* on something before it can learn how to UN-push on that same something. One cannot UN-touch something that they haven't already touched (in order to make the contact with it). Correct?

This essay harkens back to our understanding of both the OS-5-to-9 Oscar Scores and the Porcupine Skill of Chapter 4. But here is another way to say the exact same thing again... This essay is about how to use the exact same Oscar button you have been using all along, but just in the opposite way, in order to create the equal yet *opposite* choice inside Oscar's brain. And this new kind of choice happens almost as quickly.

While it is very true that most of our goals for our animals (especially the rescued animals) stem from wanting to create a more comfortable interface, sometimes what we want from our animals is *less* of that comfortable interface. Sometimes, we need the animals to learn to not be all over people. For instance *not* jumping on the elderly or *not* jumping on the pregnant women or *not* bopping toddlers in the face, those are all good ideas to build in our animals. Sometimes even, we just don't want claws to be delivered to our leg when we are trying to read.

Sometimes we want less of our animals' body parts to be launching onto us, thrown onto us, knocked into us, bumped into us, handed over to us, lain over us, sprawled over us, smeared onto us and the like. The funny part though is that humans, just like any animal, are a very inconsistent species, and we often do unto them what we don't want them doing unto us. Still, our inconsistency is not the bad part about us. In actuality, our inconsistency is the *good* part about us.

I am definitely no fan of the cognitive evil we call "consistency." When we can tap into different expressions for varying social requirements, that's where all of the learning flexibility and the good family bonding with our animals comes from. The fact is that sometimes we *secretly want* our animals to do all of those improper things to us and for us, because it's just like when we do all of those "wrong" things to and for them! During times of play, fear, medical treatment, emergency, and any other of the extremes of daily life, what we actually want and need from our animals is for them to be both very flexible *and* instantly adaptable.

But in order to teach any animal that there are times and places for things, that the rules can change on a dime and in an instant, and that they shouldn't jump to the conclusion that all new people they meet can be jumped on, then what we really need is to be able to teach them to *feel things out*, literally. What we need to do is to teach our Oscars that sometimes it's best to UN-touch a button... even before they touch it in the first place. So... what we need to teach them is that some people are *sticky* people.

If there is anything that we all know we wish we hadn't touched by mistake, it's the things that stick to us. Gross! Yuck, I get grossed out even writing about it! Whether they be the sticky raw eggs, sticky tape, the sticky burrs, or the sticky gum on the bottom of your shoe, the things that stick to us are the things that all of us animals are grossed out by the most.

Whether they were the mammals, birds, amphibians, reptiles, fish or any of the other animals that live among us, I've watched all of these different kinds of animals be grossed out by something that got stuck on their fur, on their feathers, on their scales, or even on their slimy or not slimy skins. If there is something that's not supposed to be on them and they can't get rid of it, then all they want to do is get it off. They want to *exit*, and leave that sticky thing behind.

So when Oscar just happens to be giving you too much of themselves, whatever and whenever it is that you don't want that much, and/or in any situation that you *never* want that much of, all you have to do is let Oscar get unfortunately and regrettably stuck to you. This is achieved just by playing the following game. However, note that you can really blow it on this one if you don't allow Oscar to learn that making the right choice is what *immediately* gets him or her unstuck.

The game to play is the game I call the clothespin game. Hopefully, most people still know what a clothespin is. It's that little clip that clips the laundry onto an outside clothesline for that fresh, dried-out in the sunlight smell. But... do not try to mimic the size of this clip, mimic only exactly what it *does*. These "weak clamps" hold a shirt in place, but if you really pull on that shirt, the clip/clamp will open and the shirt will "spring itself free" from the stuck place.

Whenever Oscar, or even just any part of Oscar, is too close for comfort, just turn into a full-body or a full-arm or a full-torso large clothespin, and you will put Oscar into "a lockdown," a stuck place. Do whatever you have to do so that Oscar feels stuck to you in a way s/he never intended. And wait a second for Oscar to realize that they are now stuck. Pretty immediately after that, Oscar is going to begin to try to wriggle free from the gross, unintended sticky thing that you have just become.

To make sure you are "clamping" in the safest way possible, try to catch ONLY whatever large body part is literally thrown AT you. Causing pain is too much; pinching is too much; scruffing is too much; jerking is too much. Usually, you don't need a full body restraint; you just want to lockdown whatever Oscar is smearing you with. And then, AS SOON AS s/he makes any move at all to remove ANY body part AWAY FROM YOU, that's the right answer, so just let them slide through your clamp as they exit! Oscar must always have an easy way out.

Just like with a clothespin, the second that Oscar is trying to exit, you must let Oscar slip right through your fingers and exit. After all, Oscar is doing exactly what you want: Oscar is leaving you instead of being on you. So let them leave! Let them exhale about their new discovery that sometimes you're sticky, in a disappointing way. You've just taught Oscar that there are sometimes limits in social interaction. This opens the door for them to learn that there are also other choices they can make that are better, safer, more fun, and...

I bet I know what you were thinking. I bet that you thought I was going to say "more rewarding" or "rewardable." If you *didn't* guess that answer, then you probably know your own Oscar very well. But if you did think that you should reward Oscar for leaving you, then I have one last thing to tell you about how to teach animals to NOT touch you in the ways or times you don't want.

Okay, so for the readers who think that you should reward that animal for removing himself/herself from you, you just have to remember the *cognitive* part of the original OSCAR Theory that all of this learning is based on. IF you reward an animal for un-touching you, then logic dictates that they will *learn* to try to un-touch you *again*, and more and more. Because Oscar is not dumb, and because Oscar observes, deduces, and plans, rewarding Oscar's exit from your clothespin will backfire.

Every time you reward Oscar's exit with praise or treats, Oscar will learn that they need to initially get ON you, so that you'll reward them for getting OFF of you. See how that works? It works the same way with runaway animals. If you give them a treat for coming back, they will then run away again in order to get an extra treat for coming back again. Try to remember that in the same circumstance, we would be choosing exactly what they are choosing. And we'd be learning the same unsavory habit. If anyone (inadvertently) rewarded you for being wrong, you would learn to try hard to "be wrong" every single day of the week and twice on Sunday.

The very most important point in understanding why this clothespin game works so well is because it is none other than the very same OSCAR game that you've been learning throughout this book. Any and every button is one that Oscar can either push on or *pull away* from. They find out from us which one of those two options is going to lead to predictability and thus understanding. Through one of those two simple options, they are going to be able to quickly figure out exactly how they can win at any game. It's as simple as the 0's and

1's of any computer code or the ON's and OFF's of a light switch (or an OSCAR button.)

But I'm not exaggerating here. Nearly every single thing we need our working animals or our companion animals to do to be the best pets or partners possible can be totally explained and achieved through the touching or the un-touching game. Because remember, every point of leverage also involves a locus (a point) of touching. Whether it's a harness, a collar, a leash, a rope, a rein, a leg, a saddle, a door, or even a squeeze cage, any of the equipment we want our animals to learn how to "use," they can learn how to "operate" by either pushing on it or UN-pushing on it at the appropriate time.

All of those pieces of physical equipment are nothing but a thing that Oscar can touch or un-touch with a specific body part. And the un-touching is just as important as the touching. If you really put yourself in Oscar's shoes to see this conversation from her/his perspective, you will see how important the concept of un-touching and retouching and un-touching again actually is. The animal learns about cause and effect by experimenting with this simple ON and OFF switch, because both of them will cause certain choices (effects and results) to then come out of *you*.

5.4.c Teaching Oscar to Mentally Absorb: Building a Mental Catcher's Mitt

Think baseball for a moment. Who is the most underappreciated player in baseball? The most unloved, as we all know, is the Umpire. But *underappreciated*, that honor goes to the catcher. How about hockey? The goalie gets the same disregard. We look at these players and we think, "I could do that. Their job is just to stand there, right?" Not exactly. The goalie's and catcher's job is to be a sink, and it requires special know-how to be a sink.

Kitchen sinks and bathroom sinks are just glorified funnels. But imagine having a kitchen sink that has legs. Imagine having a sink that follows you around through your day, and no matter where you throw your banana peel, your "outfielder" sink runs over and catches it. That's what an individual with a catcher's mitt (and the intent to absorb and neutralize all pop fly's, upsets, affronts, insults, and offenses) is capable of. Being a sink means having that key *absorbance* skill, which is an all-important skill.

An Oscar who feels out of control of herself/himself usually needs to *do something* to help them feel IN control. So I teach all Oscars the tool I call the active pause or the catcher's mitt. And just like any baseball coach, I teach Oscar to have solid balance, with flexed joints. A half-cocked stance is never bad either; it's always good, because it is how best to absorb shock, chaos, and anything else that comes Oscar's way, either from out of an unexpected "Left field" or from any other unexpected place.

Clamping eyes shut and hoping for it to be over is not an active pause. But planting feet in the ground with the dead weight of a tree trunk, now that is an active pause, and having that tree trunk be ready to spring like a rabbit to catch that flying banana peel, that's an active pause too. An active pause sets

Oscar up to begin to purposefully wait and to listen for the next something, and the cool part is that Oscar still feels like s/he's *doing* a whole lot. *"Oscar, it's your job to do nothing better and faster than anyone has ever done nothing before!"*

Teaching Oscars to use the mental catcher's mitt is pretty fun actually, because the tool comes as such a welcome surprise to Oscar. But just like everything else an Oscar ever learns, it must be learned *actively*. It must be sought by Oscar, not crammed in there by you; anything you try to cram in to someone else's brain won't stick. Following are the types of moments in OSCAR Therapy that you'll want to jump all over with a lot of very specific, staccato, and slightly early Approval Yeses.

To build the *mental* half of the catcher's mitt (the active pause), approve of *the end* of any sentence. Right when Oscar is in the process of the wind-down of any one "expression," before it oozes into the next expression, grab onto that wind-down moment. Also, any and every time in her life that she spontaneously exhales a heavy sigh with a "whatever, is it lunch time yet?" you need to jump up and down about that with exuberant rewards. Every time he says, "Can we just take 5?" you should say, "YES, and here, have some money too!"

If you draw out (expand on) those little toe-holds of pause in any chaotic Oscar (AND in yourself), pretty soon you will have an individual who is volunteering periods of "an emptying brain," where Oscar's planning brain has ACTIVELY shifted into idle because they now have experience that the *decision to pause* leads to approval and rewards. The empty brain is not a dopey, zoned-out entity. It is the brain that has just learned, for the first time, to *actively* listen. And brains that are actively listening are now in INPUT mode. *Now let's see, what shall we input...?*

5.4.d Teaching Oscar to Physically Absorb: The Oven Mitt Sessions

Once Oscar's body map has been "rebuilt" and the main traumas have been expunged, it's time to turn Oscar into a Superhero. Or at the very least, Oscar is now ready to don the proverbial oven mitt and go "all in" in trying to catch some flaming cannonballs, of whatever you've got. These are the things that are challenging to absorb on multiple sensory channels all at the same time, like things that look weird, sound weird, and act weird or feel weird, all at once.

After the "used to be terrified" body part(s) has been brought back online, I always then ask Oscar to strengthen it. I want the old "useless part" to become the strongest part of the body now. And if I am going to start throwing flaming cannonballs at Oscar, then s/he is going to need a catcher's mitt (which we just talked about) that now also doubles as an oven mitt, because multiply scary things are like hot potatoes that are hard to catch without getting burned.

For an animal of any body shape or size, donning a mental oven mitt means that no part of the body can be left behind when they are trying to "lean in" to meet the scary thing. For instance, when I teach needle-phobic animals, who are afraid to have someone jab a needle into their neck, I first teach the animal to "Oscar the needle" by reaching out with a front leg and shoulder stance so that they are balanced, braced, and steady, just like having a kickstand on a bicycle.

Then I teach that needle-phobic brain to lean in with their neck, toward the sharp thing, a little bit. There's nothing like self-impaling to give you a greater sense of control over being impaled. But in this game, those two parts are not enough. The final part we have to build in is a hind leg, the one that is still hanging back, behind the animal. Because this animal is only 95% committed to the role of inject-ee.

I focus right in on that hind leg until we get it stepping forward too, and doing its part of "pushing toward the needle." Because any body parts that are holding out and holding back create a "stuck in the mud" or "out-of-Oscar's-control" anchor that works against the rest of the system. A working body needs to be able to fully float like a hockey puck on the ice, and not be locked down (by phobia) at any part of them. One hundred percent "all in" commitment from all body parts is what Oscar must practice bringing to the game.

And my "oven mitt sessions" do look exactly like I'm playing a slowed down "game of catch" with these individuals, "swooping in" with a scary item that never leaves my hand. The better they learn to reach out to touch it before it touches them, to catch, absorb, and diffuse the scary thing, and come back for more, that's my green light to turn it up a notch and increase the speed, sound, or chaos of the item so that we can simulate what might happen in real life, on a bad day, during a dark and stormy night. They might need to gin up some quick courage for the unexpected angle of my hot potato, but I never give them more heat than they want to try.

In order to challenge these brains, I am really trying to scare them, but in half-speed slow motion. Heaven help the person who walks in on a late-stage oven mitt session, having never seen OSCAR Therapy before. Usually, I have to tell the animal to "take 5" while I explain to the newcomers that "it's not what it looks like" so that they don't call in the ASPCA to have me arrested for theatrical "animal abuse."

But even when I don't get to explain it to them, any and every onlooker is usually also instantly bewildered at why the animals (who are at liberty and free to leave) keep coming back for more of my "faux attacks," of their own volition, and even looking like they are having a blast in the process. Fake attack (otherwise known as "play" in the natural world and "stage fighting" in the human world) is all part of the game, and these animals are unmistakably and undeniably proud of their newfound super power abilities to "catch" my "unexpected" flaming cannon balls of scariness that they can now just *reflexively* absorb.

It's true that some of the animal owners I work with do initially contact Willing Results, LLC because they have an animal with a specific dangerous behavior or an inconvenient known phobia that disrupts normal life. Their problem is localized to a specific trigger like, say, a fear of black hats or rolled up newspapers. What these owners are obviously seeking is a "less reactive, and more rational" animal.

But even more typically, by the time a case meets me, the originating problem has generalized out so much that the owner can't even tell what is setting Oscar off. These animals are reported to be anxious about everything, more or less. And so my OSCAR diagnostic tests are what give me the most information about who they *are* as unique individuals, so that I can then give them what they actually need as unique individuals.

I have met individual animals of many species who were: afraid of rain, afraid of grass, afraid of animals, afraid of electronic noises, afraid of mechanical noises, afraid of only men, or only women, you name it. I have met dogs that were afraid of steps, afraid of stone patios, afraid of ceilings, afraid of food, afraid of the great outdoors, afraid of you name it. As long as I am staying out of their way while leading them through an OSCAR diagnostic exam, the OSCAR-complexed phobia is pretty easy to diagnose.

But later, after treatment is complete, when our case animals go back to their normal jobs in life, no matter if they get dealt an unexpected lowball, a pop fly, or a line drive, they have a newfound ability to absorb the insult, even with the part of the body that was previously scared to death of everything. My goal is for Oscar to react to the stressor *not* with a "grin and bear it" approach but more with a real "hit me with your best shot" attitude. The oven mitt sessions teach Oscar to be a *very active* participant in his or her own reaction.

When Oscar's Will is driving, the brain just has no room for irrational and flightiness to take over. Oscar will catch a canon ball if he has to, and he will drill his own body into the ground before he'll let any storm blow him away. When she's using an oven mitt, Oscar does not learn to habituate, tolerate, ignore, or internalize stress. She learns to *absorb* the heat and diffuse its energy so that the pesky "thing" won't distract from the ultimate mission of being in control of herself.

Mental Catcher's Mitts that also double as Oven Mitts should be standard-issue teaching in all kinds of schools; they should be thought of as necessary equipment for all of us (and not just our animals) in an unpredictable world.

5.5 Superhero Goals – Advanced Level

5.5.a Sensory Phobias You May Encounter During OSCAR Sessions

In OSCAR Therapy sessions, it's pretty common that we come across other phobias in addition to the reach and recoiling through "social space" phobia. And these other phobias come in a variety of flavors, dictated predominantly by the senses we already know about: touch, sight, hearing, and taste/smell.

Visual phobias (fear of heights, spiders, snakes, black cowboy hats, etc.) need Oscar to reach out and touch blips of a visual picture. You may have to provide quick flashes of a thing, which build into longer and longer times where "it" is on stage in Oscar's visual field. Exposing the peripheral vision first, in my experience, is what works best as a starting place.

Audio phobias (fear of sounds, or certain volumes, pitches or frequencies etc.) need Oscar to reach out and touch you during blips of the sound coming from *behind you*. A quick burst of the sound, which builds into longer and longer strings of single bursts, are where to begin. Then some of those single bursts start dragging on and stretching out into longer versions of the sound. (Audio phobias often combine with this next phobia type.)

But there is another sense that often stockpiles phobia in some Oscars, and that's Oscar's sense of the passage of time. This one is important because patience, waiting, and flexibility are all traits that are unavailable to an Oscar with a temporal (time-related) phobia. This most interesting phobia is one that you won't be able to observe during other kinds of therapy. But because it requires that the brain be creating a *new* physical intention, temporal phobia is readily exposed by OSCAR Therapy. I never even knew time-based phobia existed until OSCAR sessions with many brains made it apparent.

"Temporal (time) phobia" is an insidious phobia; it strangles Oscar's ability to learn through trial and error. For example, an Oscar will try hard the first time but is phobic of every second try. Or two times are ok but not three; or three times are ok but not four. Or, a "known number" of times are ok, but not a "flexible" number of times. A temporal phobic brain has learned that transgressing past the allowable number of tries brings someone's wrath upon them, or it invokes a memory of a life threatening situation where counting in a series was involved.

To blur out Oscar's previously learned expectation of attempt-oriented or minute-oriented or number-oriented pain, and to help Oscar become more flexible and sensitive to change, you have to reverse Oscar's temporal phobia. To do this, just pretend you are drunk enough to lose count sometimes. Maybe you forget the difference between two and three. Maybe you get "inadvertently interrupted" in between Oscar's tries. Be creative with your pretending. Help Oscar get out of the rut by you not focusing so much on the count or on the time passing in between the tries.

There will be a great number of exhales when repairing a Time Phobia. Reward every single one. Immediately after treating/reversing a temporal phobia, the OSCAR Therapist will also observe an extremely exhausted Oscar; the brain of the animal will seem to shut down completely or go into a deep sleep, sometimes even while standing up.

Each different class of phobia requires a slightly different kind of exposure in order for Oscar to re-experience the trigger and learn that they are not trapped in/by it. But with any and every kind of additional phobia you are also tackling, the solution to all of them is still OSCAR Therapy. "Can you intentionally touch this button with this body part while you hear that noise or see that thing? And can you touch it for an unpredictable amount of times in a row?"

When OSCAR can finally do *that*, then that's proof that the intentional Will is not only intact, but that it is more important to Oscar than their fear of the trigger. The fear is getting relegated to a place of much lesser importance, for the reason that intention is now taking over.

5.5.b Button Difficulty: Use Inconsistent Targets and Phobia-Inducing Targets

The "thing" used as the button-to-touch doesn't always have to be your hand. Once your hand is easy for Oscar to touch, then you can add a bunch of "stuff" to your button hand. Of course, some things are easier for Oscar to reach out and touch than others.

Below is a list of increasingly difficult buttons you could teach Oscar to touch. Obviously, the OSCAR practitioner should be starting out on the easy end of the list, and working up to the more "courage-requiring" end. You can be holding a wide range of items.

Unlike, the "station targets" of marine mammal trainers and other positioning-based training practices, the OSCAR button is quite different. In stationing, the animal is taught to go to and remain holding onto a safe button/station marker and to "stay on target" in order to control that body's location in the room. But the "OSCAR target" is used in the exactly opposite way.

An OSCAR target (button) is not for "grabbing onto this benign thing." It's for "trying to muster the courage to engage this thing." Remember the tarantula challenge from Chapter 4. OSCAR buttons are about building the skills of choice, courage, and rational assessment inside your Oscar's brain. Once Oscar gets that these scary seeming buttons are still just fun games, Oscar's courage goes through the roof. It's wise to hide your "flaming hoops," because Oscar is likely to jump right through them before you even ask.

Some Categories of OSCAR Targets - From Easy (a) to Difficult (k)

a) Empty Space with practitioner at a distance
b) Empty Space with practitioner close by
c) Target on Furniture that is "over there"
d) Rubber Bell of a drain plunger that is "over here"
e) Human Hand
f) Tiny *Visually* Scary Object in hand
g) Large *Visually* Scary Object in hand
h) Tiny Scary *Sounding* Object in hand
i) Large Scary *Sounding* Object in hand
j) Tiny Scary *Moving* Object in hand
k) Large Scary *Moving* Object in hand

5.5.c OSCAR Therapy IN MOTION: Tandem Partnership with NO Restraint

Motion is a funny thing. What's funny about it is that we humans forget to even consider it. But don't forget. Always remember to ask the question: is Oscar experiencing motion right now? Animal bodies move not only right and left and front and back, but they also move up and down, so just like you would, Oscars also experience torque! Oscars often have memories of things that happened to them *only* while they were *actively* in motion. And motion is not only something we do, but sometimes, motion is something that is done to us!

Sometimes "the ground" under Oscar is even in flux. Oscar's often need to learn that they can be *motion-absorbent*. Just like you'd feel on a skateboard or on the floor of a bouncy house, Oscar sometimes get moved by motion that's not under her/his control. When Oscar is in a vehicle, is that vehicle standing still? Or does it partially rotate on every possible axis? At best, being in cars feels to an animal like being on the tilt a whirl at the amusement park. At worst, the OSCAR-positive animals feel like they are more like sneakers in a washing machine.

Since this book is an *introduction* to OSCAR Therapy, most of it describes OSCAR at a stand still. But what you can do at a stand still, you can also try at a walk or at a jog or a trot. You can try it with you on one side of Oscar and then you can try it with you on the other side of Oscar. And then, it can be done at a canter or lope or skip with you on one side of them and then with you on the other side.

This is one of the sections that could be expanded into its own separate book. But the quick summary is that when OSCAR Therapy is done while the animal and you are in motion, it employs the exact same principal as doing OSCAR at a stand still; but it's just done at some increased speed and at some distance so as to prevent collision. Why do we do OSCAR Therapy in motion? Because our animals often ARE in motion! They are in motion for us, with us, and around us. In fact, you could say that when it comes to motion, our Oscars have basically different categories of jobs.

In the first category of jobs, both you and Oscar are basically not moving around much. Couch surfing, grooming, and playing the early-on OSCAR game are all jobs you can both do without moving your feet around much, if at all. And even though the feet aren't moving, we've already proven that the animal's body and brain are plenty involved.

In a second category of jobs, you stay put while Oscar is in motion. Often this job involves some sort of a "send" cue, where you send the animal out to go hunt, go catch, or go herd. Just like the OSCAR game means, "come touch this thing right here," the send cue means "go engage with that thing over there" or "go hunt for something," and even the prey species can learn to do this too, just like predator species, if a little less quickly.

You can even send animals out to do work far away from you. Retriever dogs, search dolphins, working herding dogs, sniffing dogs, search and rescue dogs, falconing, all of these animals are sent on a mission while you mostly hang back and wait. I would send my roommate's dog out to the kitchen to open the fridge and bring back cold beverages.

But in the third category of jobs, not only is Oscar moving but, this time, you are too. You are both in motion together. Examples of co-movement would be pairs figure skating or dancing (in humans), horseback riding, and dog agility or horse agility sports. There's a tandem nature to this category, with everyone moving together like in a chorus line, or like in a flock of birds, or like in a school of fish.

So OSCAR Therapy during movement isn't rocket science; it's just doing the same old OSCAR game, just at a little bit of speed. But what OSCAR at speed always requires for sure is that you wear a safe pair of running shoes whenever you are alongside!

The reason we do OSCAR games at ever increasing speeds and gaits (walk, jog, trot, skip, canter, run, gallop) is because, often, speed and arcing movement harbors within it its own phobia triggers. Just like humans can acquire phobias of going too fast on a bicycle or on a snow sled, animals who have experienced "in motion accident" or in motion abuse or in motion trauma or job-related in motion injury can acquire phobia of being in motion. Oscar can understandably become phobic of his/her own body (around others) when it achieves the particular body shapes that are *only* experienced in tandem motion. [As evidenced by NASCAR's immortal Ricky Bobby, if at one time there was a crash while going fast, then going fast can be its own cause of phobia!]

When muscles are in motion, the brain remembers that bad stuff has happened while in similar motion, and the brain tells the muscles to be on guard and get ready to flee. And so they are. Until OSCAR Therapy teaches them that movement with and around humans, all by itself, is still a game at which they can win, Oscars will remain afraid of their very own movements around us. To reverse the phobias of social motion, we ask them to lean into our OSCAR buttons. In doing so, they learn that even in motion they still have cognitive control over themselves. They still get to make choices, and they will be safe.

It amazes some veterinarians to learn that problems with movement aren't always physical in their origin, …and in fact that real physical problems can be traced back to sequestered, held-back, restricted "un-round" movement. When one hip joint believes it cannot swivel, for instance, then the whole back end will put undue stress on not only itself but on the other hip, causing the other leg to have to swivel twice as much, twice as often, and twice as far!

Think about which scenario is more likely… Did an erupted knee on one leg cause a scared-to-interact OSCAR hole on the other good leg? (This good leg may even need to lean on things like furniture or people when it gets tired.)

Or did an early-acquired OSCAR hole on the good leg cause the eventual erupted knee on the first (injured) leg??

Many of our cases have shown the later. When an animal is missing a whole side (evidenced by a lifetime of nutty behavior), the knee that is likely to structurally fail first (with positive x-rays) is often the other knee- the one on the *socially normal* side. When the socially abnormal side is always sailing around like an untethered kite, the more normal side has to do all of the swiveling and grounding, counterbalancing work. Masts on ships that hold the sails have to be big and strong and overbuilt for a reason.

When it comes to suspected physical breakdown or physical restrictions, OSCAR diagnostics should come into play. If the originating problems-in-movement were actually physical in nature (like if the animal had a small and undiagnosed tiny bone spur near a joint or a sprained muscle) then those physical restrictions wouldn't just *disappear* a few days later.

But it is not uncommon that movement problems often *do disappear* after and even during OSCAR Therapy work. The reason is one of misdiagnosis of the presentation: when an animal is *afraid* to use a certain limb in certain contexts, you'd swear that the leg sometimes looks lame, busted or painful.

For example, some animals have a hard time arcing to the left or to the right in the presence of another person or animal. And then after movement-based OSCAR sessions *at liberty*, they realize that they can. But while they are discovering it, there is a lot of deep sigh exhaling, wide-saucer eyes, being "out on Neptune," in memory flashback, and then tripping over their own four feet when they attempt to finally use them, even on flat, dry ground.

Now, if you were to tackle such a case with only physical treatment, you can achieve increased freedom of movement by freeing muscle bellies with sports massage specialists, acupressure therapies, and others that target soft tissue, fascia, neural nodes, and other critical junctions. But what you cannot automatically repair in a muscle is the animal's *intention* to try to use it, and such choices in an animal (just like in us) are NOT necessarily automatic. Just because you want them to try it doesn't mean they are okay with trying it.

As it turns out, you will always achieve the best and most complete physical ability by leveraging the *intentions* in Oscar's brain. For example, if a dancer *wants* to figure out a new dance, they get stronger in the muscles they need, while releasing tension in the ones they need *not* to get in their way.

The same is true for OSCAR-built animals. No matter what we think we humans are in control of, animals will always achieve the best versions of their own physical ability, as they are the ones in charge of every one of their many supporting muscles. As long as we can get them to choose what we want, it's Game Over for the competition.

Regarding the ultimate cause of an Oscar's physical lockdown, from what I have been able to ascertain from a number of equine cases (where everything is bigger and easier to observe), speed phobia seems to often be tangled up with visual phobias, especially from what they see in their hind view or "in their rear-view mirror."

The things they see behind them are what seem to be a major culprit much of the time, so much so that they just will not let their eyes look back there. The eyes work just fine when Oscar is not working in tandem with someone, but when someone IS back there, their imaginative memories are wreaking havoc with their eyeballs. If these animals had hands, they'd be using them to cover their eyes like when you're watching a horror movie. You shield your eyes from *what is about to happen* so you won't have to see it; because seeing something you cannot prevent is emotionally unbearable.

To repair visual phobias during movement, I often teach the practitioner to use their nearby hand as a "flitting birdie" held at different compass points around the animal's visual field. We want Oscar not only to know that there's something weird moving back there, but also to actively seek it out with their own peripheral vision, as if they are actively looking/seeking in a rear view mirror. The more Oscar can assess and react to what they perceive back there, the more we approve. Sometimes we teach Oscar to rule that crazy stuff out, and sometimes we ask Oscar to rule it in and use that birdie information to consider a different choice. In this work, animals let out many deep exhales, presumably of deep, pent up memories of bad times.

The coolest part, though, about OSCAR in motion, is that it provides the opportunity for very safe psychological rehab. You get to help the animal work out 95 percent of the animal's kinks from the vantage point of just walking or running along side. It's so much safer than normal in-harness rehab, when you're getting "the job in the mind" done way before you ever attach any leverage, any harness, any saddle, any carriage or what have you. [Later, the animal never has too much trouble with the addition of all of that stuff. If they have acquired a phobia of clanking metal sounds or snappy–sounding straps, you can reverse those phobia triggers back in the barn or the living room.]

But back to your Oscar in motion: the animal is over there, learning about combined tandem movement almost exactly as if you were on top of them in a saddle, or behind them in a carriage, and yet you remain safely on the ground. Most of the bucks, spooks, jumps, etc. will be worked through and dissipate without ever having to put your life and limb and expensive equipment at risk. When doing this kind of rehab, there are less cowboy yahoos but there are also less cowboy injuries, like broken bones and head traumas. As a metaphor, the OSCAR in motion rehab process is like the best parts of football without any of the unsavory pig-piles and head concussions.

Even if the animal is many yards away from you, you can still elicit or uncork any bottled-up freak outs, *as if* you were close at hand or even on Oscar's back.

Even with no physical contact at all, you can let the pop ups, bucks, and flees come out and wash away, *merely by moving AWAY* from Oscar at particular social angles they have been too afraid to use or engage in. The first times they try, Oscars often look all around, like they're contending with a ghost.

For example, imagine running in a wide-open space with your animal, like in a flat, empty arena or on an enclosed tennis court with no net. You run; they run. Oscar is on your right. You're both headed in the same direction. You bank to the right; they arc to the right with you. Then you both straighten out. You stop and now put Oscar on your LEFT. You run; they run.

You then bank to the LEFT; you look for OSCAR behind you and off to your LEFT, but s/he's nowhere to be seen. Not only did they not bank to the LEFT, but they ditched to the Right and left the scene entirely. When the horses leave, abandoning an angle they either cannot imagine or are afraid to use, they often jump and buck and kick out in self-defense. When dogs do it, they often wipe out; they lose their balance and fall over, even while in motion.

"We BOTH go left, when you bring your butt to me..."

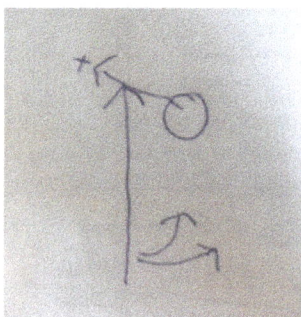

Figure 22. An example of "OSCAR in Motion" as written in a horse record; the circle is the human.

What you have discovered by the weird and unexpected occurrence is that Oscar either can't or won't bank to the Left. He does it by himself while chasing balls, but if you're there, s/he just can't or won't do it. What you've found is an OSCAR hole triggered by motion. To rebuild the hole, just use the same OSCAR language, the same OSCAR buttons, and some faith that Oscar will try their best to finally try it out.

5.5.d Building Oscar's Independence: Pitch a Wisp

Very often, we want or need our animals to choose to come to us, choose to stay with us, or not leave our side. But sometimes what we need instead is for our animals to give us some more room, to give us some space and time, and to go out there and do their work without us as we hang back and watch.

Traditional and "natural" trainers have an answer for how to achieve this. They get big and scary in order to cause the animal to choose to leave. That's one way to get the job done, but now your animal is hyper focused on you and not their job. They can't let you out of their sight, and they are now somewhat anxious, feeling like they've done something wrong. So this is not the smartest choice the part of the human.

The smarter choice is to pitch a wisp. What is a wisp? A wisp is merely an idea that's trying to get someone to follow it, just like the wisps in the forest of folklore legend that lead travelers off the trail. Just like the fireflies that beckon you to follow them just a little farther into the woods, we can beckon Oscar to follow an idea, no matter where it is located. So, we can start widening out the idea of what it means to look for, to find, and to make contact with, "a button." If coming over here and touching this real button you can see and feel is a perfectly good idea, then looking over there to touch a button over there is another perfectly good idea.

Just like an animal tamer at the circus sends each animal back onto its chair to wait there while a different animal is brought in the spotlight, we can send our animals "over there" to a physical station. But we can *also* send our animals out to an imaginary station. If there were a chair there, go sit on it. If there were a person with a button hand over there, go touch them. And when you reward Oscar for looking out there for something else to touch, that's when you get the opportunity to reward them for putting more space between them and you. Oscars will pick up on this imaginary button intention within minutes.

Do they know what they are supposed to be seeing out there? No. Do they know what you are imagining out there? No. But they know that your focus has changed. They know that you want their focus to expand outward, to take in the scenery of the sights and sounds of the world outside you both. If you then imagine that their searching has gotten them to some midway button and reward that, that's when Oscar will go looking some more. If you reward them for creating more distance between you for going *toward* an "*externally caused" reason* instead of going away from a noxious you, then they will easily give you as wide a buffer as you can imagine. Oscar will put a hundred yards in between you if you wish.

All brains, all children, all animals, and even all adults, all of us love playing the hot and cold search game. And the warmer we get, the more we like it! If we are being rewarding for searching, then we will search till the ends of the world. So if you think of yourself as having a handful of wisps in your pocket, wisps that you can pitch around just like you can throw imaginary stars up into the sky on a dark night, then an amazing thing starts to happen. The limitations of your physical location and even the physical shape of your body start not being limitations anymore.

It's easier to imagine a wisp than it is to imagine an entire other person standing over there holding up an Oscar button. An imagined wisp, just like a lightning bug flash, can be "placed" anywhere. You can imagine them not only 360° around you but also 360° overhead. It can be very far away or very close by. But the more wisps you picture, when you need them, the more you will be able to talk to Oscar in very exacting ways about exactly where they are in relation to not only you but in relation to the room, in relation to the field, or in relation to the mountaintops. The sky's the limit.

5.6 Zipping a "Newly Round" Oscar Into Necessary Life Skills

When you think about an entire case from start to finish, the building of the animal's OSCAR clock only gets somewhere between 70 and 95 percent of the work done. The last 5 to 30 percent of any case is spent on re-acclimating to their job or their trigger. And since re-acclimation is a separate phase of the work, the lingo I use to describe this last phase of the casework to my client is either "*wiring* the animal for _____" or "*zipping* the animal back into" their normal life or their regular job.

If the case started out with a just plain *abnormal animal*, if your goal for them was that you wanted normalcy, normal happiness, normal play, self assuredness, and/or less anxiety, then using just OSCAR Therapy sessions alone will get you to where the animal will get better all by themselves as they practice daily living. There's no need to zip the animal back into life or wire in some special skill they need to use for their special job. But if your goal for the animal was something that is beyond normalcy (like a job, a skill, or to play a particular role, then you'll need some additional tools because you'll need to zip this now-round OSCAR back into that goal, that role, or that skill.

This is when you start teaching Oscar the actual skills of the job. If Oscar has not already taught *themselves* how to achieve said goal (or goals), then this is when you snap right back into normal positive reward (operant conditioning, Chapter 6) language to teach this animal as if s/he were any normal young or inexperienced animal who just hasn't learned that thing yet. But... any OSCAR-built animal has many aces up his or her sleeve that make learning *anything* new a piece o' cake. OSCAR-built animals are so much easier to teach than the normal and healthy, perfect animals.

If they get confused by or fearful of any part of the new information, we just use all of our pre-built OSCAR marionette strings to explain the specifics: this neck goes here, this leg goes there, bend your own spine this way to fit into this space, etc. The "OSCAR strings" literally do the job for you.

Can't jump in a vehicle? Put your button in the vehicle. Can't be with other animals? Put the button between Oscar and the other body/animal. Needle phobia? A shark object becomes the button they should push on. Saddle phobia? Same.

Whatever the job, in the final stage of any OSCAR case, the animal learns the whole (previously terrifying) job within a few hours, and often the job is learned even within just a few minutes. Most any job can be fully explained to an OSCAR-built animal inside of two sessions. Phobias reverse within not much more. Because unlike what happened in the animal's backstory, this time, they have a fully functional ready, willing, able, curious, motivated, empowered and courageous brain with which to learn the same old easy job.

But no matter how small the phobia or job, you MUST do the work of "folding the scary old raisins back into the new OSCAR dough," as one client said a while back. We HAVE TO zipper the new animal back into the old situation, zipper tooth by zipper tooth. We have to wire the animal in to make sure s/he is now using all of her/his *new* parts to take on the old monsters.

To wire Oscar in to the job, create a simulated or made-safe, low-risk version of the next encounter with the troubling thing. By playing OSCAR games within sight of that thing, or near that thing, or extremely near that thing, or right directly into that thing, that's how you give Oscar a chance to play the rational game, earn rational rewards, and exhale and rehydrate in rational ways. This all gives Oscar the avenue on which to come back from freaky town. Oscar will come back from fear far enough to finally be able to see the "scary yo-yo" for what it is. It's just a yo-yo. Give Oscar many, many chances to find that out! If s/he doesn't want to realize it yet, just make the yo-yo even less scary, to start.

An OSCAR-built animal is primed and ready to be re-exposed to the triggers that previously set them off in a dangerous way. But you can't just throw them into that deep water of "memories of drowning" and expect them to realize that they can now swim, without incident. For a little while, you have to be there to reward and support Oscars as they realize it. Just like you can't go from just learning how to float in a pool to jumping overboard into the ocean at night, there are a few necessary learning steps in between that ought not be skipped.

For instance, if a dog has been attacking other dogs, you cannot go from the last OSCAR-angles-building session straight to letting the dog off leash at the dog park. They first need to be off leash around dogs on the OTHER SIDE of a tall strong fence, preferably chain link. And yet, the OSCAR-built animal will be the strongest and fastest and safest re-learner, when it comes to finally learning the life skills they were failing at before OSCAR Therapy.

When you finally let the dogs in together, add a muzzle to any previous biter, just to take the teeth out of the equation. This gives you more winning moments you can reward the dog for without worry. And if you've built Oscar well, most of what you'll get will be winning moments.

Wiring them for _____ is just my generic description for what it's like to introduce "trigger re-exposures." After an animal is fully OSCAR-round, it's a relatively minor job to wire them for riding in a vehicle or handling the vet visit or whatever caused that animal to hire us in the first place. Metaphorically, after you've got electricity going to every part of your kitchen, it's pretty easy to then wire in (just plug them in) all of the machines that do all of the jobs you want done in your kitchen.

When I say that an animal needs to be zipped back into their life, that just means that there are a bunch of wiring exposures that the animal needs to generalize. The animals that need a little more time to zip back in are the ones that usually had more *generalized problems* all around. There wasn't one particular trigger but a whole array of chaotic and unpredictable behavior, including under- or over-reactions that generally didn't match what the scenarios called for.

These more involved cases need some specific exposure sessions. The animal's owner needs to be taught some supportive language to follow over the next few weeks, and the animal also needs a little bit of time to re-orient to a new level of overall happiness. In fact, happiness and well being cause their own supportive forward momentum. But happiness doesn't just mean reduced anxiety; it means contented exhales, instigating of play, self-assuredness, instigating games, and deep recuperative sleep.

Just like with kids or adults or anyone, once exposure is safe, you can start building all of the normal skills that are part of Oscar's normal life. When s/he can get in a car, you can finally practice being a therapy dog, or a trail riding horse or whatever job that animal may have in life.

When we put on new glasses or new goggles, even if they are helpful, vision-correcting ones, there's always an adjustment period. In the same way, it takes a few weeks for any Oscar to get used to their own newfound areas of exploration; everything will feel new to them for a while.

In this final time period, (we might as well call it the "baking time"), grant your Oscar a little slack while s/he gets his or her new 3-D goggles situated; it's about getting used to a new normal for them. While in this timeframe, any new actions that look like their "awareness is rebalancing" shouldn't make you nervous; those are very good signs of reintegration, healing, and becoming almost super-normal, or very, very hard to fluster.

Whenever one is offered up, don't be afraid if an OSCAR game "just comes out of nowhere" and finds you! Remember that when an animal knows there is value in reaching out to engage a button, they are likely to now try to reach out and gently touch many things in the big, wide world, just to see what will happen next. Just like with any baby, this is how all brains of any age learn. In actual fact, OSCAR Therapy is what gives Oscars their "childhoods" back, quite literally. It allows them to reach out and bonk the world, just to see what it does. When life is both fun and funny this way, that's when everything is both learnable and re-learnable.

Here are some examples of zipping Oscar-built animals back into normal life:

1. If a horse is afraid of black cowboy hats, then put a hat nearer and nearer to (and then in) your hand button.

2. If a dog is terrified of sticks in your hand, put a little and then larger stick in your button hand.

3. Needle phobia? Rubber dental tools at first then a tiny 30-gauge needle goes in the button hand.

4. Dog won't put on collar or harness? Dog, please tuck yourself under and into these clothes I'm holding.

5. Horse saddle? Horse blanket? Horse, please touch this with a nose first, then shoulder, then please tuck yourself under and into these clothes or this gear I'm holding.

6. Sheep or Llama or Alpaca afraid of sheers? Please lean into this vibrating hand and later, these vibrating clippers.

7. Husband afraid of spiders?

8. Wife afraid of snakes?

9. Kid afraid of zombies?

10. It's all the same.

5.6.a No Need for Repeating

They say you never forget how to ride a bike, and yet you forget the names of the American presidents right after you learn them. The difference is that one priority is created by you, and the other is merely a mimicking of the teacher's priorities or a book's priorities. Review is necessary before the test on the presidents, but review and re-practicing are not necessary in OSCAR Therapy or any Approval-based learning. *What is learned is now owned.*

What is learned does not need to be relearned and re-practiced because Oscar has built the whole thing, up to now. You didn't do hardly anything. You didn't change their universe or become part of the solution. You just made their universe really small so they could see it in more and clearer detail. It was not your work to do; it was theirs to do, because they were going towards something they wanted at every step of the way.

OSCAR Therapy learning is like figuring out the key to a treasure map and then finding a million bucks in gold doubloons. You can't carry all the heavy gold to the bank, so you have to go back tomorrow. But when tomorrow comes, are you going to have to relearn the secret codes again? No! And how about next month, will you have to relearn them then? No! And how about when you are old and gray and entrusting the map to your grandkids... Will you have to relearn it fifty years down the line? No!

And how about trigonometry? Twenty years later, or one year later, or one semester later, or ten minutes after the final exam? Do you have to relearn your trigonometry? Yep. It's because you never wanted to learn it in the first place. So you really didn't. Trig really didn't change you. But that treasure map did. The treasure map shaped you. An OSCAR map, as it's being attained, shapes a brain.

5.6.b Who Can Initiate?

Obviously, most of the time, it's us humans who will be initiating the OSCAR conversation, when we can. We have goals we want our animals to meet, but we also have schedules, errands to run, appointments to keep and responsibilities. We have certain times of the day where we are available to/for our animals and certain times when we just aren't.

And yet very often, whenever you are around, the animals themselves may sometimes try to initiate the OSCAR conversation *with you*. Not because they are starving for food rewards but because they want the exchange and a fun game play, just to change things up in an otherwise boring day.

If you are not in the mood to converse or if the animal needs to be focusing on another job, then just give your Release cue and continue about your business. Oscar will take the hint and walk away only maybe two attempts to get your attention.

If you DO choose to accept the invitation to converse, then *hang back a bit*. Wait for the animal to show you what they want to talk about... tell you about... show to you... show off... or just plain "say." Sometimes, you'll be amazed at what your animals want to discuss with you *today*, via the OSCAR game.

5.6.c Oscar's Learning Curve Is Always An Exponential One – Yours Is Too

"Exponential" change is a big descriptor for a simple idea. Exponential change is happening slowly all the time, even in things that you think are not changing at all, like "stagnant" things. Likewise, exponential learning changes are happening over a long period. But just like any slow process, most of our internal "Richter scale" sensing meters are just not sensitive enough to see the first 90 percent of an exponential growth curve!

Imagine a towel lying on the back of a chair. It's sitting there and sitting there and sitting there while you are reading your book. Half an hour goes by but then all of a sudden, even though no one moved an inch and there was no breeze inside the room... plunk! That towel falls off the chair. Now- why did that happen? Was there a ghost? Was there a change in the earth's gravitational force but only in your room? It probably wasn't that.

When you flung the towel down, it was not quite balanced and it immediately started to slide. It slid about 0.1 millimeter, and so it was a little more out of balance. It slid 0.2 mm this time and became even a little more out of balance. Because of that it slid 0.4 mm and this time it was sort of more out of balance. Because of that it slid 1 inch, and because of that... plop- on the floor, like it was *flung* to the floor. That's an exponential change.

The path of the towel was just so short and small in the beginning that you didn't notice it, and that's why bad behavior just "shows up all at once, out of nowhere." It's not out of nowhere; it's been growing for a long time, but the learning path was exponential, and during the first 90 percent of the curve, you didn't notice it happening. Exponential change is why a watched pot never boils and a steak on the grill goes rare, rare, rare, charred.

Small changes do not add up to *change* the world. They add up to *cause* the world. One causes one for a while. Then out of the blue one day, one causes two. Then two causes four. Then five causes twenty-five. Small ideas don't change one at a time. Small ideas change in exponential fashion, because each small idea *has influence* on all the other small ideas.

The learning curve is Oscar's curve only- not yours. You are not the one paving the road to your goal; you are only setting some compass points. Attempting to predict the speed of progress or the slope of the curve is not something you can do since you have no idea what Oscar's path forward is going to look like- what his tools currently are or are not. Her/his path to greatness could be a 30-degree curve, or a 60-degree curve, a 90-degree curve, or a coiling curve; we just have no idea.

Whether you're building a new skill, rehabbing a phobia, or whatever, things are truly *not learned* through linear baby steps, except for just the beginning acclimation part of any learning curve. Real learning always happens over the timeline of one of these exponential curves. If Oscar's learning pathway is *not* exponential, then what you have there is a gap *or many gaps* in your teaching toolbox. When s/he is trying to learn, any learner will always make exponential leaps. If they leap wrong, that's direct evidence that you have missed a step in the teaching. If they have not learned what you think you are teaching, then you are not asking the right questions.

If a learner has no teacher at all, it may take many years to identify and master a new skill. It takes many *more* years than that if they have a bad teacher. But it doesn't take many years to learn something from a good teacher because their very effective will-based teaching process is never linear. It's always exponential. If you're a good teacher, eventually, the student may even kick you off the curve because you cannot keep up with his or her learning speed, and you are holding them back. That's no one's fault. It's the nature of the evolution of ideas.

5.6.d Allow Difficulty to Deflate

Once brains are in the OSCAR zone, change can happen very quickly. Things you thought would never happen indeed happen. What you previously thought would take Oscar a whole weekend to learn often takes about 20 minutes for them to learn solidly. What you previously thought would take a year, can take two weeks.

Just keep putting one OSCAR foot in front of the other, one step at a time, and you will find that the steep hill of a difficult learning curve, or the difficult communication challenge that you thought was so insurmountable, just simply and unceremoniously self-deflates and melts away. It's the exponential aspect of the OSCAR learning curve that is the reason why this happens. Here are some quotes from clients:

"The huge problem just isn't there anymore, and we hadn't even practiced."

"Even though it took some time on the clock, it felt like no time at all."

"What I thought would take years took just a few sessions."

"I'm astonished at how far we've come in such a short time."

When you're nearing the end of troubled times, it's time to remember why you started this whole OSCAR conversation in the first place. It was to help

Oscar to help change himself/herself. And now that s/he has done that, you must let him/her be changed. All by himself. All by herself. Don't own anything Oscar did or became. Don't take credit for anything Oscar learned. You learned things about Oscar too, on this expedition. Still, you probably learned the most about yourself.

So the most important thing at the end of any Approval-based OSCAR conversation is to let Oscar be who Oscar is. Remember, you are still two different and independent individuals who just happen to know, now, how to create something *together*.

For the first time ever, Oscar is willing *and now able* to create the concept/behavior/choice that you hoped s/he would. Animals are clearly proud of the thing they are now doing, the thing that up until recently was terrifying to them. Pride just radiates off of them while they are participating in the thing they were afraid to even imagine before. And if Oscar has met your goal, and can replicate that goal maybe two times, upon reasonable request, then there is only one thing left to do...

Go have fun with Oscar! But also, please let the animals go have fun too, especially if they insist on it. After all, they earned it.

After OSCAR Therapy, a few of the OSCAR-graduate horse cases have literally knocked a fence down in order to go play (for the first time ever) with neighboring animals. After a lifetime of social isolation because they were too fearful of, aggressive with, and a grave danger to the others in nearby fields, their new (and long overdue) play drive was so strong that they apparently couldn't contain themselves. Oscar's previous trepidation about interaction with others just plain disappears, and they want to try out what *being next to others* actually feels like.

After the witnessing owners had their heart attacks, they caught some of the play on video to send to me. The decision to "try these animals in together" was made for them, and much earlier than planned. OSCAR-rebuilt dogs do this jailbreak play too, *if* they get the chance.

And just because an animal used to be a real danger to others of its species before, it doesn't mean that the same danger exists now. After OSCAR Therapy for the previous offenders, animals can be cautiously reintroduced, but ONLY at liberty and ONLY with separation fencing between them for a few weeks minimum. If Oscars want to play and interact more like "normal folk" (together) that will become clear over time. On dogs, a soft muzzle can add a level of insurance until you see that it's no longer necessary.

Isolation is always an unnatural and stress-inducing state in any social species. When an Oscar has become fully rehabilitated, observe what that animal is telling the other animals. If they clearly want an opportunity to rejoin society again, let them try it. Don't hold their past against them. After they've been built by OSCAR Therapy and zipped into their new awarenesses, they are now not who they used to be; they have become whole.

Rejoining society is an opportunity *you* would want if you were in the same boat. Start slow, and don't take your eyes off the scene, until you just don't need to anymore. When in doubt of a potential reintroduction, you can always consult us by live-streaming video. We assess the functional versus not functional OSCAR clocks in real time, within minutes.

5.6.e When an OSCAR Animal Moves to a NON-OSCAR Home

Animals, who have finally learned about their own bodies in space, and how to use them in tricky and unfamiliar situations, are just plain safer animals to be around. OSCAR Therapy is excellent at teaching animals how to understand us humans in a more 3-D fashion so they can more easily habituate to our strange habits.

Many people tell me that they don't want their new language-speaking animal, who has finally been heard and understood and taught to relate, to have to move on to new owners who will treat them like they don't have a brain. I have to admit that, when I started out, this was my main concern as well.

But in the handful of stories I have heard about the OSCAR-graduated animals who have moved on to non-OSCAR households (for whatever reason), they are all better off than even I imagined they'd be. OSCAR recipients not surprisingly bring their learned awareness with them wherever they go. They quickly learn to blend in to their new families and new jobs. The funny part is that the new owners can't quite believe that their new animal ever had "the history" they really did have.

Nowadays I try to reassure clients that the animals don't need someone who speaks a clear language in order to be happy. They have become more balanced and they will stay that way no matter whom they live with. Animals got along just fine without us for millennia, and they will continue to do so. We can all understand that we miss our beloved teachers, but we also know that we don't need to see them everyday once the lessons have been learned.

Just yesterday, Stuart's owner told me this story:

"So the horse next to me at the show was supposed to compete next, but it didn't want to go forward into the arena and it started running sideways super fast right into us, and I really thought Stuart was gonna bite it 'cus he made the "invisible ears," ears-flat-back, "I hate you" face and snaked his head, but he stopped just short of attacking.

Even in his rump... I felt Stuart's leg come up like he was going to kick that horse, and that's what I was expecting, the kick and the bite and the strike and some bleeding flesh hanging, but none of that happened! I was stunned that he did NOT bite or lunge like I'd seen him do to horses in the past; this time he just shifted himself away, sideways. He did make the face though... I don't blame him; that horse was crashing into us. I wanted to punch that horse myself to get him away, but I was in the saddle. And it wasn't that poor horse's fault that he was so scared of whatever it was.

On *three* separate occasions, when something like that happened, before OSCAR, Stuart took a chunk out of someone's horse (three different horses); there was blood everywhere. Stuart was famous for biting other horses, and that's what I was expecting. But this time, what was shocking was that all of that *wasn't* what was happening. Back then, he was scared and would lash out, but this time he just absorbed the chaos of the scene in his body and in his brain. It was just like you say; he absorbed the energy of the asteroid and diffused it. It was amazing..."

The whole point of co-creating OSCAR Therapy in the first place was to help *the animal* turn things around; I am primarily a biologist after all. OSCAR recipients get along well with other animals in the family so much better than they used to, and they blend in better with just about any *other species* of animal too, in addition to the humans. The fact that it also helps the owners in countless ways... is just icing on the cake.

5.7 Reviving Tinker Bell: The Biggest Barrier to An OSCAR Therapy Full Recovery

"There is a hump of disbelief, and if you can make it over THAT, then you win...

It's like reaching through the mirror." – Stuart's owner

Losing a potential success story is a loss to everyone... to you, to the human family, to the animal family, to the practitioner, and not to mention, to Oscar! In OSCAR Therapy "the patient" is *never* lost, but in real life, *the case* may indeed be lost. And odd as it may seem, the owner's *fear of success* is quite often the only monkey wrench in an otherwise successful treatment approach. So this section is about self-realization among the owners.

In reversing phobias in animals, the only slippery slope I know of lies in the owner herself or himself. Far and away, the biggest problem in my multi-species behavior caseload is what to do about a certain subset of the humans –specifically, the humans who "don't believe in fairies." And they don't believe in Oscar(s) mainly, I must presume, because they've been taught not to.

In the *Peter Pan* stage play, Tinker Bell can't come back to life until the people in the audience clap loud enough for her. They need to believe in fairies, and some people still won't. And if not enough people *make the choice* to clap for Oscar, EVEN AFTER they've seen Oscar's magic begin to work *in real life*, now *that* is a real tragedy.

Even though I see nothing but forward progress, and even though the owner *does* see the wheels turning in the animal's brain, owners can still be at HIGH risk for not allowing success to happen. One reason owners don't believe the OSCAR Therapy results that are happening right before their very eyes (nor do they believe the lengthy testimonials on the OSCAR Therapy website) is that they just can't believe that *anyone's* brain can change so drastically, or can repair so completely. Even the most well-intentioned horse and dog owners can be too stuck in the past to let good recovery happen.

Others are in worse shape; they are absolutely invested in failure, self-sabotaging every good move they make. Stealing defeat from the jaws of victory is what some people choose. Either they need the problem more than they want a solution, or they can't seem to bear the responsibility of the existence of the very idea of "choice/will" itself. And if *they* don't have *that*, they have a hard time seeing it *or its value*, in another.

Normal anxiety around learning any new paradigm is understandable, but I hope the following section will be helpful to all of the owners who also do find themselves in this anxiety-riddled, abandoning-of-Tinker Bell boat.

And if you can't wrap your head around just how it could be that a caring guardian might not be able to muster enough faith in the possibility that a glorious phoenix can rise from mere ashes inside their troubled Oscar's brain… then…

Oh, let us count the ways…

5.7.a The "Crash Cart" Quiz at Willing Results, LLC

Humans, across the board, are much more invested in an animal not changing than the animal ever is. And that's true even when we humans think it's not. Human brains are invested in winning, but human brains also become invested in loss; they get used to the status quo of how it's been, and then even change for the better takes "too much effort."

Some owners harbor their own learned phobias and or learned helplessness. Some have already decided not to even try their homework since their efforts with other approaches in the past (before OSCAR) were mostly dead ends. And even though the whole case is about to fall apart without their participation, owners OFTEN are too afraid to talk about what they are feeling, without the practitioner preemptively begging them to show up. (Exactly the same as the OSCAR problem itself.)

When a plumbing problem hits, like with a bathroom toilet explosion, we call the emergency plumber, and he brings in his plumber's emergency plumbing kit. Similarly, when a doctor is losing the patient, the doctor pulls out the emergency body Crash Kit that has all the quick testing gadgets and fast-acting systemic meds for that body emergency.

But when an OSCAR patient's future is on a slippery slope because an owner's emotional sand seems to be slipping through their own fingers… that too is an emergency. It's an emotional overwhelm emergency; so we OSCAR practitioners had to build a crash kit for that. It's our "owner emergency" quiz, and the owner is to circle all of the statements that apply to what they are feeling and thinking right now.

We know that if we can just get these unspoken concerns out in the open, we can work each one of them out with some additional owner orientation, education, and maybe even some support from previous owners who have been in their shoes and had the exact same concerns. The following is a compilation of all of the fears we've heard along the way, from many *if not all* of the SUCCESSFUL cases who got all the way over the rainbow.

If you're an owner who feels any of these below, you're in very good company, and might I add, courageous company. We have collectively decided to share our compiled list of clients' doubts here so that others may use them to at least have some concrete words for the feelings. Talking about it is always the first step to feeling less confused, scared, and/or alone.

"I feel... _____"

1. like I'm re-living memories; I can't get bad images out of my head.
2. like hyperventilating, when my animal gets nervous
3. paralyzed, shocked, petrified
4. afraid to do my homework. It feels unsafe for me.
5. afraid to do my homework. It feels unsafe for animal.
6. like Casey doesn't understand why I'm afraid
7. confused about WHY Casey is doing...
8. confused about WHAT Casey is doing
9. like Casey doesn't understand the real problem
10. confused by my homework
11. like I don't have enough_____
12. not quite ready to do the homework on my own
13. unsupported by my family and other decision makers
14. like this process might take forever
15. like this requires too much attention
16. like I will run out of funds before it's finished
17. I feel stuck between _____ and _____
18. like I wish I knew about _____ ahead of time
19. like I keep losing momentum with _____
20. like I will be the reason for _____'s failure
21. like I'm making excuses to avoid working with_____
22. like I really want to get rid of _____
23. like my animal cannot handle learning
24. like my animal hates me
25. like my animal is just being evil
26. guilty that I didn't see his/her problem for what it is
27. like I'd rather just cope with his/her problem
28. like I have decided not to know who this animal is
29. like I'd rather not see reality; it's too much for me.
30. frustrated that the *uninformed people* treat me like I'm a gullible idiot for looking into something that is foreign to *them* (even

though they have no concept of what it is, because they have never had to / chosen to tackle a problem like this one before. They just euthanize.

5.7.b The Forgotten Victim of a Troubled Animal: Opportunity Knocks

We see it in almost every case. When an animal was "under the thumb" of a past abuser, they learned quickly not to express any emotion at all. But once free and safe in a loving rescuer home, it only takes a few months for a whole history of pent-up pain to begin to pour out.

When troubled minds finally find themselves in safe environments, their whole hurt-filled history tends to start bubbling forth so that the long-held pain can finally be addressed. Try hard to take this phase as a compliment, that an animal feels safe enough to reveal to you the inner pain they've been hiding from the world for so long.

Loving owners are convinced that there is a very smart and loving animal in there somewhere. They are always right, and OSCAR Therapy always finds it. And yet, for the people who didn't know that their new rescued companion also brings with him/her a scary past, then the unsuspecting new owner is left holding a potentially dangerous bag.

Usually things have begun to go terribly wrong long before I get a call. Owners have usually even experienced some very bad things. From broken bones, to broken hopes, to even inadvertent death, all of those negative experiences are not only shocking but were also (seemingly) unavoidable. And the shocks that a brain can't prevent are what create phobia in the owner, guardian, or pet parent.

Neither an animal's phobia nor a human's phobia just disappears on its own with logic and reason. We can "know" that our animal's dangerous behavior problem is fixed, but just like Oscar couldn't, our reptilian nerves won't let us actually act on that knowledge until we've actually *experienced* normal interaction with them. So it's a catch 22 for the owner. You can't find out that it's now safe to interact with your new and improved Oscar if your own brain won't even let you try!

"Zoophobia" is a term that refers to a person's fear of certain species of animals largely due to previous bad experience. But that term doesn't really cover the whole reality of the personal/intimate/daily fear of our own pets. We know our attackers quite well because we live with them. But it is in this reality that we see a lot of pet-o-phobias, or let's even say "Oscar-phobia: fear of the animal I rescued or purposefully took on."

Account of Michelle, Age 50, Connecticut

I've been a horsewoman for 30 years, but when I bought Clara and brought her home as an already competing riding horse, I got more than I bargained for. It turned out that she had a habit of "rearing and lunging at people" which put my daughter and grandchildren in a lot of danger. And this mare even scared me half to death on a few occasions too.

Kindness and time didn't help Clara's problem get better at all, and before too long I became scared to feed her, clean her stall, or even enter my otherwise perfect little barn. She picked on our little pony too, and she even lunged at wheelbarrows! Little did I know the truth behind her name: 'Clara' meant "she who brings clarity for those who cannot see, just like I wasn't able to see her and even myself clearly until OSCAR.

Being there to witness every step of the transformation of Clara with OSCAR Therapy did almost nothing to reverse my own acquired phobia of her front end; my own learned paralysis when I was near this horse was stark. And quite honestly, I was also totally freaked out by my apparent misunderstanding of all that I thought I knew about horses.

I had to hit total rock bottom before I could see the way forward for me personally. Even though I knew Casey worked wonders with us in the first session, I really just didn't believe that I could be a part of the picture for this horse's future, so I let life get in the way as an excuse to avoid her and even what was obviously helping her. I knew that if I encountered her scary behavior again, I would not be able to get that image from my mind, leaving me probably paralyzed in our advancement, and personally responsible for the failure.

During Casey's second session with us, even while trusting her judgment and KNOWING that it would be best to approach the horse at that time, Casey still had to "teach" my automatic reptile brain just like she teaches any phobic animal. Because my brain (just like any animal's brain) is wired for survival, it overrides sensibility. It was so critical that the OSCAR process helped my own *reactive* brain before it asked me to think/plan/do anything.

When trying to understand how an animal doesn't use part of its body -even if you hear it and comprehend it intellectually, experiencing it first hand *in your own body* puts it in a whole new perspective. It's like you have firsthand knowledge of what the horse is feeling. Those of us "lucky enough" to have had their own body-use PTSD have a real advantage- we have total understanding.

I just wish others could experience what I'm experiencing during these sessions and what comes from them. I know I would not have believed these results if I had not experienced it first hand. Over the years, I have seen horses be transformed by trainers, but somehow, something important seemed to be missing from the end result, like either the horse's personality *or the owner's personality* was missing in the end.

Also, I think with a lot of "trainers," even if they know how to "fix" the animal, they are still unable to figure out how to "fix the owner," and the downward spiral just continues. Had I worked with a "trainer" I would have brought Clara home to my same old fears of her. Often, the owner would still be freaked out and just going through the motions they were taught, without knowing why... Often the animal would be sold or put down in the end anyway, using some other reason as the excuse.

I cannot put into words how great it feels to truly believe that we will now be able to be a better team than I could have imagined even when I bought Clara! Again I say, thank goodness OSCAR Therapy is designed to care enough about the animals to also help their people- who are supposed to be their guardians- in the very same way!"

CHAPTER 6: OSCAR THERAPY IS "OC IN THE TRENCHES" (EXCERPTS FROM THE *WILL-ING* MANUAL)

My "trauma shrink" psychotherapist father has been doing that same job for as long as I can remember. He calls trauma therapy with people "working in the trenches" as the risks are many, the available resources are low, and the stakes are high. With such overwhelming pressures on his clients, he always has some hot ones that are on the edge of going to a place of no return.

Of course, psychotherapy and OSCAR Therapy both have a much higher *rate* of success than any real war fought in the real trenches. However, in both of these kinds of therapy, as in war, without a high degree of skill that is mainly learned on the job, things can go south quickly. With the animal cases that are phobic, angry, and reactive, standard operant conditioning and standard clicker training tools and skills are just plain insufficient to the task, in any reasonable time frame.

When dealing with the intensity, explosiveness, and speed of the primal and automatic phobic reflexes, the practitioner must bring their own high speed and high-precision participation to the table. We are truly becoming part of the Oscar's brains for a time, in order to help them heal themselves from the inside out. This chapter introduces some important upgrade modifications where standard operant conditioning has had to be customized to meet the needs of the terrain on the job with these "impossible" cases.

Chapter 6 is here to be used as our custom, in-house reference shelf. If you are stuck at a dead end, or if you want a deeper dive into some of the finer points of an Operant Conditioning conversation *OSCAR style*, then peruse the subtitles in this chapter; they will get you unstuck. And if you'd like to read a disturbing amount of essays like these, see *Will-ing*, the "mothership book" from Willing Results, LLC, as the following are just a few copied excerpts from that three-volume tome about how to leverage "the will."

6.1 Dead Horse Walking: An Eyewitness Account of a Recovery Story

Account of Janeen R., Brooklyn CT

A 12-year-old Leopard Appaloosa gelding's days were numbered. His owner loved him dearly but was running out of training options. The last two rides, he bucked her off. But his whole life history wasn't great either; Stuart was rescued from the kill pen at age 7. He couldn't be ridden into the auction arena and they referred to him as "green broke" though for good reason. He wasn't safe.

Love and money have incredible power to "solve" obstacles, so his owner spent many years and thousands of dollars on training. Eventually, Stuart was successfully shown in Western Pleasure classes until one day he plain refused to get on the trailer. His owner once again sought out expert help and tried every trick in the book including purchasing a brand new trailer. Some days she managed to get him to a show or riding event but mostly not; the stress of not knowing if he would load at the end of the day wasn't worth it.

His next regression? He refused to put the bit in his mouth. Experts were shocked at their inability to fix his problem. Hackamores are not allowed in the show ring. The vet checked his mouth and jaw and tested for any and all neurological disorders: none. An equine Chiropractor found nothing. Both experts agreed there was zero physically wrong with this horse.

So here was an owner stuck with a horse she loves that won't trailer load, won't accept a bit, won't be bathed, won't accept stall confinement, tests all fencing, can't be re-saddled between classes, and bucks her off for no apparent reason at all. Stuart did have excellent ground manners and farrier manners, but sadly, these few positives were not enough. He couldn't even be a lawn ornament as he has a long track record of attacking other horses. Stuart's veterinarian sadly broached the subject of euthanasia, simply to help the owner move on to a more fulfilling equine relationship. There was nothing left to do.

Then out of the blue, but not really, an advertisement she had seen many times over the last few years in a popular Equine handout finally jumped out at her while flipping through the pages. Stuart's owner couldn't believe she never really took note of the "horse shrink" ad in the past because Stuart clearly had every issue listed there! She went to the website...www.oscartherapy.com and read every word. She immediately had a friend pick up the phone for her because she couldn't even speak clearly about Stuart without sobbing.

Stuart needed a "whole brain rebuild" since most of his brain's body map was missing and was harboring massive amounts of PTSD. Not only that, but his owner needed the same; she had OSCAR issues too, all tangled up with the problems had by the horse.

Stuart was on death row only 5 months ago. Now, Stuart not only has a new lease on life, but he is amazingly capable. He self loads and drives perfectly; he doesn't even want to leave the trailer when we drop the butt bar. He is ridden whenever she wants with no need for drilling or practice; he looks like a dressage dancer when he does. He has even aided in reversing the owner's learned phobia of riding at speed and of being bucked off! His fears of stall and water and other animals are just gone; he accepts the bit but he prefers to perform perfectly in a bitless bridle. Just looking at him you can see that in his own mind, he is a changed horse.

I was the friend in this story; I made the initial call. I hated Stuart back then for the pain and fear he was causing; who knew back then... that Stuart was feeling the exact same way. I have witnessed the entire transformation from the outside, and what I have witnessed is nothing short of astonishing. And who knew that the answer all along was in the phone book... Thankfully, we found it before it was too late for us all.

6.2 Without Warning, Daisy Turns Into a Vicious Dog

Jack and Jill and Daisy the Pit Bull, New Haven, CT

I'm calling you today because I heard about you at my dog's vet office. Right after she lunged at one of them again, they said, 'There's a person who can fix this, it's hard to explain what it is, but it works. It worked on my dangerous horse.'

My name is Jack and, don't laugh, but my wife's name is Jill, and it's a long story about our not so storybook puppy, but I rescued her off the streets of New Haven. And maybe because she was a scary looking Pit Bull, we named her Daisy... we had hope for her. We don't know how long she had been on the streets, but long story short she's been with us for 10 months now. And I think she was happy to be rescued because she is sweet with us and with our other rescue dog too.

But with all strangers to the house or even our friends and relatives, without warning, she turns into a vicious dog; I don't know what's wrong with her. She has scared so many people, neighbors have even called the police, and now the vet... she even bit me when I got in between her and a man at the dog park. My wife is having near panic attacks from the stress of protecting the world from our dog." Daisy also loses her mind when it comes to any loud noises and anything new in her environment, so it's hard to even walk her down the street. We really want to help her, but we are afraid that we're going to have to put her down... and if we do have to do that our hearts will be broken completely.

This was my response:

"Jack, even though I've never even seen her yet, I guarantee you that I know what's wrong with your dog, and it can be repaired. All dogs like this have a not-commonly-recognized problem that most vets don't even know about, but it's true nonetheless. And better than that, it's reversible. Do you remember the bionic man? We can rebuild her! And by we, I mean me. Owner participation comes later, in the day to day of the re-acclimation phase. You don't have to become a trainer at all, but there will be homework later. However, I will need an owner to be present at every session, to witness the dog's brain progression and to be part of the team."

A post traumatic stress (PTSD) "fingerprint" or "dent" is imprinted on the brain, and it shows itself as "acute and irrational," out-of-nowhere, and/or seemingly inconsistent behavior, and yet, it's not irrational at all when you see the vectors of each brain's map. Animals that push too hard on you, "bop" you, smear themselves on you, push you into furniture or walls, or spin in tight circles, in "favorite directions," these are all clues that s/he's living with an OSCAR-affected brain. The Biting and "aggression" is just the animal's frustration and exhaustion playing out.

So let's examine how Daisy's case progressed:

Session 1: By using tiny chopped steak and chicken as reward, it was all about urging daisy to stop barking at me and take food through the holes of a baby gate with me sitting on the floor on the other side. Except for a temporary separating fence, no equipment is used in any OSCAR session; every dog is fully at liberty and is free to leave the session at any time. On day 1, Daisy was only aware of having a left front shoulder but all other portions of her body were off limits to (had been locked away from) her thinking brain; her reaction to all of her other zones was a knee-jerk reflex to attack or flee.

Sessions 2-10 were all needed to build Daisy's own cognitive map of her entire body. "Think about reaching out with your right shoulder, think about touching me with your left hip." Body parts are re-wired into the thinking brain with a simple touch game, but I NEVER touch the dog. The dog must reach out with said body part to purposefully touch me or a target object in my hand.

This courage to "reach toward where this dog has not reached before" means that OSCAR sessions are emotionally and mentally draining for any animal going through this process, evidenced by the dozen or so "big sigh" exhales these dogs let out per session. When they have no more learning energy left, I turn off the clock, the animal crashes into tuckered-out sleep, and that's the end of the session; so every session is as efficient as possible. Daisy used roughly 90 minutes of brainpower per session, which is a little less than typical, because she's still a puppy at less than 2 years old.

Even if our good intentions can't change an animal's past, they certainly can re-write the future, by merely re-wiring the present. The way out of the problem of ANY dangerous animal is to merely teach the animals to push out their own dents of subconscious memory, from the inside out. But you can't do it for them; you must teach THEM to do it for themselves. They learn to rewrite both their subconscious and their CONSCIOUS choices. When Daisy first started presenting her body parts to strangers of her own accord, Jill couldn't believe her eyes.

Session 11: was about giving Daisy a mental catchers mitt for all audio stressors (loud or novel sounds) and every day after this day, no noises have obviously bothered her. Not wind storms nor thunderstorms nor sirens nor the slamming of doors.

Session 12: began the introduction of strangers (colleagues of mine) around whom Daisy was encouraged to initiate an OSCAR game in order to feel "in control of herself" in response to the novelty of strangers.

Session 14: It's time to bring in Jill and Jack: how to introduce strangers and Daisy to each other. This step involved use of a temporary isolation fence, "the doggie cell," in the yard.

A quote from Jill: "I can totally introduce Daisy to new people now! With the help of our round intro-space, Daisy has a new best friend in about 3 minutes, every time. Even before I decide it's ok, Daisy is totally ready to play and show me how cool she thinks they are! She wants EVERYONE to play the OSCAR game with her, but if they don't want to she's ok with that too. Jack of course still loves his princess..."

I met Daisy the New Haven street dog in mid July, and by mid November the case was just about finished. OSCAR Therapy is an essential and necessary approach that every canine rescue organization and every branch office should learn, because many if not the majority of rescue dogs come with PTSD of some variety or another. Whether it be an audio, visual, social, physical, or you-name -it-phobia that leads to their anxiety and learned aggression, rescued animals have usually been through too much. OSCAR Therapy accesses the will-based, neurologic taproot that reverses and permanently repairs them all.

6.3 OSCAR Therapy Is an "Attempt-Inducing" Conversation

Animals in OSCAR Therapy love this game more than almost anything else they do. Recently, I was teaching an OSCAR horse session on the morning of the first snowfall of the year. Mid-session, all the other horses in the barn were finally being let out to run and bound about in the year's first white fluffy stuff, a yearly event which is always just as fun for horses as it is for children.

Since I didn't want to deny that special moment to the horse, I paused the session to let him go out with the others. He ran out and then in and then out and then in and then out; he was torn on whether inside with OSCAR games or outside with the first snow would be more fun... Even I was amazed by his vacillation. It was a testament to just how fun (and addictive) OSCAR sessions are for any brain who is learning it. The motivation is there.

And yet, traditionally "difficult" animals have been long thought of as difficult for a good reason. When Oscar's brain is missing some critical knowledge that the owner (at worst) assumes that Oscar already has or (at best) never considered before, then both animal and owner are just not on the same page. An Oscar isn't even on the same page with him/herself. This is a rough starting out place by anyone's measure. The problem looms large, but we practitioners do not dismay because we know where the *power* behind the OSCAR conversation comes from! (And it's not from us!)

Every OSCAR inquiry asks the same simple question: "Can you use that part of you there to reach out and touch this button right here?" Next, the answer from the individual you asked is either a Yes or a No or a large gray area of "maybe sort of."

And when Oscar is really trying hard to touch it, get ready to laugh. Because after you get past the initial tears part, you start bumping right into these clear and unmistakable reactions from the animals: imagination, embarrassment, courage, denial, jokes, lying, creativity, bribing, self-righteousness, jealousy, and true gratitude and love. At least half of those will cause you to bust a gut in out loud laughter with your animal, as they experience the vicissitudes of life just the same way you do.

And yet, it's what we practitioners say **after** that reaction from Oscar that then steers the therapy and builds its startling results. What we say *and don't say* in the process of the work will have a large impact on Oscar's future, no matter who s/he lives with or interacts with from there on out. In OSCAR Therapy, we go to great lengths to not do Oscar's learning work for him/her. Our job is to urge the "wrecked" brains to choose their way forward, all the way into becoming the "superhero" brains that we talked about in the previous chapter.

This chapter will describe the specialized *communication tools* we use to help Oscar quickly span the gaps of understanding and to help Oscar construct the new mechanics of what we call "chaos-absorbing capability." But without Oscar's coming to the table of their own free will to try to give our game a shot, nothing will be built. This first section is all about how we create that voluntary participation. And if your Oscar isn't flat out demanding that s/he get to play the game, then either Oscar has a significant medical challenge that needs to be addressed first, or there's something wrong in how you're playing it.

6.4 Positive Motivation vs. Negative Motivation

No matter what species of brain you are working with, and no matter what your goal is for that brain, I would ask you (just as I ask all uninitiated doubters) this single, simple, straightforward question:

> Of all of the physical training tools that you've got hanging on the wall, hook, or rack, which ones of those are designed and engineered to say "YES"?
>
> Note that the tools designed with quick-release features that 'stop saying No' (ex: horse kicking chains or dog bark collars) do not qualify.

Positive Motivators (that work like an ON switch) are the things that urge your brain to *find a way to cause* a good thing to happen. Negative Motivators (that work like an OFF switch) are the things that urge you to *find a way to stop* a noxious/bad/icky thing from happening. And it's not only that these two are merely different, it's that, in fact, one always works, and the other one always backfires.

When your goal is to get things created or accomplished, Positive works better.

And when your goal is to get bad things to turn off, Positive is *still* the switch that works better. Why does it work better? I don't know. Leave that to the neuroscientists. It probably has to do with the products of opportunity creation verses the products of deletion of opportunity. But just to show you how the two really operate, answer the next simple question. It's a simple taste test:

Would you rather...

a) Ignore something bad on the way to something you know is good, or...

b) Ignore something good on the way to something you know is bad.

If you were Winnie the Pooh, would you be more likely to ignore bee stings inherent to getting honey? Or would you be more likely to ignore a jar of honey on the way to storming a hive? In that second case, you'd be prioritizing getting control over a bad thing over everything else, over all potential gains.

Let's go one step more generalized. Are you more willing to ignore a fight while you're on your way to a pile of what you like, or, are you more willing to ignore a pile of what you like while you're on your way to a fight? Unless you are in a persistent state of rage, you are most likely going to pick the first one in all cases.

That's a little homebrew proof that positive opportunity is a much stronger motivator than causing the end of negative pressure. (And yes, my proof also implies that people who focus on the use of negative motivators are always in a persistent state of rage.) Negative pressure is not what the psych people of the 1950's thought; it is not the enormous motivator they imagined it to be. Negative crap is stuff we all can learn pretty quickly to tolerate.

In fact, negative pressure can be tolerated for eons without the recipient of it learning a damn thing. If you want to keep a brain switched off and under your assholian thumb, that's a pretty good way to achieve it. But if your goal is to teach Oscar to improve or even create, then you will need to set this tool aside and pick up another.

Still, many people seriously misunderstand what a positive motivator does; they use words like "bribe and weak and giving in and short-sighted" to discount/ignore the physics they don't understand. "Raindrops on roses and small mitten kittens," as my Harley-riding friend likes to describe the positive motivators, are more than just a happy place for Oscar's brain to temporarily go. Positives are actually a state of mind. Sought-out potential and earned rewards bring with them a steady state of safety, wellbeing, and *opportunity* that has the power to literally overwrite the experience of a bee sting or any other noxious topic you are discussing with Oscar. Stings have no such power to overwrite.

As an arm-waving estimate I would say that positive motivators are about 20 times stronger (that's 2,000 percent stronger) than negative motivators. Because whatever takes you one hour (two half-hour sessions) to teach using "release of a negative pressure" takes about three minutes to teach using positive motivators. Even if no other benefit is taken into consideration, using positive motivation is just a *huge* time saver.

6.4.a "Yes & No" Is Insufficient: "No"-Based "Logic" Falls Away

Adjustments to *your own will* are what help you learn the language of OSCAR Therapy, and Willing Results LLC teaches three learn-by-doing Will Classes in real time. In class, when a would-be teacher (the person who is trying to explain something to an Oscar) has not yet acquired our working language, and when that lack of ability is leading to some unfortunate events, participants tend to panic and yell out... *NOOOO!* And that's when Oscar's learning stops.

Hot/cold, red light/green light, yes/no, you can play the *No* game with whatever words you choose, but they're all the same in what they mean. Sometimes my classes get hung up on someone's dependent need for the *No* tool, and if that's what people need to learn about, it's no skin off my nose. I used to be addicted to the word myself so I love teaching about what *No* does, whenever the topic comes up.

For whatever reason, it's usually the males in the crowd who argue that *No* is "a necessary component" of Yes; they believe it's wrong to give up their *No* tool. We start with a small discussion in the class about how constructive *No* really is and then the men (and some of the women too) protest, swearing that *No* always gets any "explaining" job done much quicker and more reliably than all of this time-wasting *"Yes crap."* I love it when someone puts this topic on the table, because that individual gets to go immediately on the receiving end hot seat so that s/he can prove it to us, by doing the learning himself/herself.

When he's playing the part of Oscar, and everyone in the room is trying to explain a specific task to him using only Yeses and No's, every single *No* he hears for the next few minutes does for him exactly what it does for anyone. It leaves him in the dark. *No* is nothing. It's a void, an absence of information. It doesn't point to the useful paths, and worse yet, it reprimands Oscar for looking for them. It can occasionally clear the way for a path, like a snowplow, but it is NOT a path itself. A snowplow without road underneath it has no purpose.

No is literally like a chemical off switch for any thought process. Hearing it, Oscar forgets about all main highways of possibility and focuses only on the safety of back road dead-ends. *No literally always* backs any and every thinking brain into a corner. Always.

And since the humans who are sure they are correct are the kinds of people who especially hate being left in a corner in the dark, I try to help us all in class to change the subject quickly so that the Oscar on the hot seat doesn't have to eat too much crow. My aim is to keep him or her in the class. My aim is not to be the cause of him or her shutting down.

So I thank him profusely for volunteering to drive that point home for all of us. But before he's back in his regular seat, I ask if the *No's* that we offered helped him to understand us better. Invariably, he says, "No." And that's usually the last time we hear that word for the rest of the course.

6.4.b Motivators vs. Bribes

The age-old idea of a carrot on the end of a stick lashed to the donkey's pack is a fine example of a bribe. A bribe is an unattainable commodity that has been "attached" to something, to either a physical target or a mental target that you really want Oscar to "interact with." When you use some kind of bait to induce a specific choice/destination, that is a clear transaction. If used as a teaching tool though, to *teach* Oscar *how* to make a choice, a bribe is at best a lie and, at worst, it is confusion incarnate. Bribes can't teach.

Here is the age-old lie… your donkey steps ahead to get at that "attainable" carrot, and yet, his action also pushes the carrot farther off. But he's not dumb; five minutes of this, and not only will he stop dead in his tracks. He will also learn to never reach for a carrot again in his life unless he gains some opposite experiences where dangling carrots are actually attainable things.

What's more, bribes mainly backfire; learners get so caught up and so focused on the commodity itself that they even forget all about the "interaction thing" you tied to it. For instance, if I were to tie a $100 bill to a broom handle and then hand you the broom, the last thing you would do with it is sweep. The first thing you're going to do is start untying the knot!

However, you can tell that a commodity is being thought of as and is being used correctly as a motivator/reward (and not a bribe) when, at some point in the learning, Oscar chooses to blow right by your $100 bill *payments* in order to try harder to solve the puzzle of what kind of sweeping works best! For the problem-solving Oscar, regardless of species, any commodity earned becomes merely an after thought. Its importance takes a back seat to the value of the empowerment of the experience of learning. Oscars don't really have time for commodities—they are too busy learning how to *create* their world.

In the book, play, and movie called *The Miracle Worker*, there is a scene in which Helen Keller tosses aside every object she learns the name of, in order to quickly get to the next object. That scene is reminiscent of Oscar's change in priority. Her brain is thirsting for knowledge and can't load the information in fast enough. Information itself is the reward, not the foods or monies that helped motivate Oscar to search for it. It really makes you begin to cry with understanding when you see it happening. Payment of any kind (if you want to use it) is no different in OSCAR Therapy; it becomes less and less important to Oscar's process.

A correctly used motivator (a reward waiting in the wings) grabs your attention, but it is not pulling you toward *an action*; it's pulling you toward a choice. So the payment is eventually relegated, *by the learner/receiver*, to playing a minor role.

A bribe, on the other hand, is sort of an oxymoronic idea. By definition, a bribe is a reward that is inexorably tied to only an action, and never a choice. The inherent problem with bribes is that they are *intrinsically designed to fail* at their intended goal. Because the learners are so mesmerized by the reward, they are practically blind to the target choice that the reward is tied to. In fact, when a bribe is in use, the recipient will learn to do everything possible to *actively avoid* the target choice you're hoping they'll make for you.

Let's get back to the old carrot on a stick for a moment. Have you ever seen money that is lashed to an assignment from your boss? Did you really get paid fairly in the end? Most everyone, jackasses included, eventually learns to avoid the carrots, promises, and other moving targets altogether. In fact, what you *really* learn is to do *everything but* touch that target.

As a manager, how can you tell the difference between a motivation and a bribe? It's simple. If it feels like you're bribing someone, you are. As a subordinate, how can you tell the difference between a motivation and a bribe? Simple, if it feels like you're being bribed, you are.

How can the answer be so simple? Because what you feel is one of those original feelings that goes way back to the beginnings of the animal experience. What you are feeling is the loss of your autonomy. At this moment, someone else is trying to have control over your choices. If you feel like you have been trapped by your hunter, and like you have to get away, then what you are dealing with is a bribe.

When you want to empower someone, you should at no time lie to them about the value (*to you*) of *their choice* that you are approving of, not even in the slightest. You can bait them with a carrot, but do not then move that carrot once they reach it. Do not ever keep on moving the finish line further on down the road. You especially ought not *ever* bait & switch ANY reward with individuals who have been the victims of lies. Do not dangle a jackpot to then payoff in Kewpie dolls. Do that, and you've lost them.

You have to give every earned reward to Oscar, no matter how much it's killing you to do so, and then you have to go get another carrot. And if you're worried about conserving the content of your wallet or your garden, just use tiny "carrots;" because using many small payments works just fine.

6.4.c "Payment" Transactions

If you agree that payment is a good motivating tool (and you don't have to take my word for it, you can experiment for yourself) then there's just one more really important thing to know about making payments. You have to know how to carry out the transaction. For instance, thousands of horse owners and dog trainers and other animal trainers across the countryside will tell you that you should never feed an animal out of your hand because hand-fed animals become overly demanding and dangerous: they bite. That is the claim.

The reasoning of the reward-averse "trainer" is here:

- Bribes backfire (even though Operant Conditioning transaction is nothing like a bribe /lie)

- I refuse to "pay" for something the animal should do anyway (even though they don't know how or why to do what they "should do.")

- Food in hand teaches non-biting animals to bite hands (even though food in a bucket in hand is something that we interact with, and safely provide to animals every day).

- I don't want my animal to get fat (even though a simple subtraction from other meals or use of low calorie foods chopped small would prevent weight gain).

- I don't want my animal to think less of me, use me, think they can control me, get too excited, etc. (Even though the non-discriminating human is the one who is rewarding the unwanted behaviors).

To every one of the food-fearful people, I ask this one simple question. If some unarmed drunk moron walks up to you on the street and says "Hey you, I want all your money…" Do you just hand it over? If a human being can't figure out how to complete a hand-operated food transaction with a domesticated animal, then they probably aren't fit to provide daily care to that animal.

Additionally, as a consumer, *you* may not want to pay *that person* for their opinion, seeing that they can't understand a normal fee for service transaction in any respectful way. If any human is manipulating you and threatening you in order to get *your* carrots, and if they're getting away with it, then what you have there is a much bigger problem than money loss; you have a problem you're your own insufficient Presence.

In OSCAR Therapy, reward commodities will be used in order to prime the pump of "choice making" even whilst the most difficult and scary topics are being discussed. In most OSCAR cases, small volume but high frequency food bits will be used. But withholding of normal daily food rations is only rarely necessary, and only for the "picky non-eater" individuals.

When food use is not an option, as in cases of non-eaters, nocturnal eaters, throat or oral cavity phobias or post surgical limitations, other sensory stimuli are just fine when used as OSCAR rewards. Sound-based, visual-based, and toy-based rewards are always available options. But contact-based rewards like hugging, petting, and scratching ought to be avoided in OSCAR Therapy, because they break the first rule: Thou Shalt Not Touch Oscar.

In any OSCAR Therapy conversation, the reward itself quickly becomes much less important to every learning brain than is the shared language itself. The empowerment that comes with learning how to make winning choices is what Oscar values most of all. To Oscar, each win gains them new levels of knowledge, awareness, and control over their own selves, relationships, environments, and world.

When you feel as though Oscar doesn't deserve reward or payment for the efforts, then you can be angry and frustrated with your animals, but if you don't want to understand them slightly more than you want to dislike or blame them, then OSCAR Therapy is not for you, until you do want that. There's a bunch of double negatives in that politically correct statement above, but what it boils down to is this. You don't have to have any love for Oscar; you do have to want to understand Oscar.

6.4.d Options for Non-Food Rewards

The earned rewards that are paid out to an Oscar don't always have to be comprised of food. In teaching, OSCAR Therapists can employ motivators on the entire spectrum, starting from pecking order status all the way through rivalry competition, self expression, cross talk, commodity (food or property), play, curiosity, novelty, free time, autonomy, and last of all, relief from something icky. These motivators seem to be less and less effective, in roughly that descending order, but we can still use them all.

Whether we're talking about actual money, or the commodities that Oscar earns AS payment, payola, buy offs, rewards, payoffs, gifts, or trades, individuals are highly motivated by payment. And wouldn't ya know, animals are also very highly motivated by it, given they understand the concept of money and plenty of animals do. [A student at Yale showed that when Capuchin monkeys spend exchange coins (money), they spend it primarily on sex, food, and gambling.]

But even regarding our human-to-human payments, the value associated with *the transaction itself* is the other big thing to consider. In OSCAR Therapy, the value is not really in the commodity itself; it's in the earning of it. The transaction itself is more important to any Oscar brain than the thing being transacted. And to that end, what these animals value most is more transactions instead of less.

We have observed that, to an earning brain, being paid a lump sum feels like a single transaction, or a single win, but being paid 5 small sums feels like at least 6 or 8 wins because of the added value of each transaction. So in OSCAR Therapy we pay out the earned bits one bit at a time. To an Oscar's brain, one handful of 8 bits = 1 reward, but 8 bits given one at a time = more reward than they can imagine!

So when we feed rewards during OSCAR sessions, we feed in this style:

1 + 1 + 1. Our paying out a jackpot for a fabulous and courageous choice would look like this... 1 + 1 + 1 + 1 + 1 + 1 + 1 + 1 + . You'd stop at the point where Oscar "looses count" because payment that exceeds that is just money down the drain, unnoticed by Oscar's learning brain. You'll know when they've lost count when they seem "surprised" by the previous "additional yet unexpected" payout. As soon as you see that mildly surprised expression on their face, you've paid enough in that moment.

I've noticed that some dogs can't count past three, some horses *can* count up to seven, some nonprofit employees are overwhelmed with anything over 25, and some CEOs won't even notice a jackpot unless it's more than a million. You should Jackpot accordingly for Oscar's leaps forward. Unexpected quantity of reward really gets Oscar's attention, and what led up to it is not soon forgotten. Oscar learns to enjoy this conversation.

6.5 HOW to Say Yes: Even More Than Your Grandfather's Operant Conditioning

6.5.a Chocolate for Breathing: You Lost Me at Hello

It's true that the first moments of any conversation are the worst. But it's not because of some universal anxiety and need for someone to break the ice. It's because we have no idea how to or why we should acknowledge someone else's existence when there is, as yet, no clear and obvious reason to do that.

If that's how hard it is for two random ships passing in the night, (think two individuals that are not even the same species) to acknowledge each other, then imagine how hard it becomes when there are some expectations on deck too! Countless people have proclaimed, "But how am I supposed to even start when s/he's giving me nothing good to comment on?!"

In Approval class, I give you a small goal to teach your assigned "learner," and then I just wait in silence. When you come to the table with absolutely nothing (no clear communication of anything), I let you feel this pain. It's the pain of the communication void. It is a very uncomfortable place to be. For the first few loooong minutes of Approval class, I let the pain of that void really sink in deep. I do that so you will never again forget what it feels like to be strangled by yourself... by your own lack of voice... by your own lack of choice. And no one ever forgets it.

Most humans have a general predisposition toward holding back approval, for the expressed purpose of waiting for something better from Oscar to show itself; they suspect the better Oscar is right around the corner. But if you ask Oscar, Oscar only feels the void of where your voice should be. And it never even occurs to Oscar that there is some imaginary goal they should be working toward. Our focus on silence is *hurting* Oscar with every passing moment, and in Approval class, I let people feel that pain acutely.

The fact that almost every would-be teacher never gets this one right in the beginning is only slightly noteworthy. What is *incredibly* noteworthy, however, is how much our whole species seems to be pre-programmed to out and out refuse the knowledge that *The Better is the **Enemy** of the Good*, especially at the beginning of an exchange. The idea of giving away something for nothing *to prime the pump of communication* is generally lost on the human race. With every new client I teach, nearly everyone's first words are, "But... but... Oscar hasn't done anything good yet!"

Let those words echo in your mind a few times. Imagine yourself just walking down the street minding your own business, and someone walks up to you and says, "Hey you! You haven't done anything to deserve my approval!" In my classes, there's an easy fix. I just have you and Oscar swap roles for a minute. Two seconds in Oscar's uncomfortable shoes during any challenge puzzle, and the penny-pinching teachers get the point entirely: it hurts to be rejected right out of thin air. And for Oscar, when they are just minding their own business, even before any conversation is happening, hearing such things is downright head scratching.

As it turns out, Approval is not even the property of the mind or the plan. More striking than that, *Approval* is really only effective when applied *before* there is any plan, and before there is any result. *Someone* has to start the initial volley, prime the pump, throw the first pitch, or put in the initial activator energy to get the "relate" wheel turning, and if Oscar's not doing it, then someone has to. So it has to be you. It's *your* goal that you care about after all, so you may as well be the one to initiate the first transaction.

The top reason why people cough and sputter and choke at the very beginning of their first lesson in Approval is because that's the time when they need to approve of Oscar for plain old *existing*. This is what helps Oscar choose interaction over the other perfectly reasonable option: no interaction. All those who learn OSCAR Therapy find out in short order that if they don't approve of Oscar for his sheer ability to breathe in and out, they will get no further in this conversation.

And at the very beginning of any conversation, you've got zero other chips to play anyway, so you might as well play the only chip you have! The only chip to play is a gift for no reason; I call it Chocolate for Breathing. Another name for it is Santa Claus, a gift simply because you exist. A gift is something good and extra, not something good and recovered. A cookie is a gift. But saying, "Your house burned down! Only kiddin,' your house didn't really burn down, Merry Christmas!" That is *not* a gift. Reversing or withholding something bad is *never* a gift.

6.5.b Find Your Approve: "YES" Chiropractics

The best story I tell about what it's like to acquire this YES skill came from a Boston executive. This tall, ominous yet distinguished looking gentleman came to my one-day class because he had been threatened by Human

Resources. He was being mandated to learn how to get along with people. "No matter what you have to do, get it done!" said they in HR.

He introduced himself to our little workshop this way, "I can't tell you my name, who my employer is, or what I do. Trust me when I say it's a big company you'd all know, and someone like me doing something like this has to fly under the radar, so let's get on it and get this done. I'm a senior vice president and everyone who works for me hates me. I don't have a lot of time to piss around, I really need to learn something, like *right now*."

The class went like routine clockwork. All eight participants were getting the skills down and, as if they were on a very fruitful Easter egg hunt, they all had half a dozen new skills in their baskets, everyone except for Mr. VP. He was getting frustrated and starting to shut down. And even though he had a terrific towering presence, as partners and puzzles swapped around, people were starting to avoid him. So I focused in on him while the others were chugging along.

Mr. VP's goal was the same one I had given to everybody else: use only the single word "YES" to teach another perfect stranger from class something specific. Mr. VP's random stranger was named Mark, who was to learn to go to the blackboard, pick up the white chalk, not the yellow chalk, and draw a huge circle on the blackboard. The "Approvers" were of course supposed to teach their goal to their learner without talking or using any body language at all.

In short order, the class was starting to see why Mr. VP's employees couldn't stand him. Mr. VP waited, and waited, with arms crossed, and when Mark happened to walk near the black board, Mr. VP said, "Well....?" So right here, Mr. VP became MY student, while he was still teaching Mark.

Here's the play by play of my conversation with Mr. VP, about Mark, who he was responsible for *supervising* in our Saturday Will Agility class:
Mark: Staring at floor near chalkboard
VP: Staring at Mark
Mark: Frustrated
Me: Is he doing what you want right now?
VP: No.
Me: Is he doing something wrong?
VP: No.
Me: Is there any tiny part of what he's doing that could be useful to you?
VP: Yes.
Me: Could you say that?
VP: What?
Me: Could you tell that to Mark?
VP: Tell him what?
Me: What you just said to me.

VP: What, you mean the partial correct thing?

Me: Exactly, how could you explain that to Mark?

VP: By saying that he was right?

Me: When?

VP: Already. I mean before.

Me: What could you have said before?

VP: I could have said...

Me: (silence)

VP: Yeeessss... In the middle. I could have said yes *in the middle*... yes to something *small* instead of waiting for something big that never comes.

VP: I HAD NO IDEA IT WAS OK TO SAY YES TO SOMETHING THAT HASN'T BEEN COMPLETED YET!

Me: Yup, your YES was just out of joint, simple as that.

VP: "I truly love all of my employees, so much so that I have been convinced all these years that giving them encouragement was belittling them; they are already very successful at what they do, so what would they need me for? I thought approval was a power trip. I had no idea that it was the basis for transferring information and that it was independent of anyone's judgment of anyone. Oh my God. I've left my people in the dark my whole career when I thought I was honoring them. No wonder they hate me. I'd hate me! I don't though, because I get it now. ...But if I had to work for me, I mean."

"I can't believe it. I actually learned what I came here to learn, and I found it myself, I mean you, I mean I, I mean you helped me find it myself. And from an animal behaviorist, no less. I can't believe it. Do you understand how convinced I am that my success at work is about to change?"

"YES," I said with a wide smile.

When simple conversations turn into convoluted "Who's on First" volleys, that's your stone cold evidence that there is an active kink in your own alignment. A kink is *not* just something that's *not known*, it's something that's actively, yet *subconsciously* avoided, and usually for some very good reason. In this case, the necessary tool was avoided in order *to honor* Mr. VP's employees. *Intentions are usually just fine; it's just simply the Will's Agility (the expression of that intention) that's out of whack.*

After about 15-20 minutes of trying out his new pair of YES shoes, Mr. VP became the BEST supervisor/teacher/explainer/approver in the room, by far. He had real talent. His continence shifted, his face lifted, he became happy, at ease, connected, and incredibly in tune, possessing the fine detail attention of a spider repairing a web.

The love and respect he had said he truly felt for those around him finally got a place to perch, and before the class was over, Mr. VP was the favorite teacher, winning all of the spontaneous applause from the other participants, and then he started coaching others in the last half hour.

6.5.c Approval Is of "One Point" in Time

One of the most valuable of all of the Approval-based Will Tools is the point. You could also call it the tic or the tock or the click or the zip or the nick or the pip; I call it the Gd, which ends up sounding like Git, but the word is "Good" without the "oo" in the middle. Gd. That's the "point of approval" I use.

The point is an invaluable tool for teaching brains, because in Will Agility, and in OSCAR Therapy, saying the word YES just takes way too long. The meaning of the One Point is YES, but the audibly drawn out spoken word YEEEESSSSS can be such a non-specific white wash that it's nearly useless.

If you were performing a series of confusing dance steps, and your teacher said, Yeeeeeeees, then how would you know which step was the good one? You didn't get precise enough information in time, and you'd have to conclude that all of your steps were correct. To avoid all of the confusion that can be directly caused by your own Approvals of Oscar, keep them short; saying yep or yip would be more precise than Yes. Sharp. Staccato.

In fact, when you are really helping Oscar understand you, you will often find yourself murmuring repetitious Yips that sound just like the enchanting but elusive Sesame Street Yip Yips created by Jim Henson. These infrequently seen but much loved wide-mouthed Muppet aliens are often faced with the uncertain task of identifying Earth species. The Yip Yips never go so far as to try to mind-meld with the Earthlings (thereby teaching us their monosyllabic yip-based language) as well as we do in OSCAR Therapy, but maybe they will in Sesame Street, the Next Generation. Regardless, if you are approving effectively, you'll know it when you begin to sound as ridiculous as those fuzzy Martian Muppets. Yipyipyipyipyip.

Approval is a moment, not a statement. It's a look, not a sentence. Approval is a wink, and not much more. More would be an infraction, a judgment, an over-stepping of bounds. The idea of YES is most useful when it is conveyed in no more time than the tic of a second hand as it jumps. A whole second is much too long.

Approval needs to take place in the fastest chunk of perceptible signal possible. Anything more ends up being inadvertently belittling as a waste of Oscar's time because s/he *hears* you in micro second speed. If you want to catch a fleeting thought as it flits by, you have to be quick with your net. And that's why a quick and sharp "good without the oo's" or "Gd" (pronounced like Git) is more a *physical* skill than a conceptual one. If your communications are sluggish, they cannot be agile.

If you miss one once in a while, it's no big deal; Oscar will be very forgiving of you as s/he keeps trying. But if you do not fully believe in or fully commit to your YESes in general, even a microscopic "hold out" puts a chokehold on your Approval skill. The friction you've introduced there then gives you a 1/3 of a second delay in your timing of your YES, so for the learner it's like hearing a hesitant "yeahhh" or an *echo* of you instead of hearing you directly.

Watch a second hand click on a wall clock and you can see exactly how long 1/3 of a second is. Sounding like that echo is enough to slow down your conversation with Oscar about 60 percent. So, getting rid of the delay will push your conversation with Oscar to be 60 percent faster. You'll get things taught in less than half the time.

When your will to hold back is fighting the gift of your approval, your points of approval end up sounding like they have qualifiers, or… punctuation. Here are some examples of how these long, drawn out, and sloppy approvals or "approval hold outs" sound to Oscar:

"yes, but"

"sooooo, yes"

"and yes."

"yes, yes… yes? yes"

All of these would-be approvals are getting jammed up or gummed up. They are like peanut butter or thick clumps of mud on your telephone line. Make your approval Gd's sharp like staccato piano or like Morse code or like a Geiger counter. Every single Gd must have a period or an exclamation point on it, because those are the only kinds of verbal approvals that keep your telephone line to Oscar clear and understandable: Gd. Gd. Gd. _____ Gd. Gd.

6.5.d Lingo: Flexible Works Better Than Consistent

Question: *"So what's the lingo? What's supposed to actually come out of my mouth when YES is what I mean? Casey, you should do it first so I can hear what the hell you're talking about."*

Answer: It doesn't matter. Like, at all. It just doesn't matter at all. The lingo you should use is "any sharp sensors received change that you can turn on and off," meaning that if Oscar notices it, it's good enough. Personally I use a tone changing "snapping gum" tongue snap that varies by 7 notes on a musical scale. I teach my clients to use the word Good, with no oo's it in. "Gd." Just until they find something they like using better.

But really, it's your pick and you can even change 'em up on the fly whenever you need. Your YES can switch between sound, a volume change, visual items, a flash of light, whatever; it just needs to be a quick perceptible change. What you choose to use is so *unimportant*, that the sensory mode you pick *can even be changed from minute to minute* if you wish, and Oscar will follow right along and won't miss a beat.

To help Oscar learn to follow along faster, just start overlapping your signals a bit. For example:

If A=B, and B=C, then A=C, right?

If scary sound = opportunity to hit the button…

…and if hitting the button = good,

...then scary sound = good. Right?

An Oscar's brain makes the same leap within a very few exposures to that scary sound.

If a click = good, and then a click means a handshake, then a handshake = good. Right?

That's how you can "retranslate" a Yes to mean a touch, by leapfrogging the idea. It's like using an electric socket adapter, if you want to think of it that way. You're just saying to Oscar, when you feel this, it's like you're hearing *that*. Your talk just needs to be fluid and not really planned out. All sensory signals are the collective words that can make up your new OSCAR Therapy language: use 'em all and mash 'em up.

The reason Oscar can and will follow your YES from a finger pressure to a clucking tongue to a flashlight turned on is because the change links information that is *generically new* to the generic idea of *new benefit*. Oscar learns that, "Whenever I sense something weird and unexpected, that means I win." That's a very powerful thing to learn about the idea of being flexible *on purpose.*

Operant Conditioners have made "The Bridge Signal" (the sensed signal which becomes the idea of YES) out to be a message that is technical, sterile, binomial, and robotic. Whether it's Pavlov's bell or the child psychologists' clicker device or the dolphin trainer's whistle, these consistent and technical "bridges" that always sound the same, in my humble opinion, are lacking. Just because an animal is taught in Japanese and then is passed on to a Spanish speaking family, that doesn't mean the animal will forget the Japanese word for "come" or for anything else.

Anyone's assumption that Oscar *cannot* follow the bouncing ball as it is changing color and changing shape is *just so untrue* that it ends up to be quite limiting to the conversation. What cross-talk could be happening at lighting speed is happening instead at a crawl because we've gagged our four other means of communication, our four other means of sensory perception, in favor of the one we have isolated out.

If the dolphin is across the pool, blow the whistle. But if he's a deaf dolphin, use a flashlight. But if he's on stage with you, just OSCAR button him. Oscar is never a dumb individual, and extrapolating is what animals do best, anyway.

My favorite marine mammal trainer (who shall remain nameless and genderless) was also quite often hung over from the nightlife. And some days that whistle was just too damn loud. Instead of using "the approved communication equipment," this trainer would just raise one eyebrow and raise one index finger half way. Anything else gave this person a headache but that approach made the communications with the dolphins and whales and sea lions and seals so fluid and seamless that it looked to me like all of the animals liked this human best of all because of it.

It's a terrific thing to use different textures in your Approval, just like a paintbrush. What is baby talk if not the whole kitchen sink of tones, speeds, pauses, and pitches. Instinctively, that's how we teach a newborn how to *hear* us. You and I may hate baby talk as adults, but ask a baby if s/he hates it. The variations on a theme make perfect sense to them; they're not dumb either.

The idea here is that YES is *not only* a marker in space; it also includes conceptual information. It is not only a time marker- it draws an EMOTION IDEA out of Oscar. It serves as the IDEA of, the empowerment to, and the acquiring of things that have value. YES can mean you are done, or it can mean keep going, or it can mean you are done *and* keep going! YES can be in your control OR the YES can be in Oscar's control if you decide that the yes is something that Oscar is invited to draw *out of you*.

A YES will backfire on you if it's *late* (including if it's too loooong); but other than that, any other "rules" about how to use it just make things worse. It's fine to get familiar with "the signal" using the kindergarten basics of "consistent operant conditioning" at first, but then, as soon as you can, start adding in the wide variety of ways to say yes, ways that are available to us all. To fold in the new ones, just use a string of the known Gd's and sprinkle in a few of your new signals followed by reward.

Remember what you are ACTUALLY doing this for. The bridge literally means, "YES, you ARE RIGHT." If you are getting that idea across, don't limit yourself to how you say it, and don't limit your counterpart to acting like a dumb robot, no matter what species, breed, gender, age, or other classification you think you're talking to.

You are not working with a beta-test lab robot here, where you have to use correct pronunciation or else the computer doesn't understand you. You are working here with a whole brain designed over eons of trial and error to survive the chaos of the natural world. Let's give it the respect it deserves. The way to help that brain most is to say yes in as many ways and modes as you can.

6.5.e Jackpot for Oscar's Questions, Not Just for Answers

In Operant Conditioning, "jackpot" is a technical term. No kidding. When the chicken pecks the right key in the psychology lab, she gets what the scientists call a "jackpot," where a whole lot of food pellets come out of the chute, just like a slot machine hitting three cherries.

How many pellets? According to OSCAR Therapy, the amount of Approval you hand over in the jackpot just has to be "more than Oscar expected" at the moment, but doled out one at a time. That's how you know there's enough Approval or reward in your gift to make it a jackpot. "Oscar, that try was so good that you earned not only this one, but here's another, and here's another, and here's another, and here's another, and..."

But in OSCAR Therapy, the work is usually about phobia of social body use. It's hard for an Oscar to guess wrong when their body doesn't know how to guess at all in the first place. So a right or wrong answer is not what you're going to get a lot of. What you're going to get a lot of is Oscar's own imagination, and the beginnings of asking the questions about possibilities.

Imagine a way that they might be able to try to move. Rewarding that imagination is even more important than rewarding a job that is perfectly done. Because without a wisp of an initial exploration, no body parts will be going anywhere new.

6.6 WHEN to Say Yes: Much More Than Your Aunt's Clicker Training

You can pick up good operant conditioning, clicker training, and nose-bound target training type teaching skills through any number of routes these days. Short free videos can be found on a zillion Clicker Trainers' websites as well as in probably dozens of books at your local library. From professional behaviorists to exotic animal specialists at zoos and aquariums to the backyard barns of just about any species large or small, it seems you can't open a car door without hitting somebody that can get you started in good solid operant conditioning language.

With this easy to use language you can both civilize your animals and teach them myriad party tricks. You can even mold/shape your human family members, unbeknownst to them. But OSCAR Therapy uses that same approach as a springboard launching off point, with the aim of diving into a new and deeper level of understanding, rehabilitation, healing, and brain repair.

6.6.a Myth: "Oscar has a short attention span."

Whenever possible, OSCAR Therapy teaching sessions should last as long as the attention span of the client. Most humans last about two hours before their brains max out. But the animals, they usually outlast their people by a long shot.

Have you ever wondered why the "slackers" in society can learn how to improve on the video games for 20 hours a day on the weekends, and then get busted at school for being unfocused? It's because their game world matters to them. Their school world doesn't. When Oscar is invested, s/he has a long attention span.

It is my experience that horses have an attention span of roughly 2 to 4 hours, repeatable up to three times a day (in an emergency), allowing roughly 6 to 9 hours a day of teaching time. Dogs can go for 2 to 3 hours, repeatable up to two times per day. This amount of focus and focused learning rivals both the human's college lecture format and also the human's intensive immersion format.

Typically, the riding horses who are "in work" work hard. Training is serious and physically demanding, so a typical horse "in work" is happy to be done when they're done. When the saddle comes off, they exhale big, and then the horse is allowed to eat a few bites of grass or a few bites of hay while walking around and cooling down. Trainers usually have to ride a few horses in a row, so the saddle switching time is when the rider gets to take 5 to hit the bathroom. And just last week I was reminded of the stark change in life that follows when brains are engaged versus when they are not.

The clients of mine who are trainers themselves keep complaining to me of a new problem they have to contend with now, ever since they met me: horses in the bathroom. Even though Will-based riding can be sort of a workout for the horse's muscles, it's their brains that get so engaged that they won't let their communication partner out of their sight. The horses start sticking to the dismounted riders like glue. Riders head off to the bathroom as usual, but the horses, who are supposed to be happily eating grass, attentively watch the person out of the corner of their eye.

When the rider goes behind closed doors, the horses usually go trotting over to that door and start using their big heads to push the door open. And it's a little more un-nerving than when your cat or dog does that same thing in the house because, since the horse also tries to come in there with you, a big horse in the way makes certain that the door won't be closing any time soon, even though you're on the toilet. And in the community barn, you'll usually have a bunch of human non-family members watching your struggle.

Oscar's "coming out of the wood work" is not something of which Oscar is in very much control. They haven't exactly decided, consciously anyhow, to engage with you in this new ultra-attentive way. They just end up doing it, out of play instinct mostly. Good communication, for Oscar, is like seeing themselves in a funhouse mirror for the first time. When you see one, you kind of can't help yourself or stop yourself from waving your hands around in front of it.

Oscar's new attention on you is an effect of your change of priority. When Oscar believes that your approval of Oscar's own self expression is real, Oscar will most definitely emerge or materialize with unprecedented intensity, and in ways that you cannot predict and will not expect. Just get a strong latch for the bathroom door.

6.6.b It's Safe to Put Oscar On Hold When You Must (Ipanema)

The Blues Brothers is a classic cinema movie masterpiece, and a perfectly will-balanced piece of art for too many reasons to count. But one of the most instructive juxtapositions in the 1980 film is toward the end. Jake and Elwood, our renegade do-gooders, are making a mad dash for the clerk's office to pay the property taxes on the orphanage that raised them, having themselves raised the money in a slightly illicit manner.

On the one hand, they are being chased through the city of Chicago by maybe 1,000 law enforcement representatives all heavily armed and descending on them from every direction. On the other hand, they have no choice but to listen to the soothing elevator musak bossa nova classic, *The Girl from Ipanema*. A veritable army will catch up with them momentarily but right now, they are in "on hold" limbo.

Since Oscar's progress pathways are instantly hard wired; what is learned is learned. That means that you can time out of the action just like Jake and Elwood, hear some elevator musak, and then time back in to the action almost without limit. Oscar will not lose his or her place on the page no matter how much on hold musak they hear. Right in the middle of OSCAR Therapy sessions you can give Oscar an "on hold" cue and run to the bathroom, take a short phone call, attend to another animal or do whatever you gotta do; Oscar will be ready to go as soon as you get back.

6.6.c Over-Acting: Photonegative YES Teaches Oscar to Dial It Back

Just for a second, think about Morse code. Imagine the dots and dashes representing the language you use to approve of Oscar. Imagine that the long dashes represent you watching and waiting, and the dots are what represent the Yeses you dole out when Oscar does something you like. What you "say" to Oscar might generally look like this:

---- • --------- • • ---------- •------ •------- • • --------- •---

That's the typical style of your typical teacher, right? A lot of waiting with a few 'attaboys peppered in.

Okay, now, imagine getting out an old camera, one that used real film. Imagine taking a "photo" of that line of dashes and dots. (If you've never seen a real camera before, just hit the Negative button on your smart phone's photo filters.) Imagine the negative roll, the photo-film negative of that dots and dashes line above. The negative would be something like this, below. The dots became now dashes and the dashes are now dots.

•••••••••--•••••••••••••----•••••••••••••--•••••--••••••••----•••••••••••••--••• !

Translated back into the language of Approval, that code, in English, would sound like this:

Yeseseseseses333—yeseseses—eseseseseseses—yesesesesese—eses—Done!

or

Goodgdgdgdgd—goodgdgd—gdgdgdgdgdgdgd—goodgdgdgdgd —gdgd—tada!

And that there is the tool I call "photonegative yes or PNY." It can be a mouthful, but once you realize how incredibly powerful it is, you'll learn how to use it with less verbiage. As long as you get the message across, "yes to everything *except* that tiny little bit from Oscar that spilled over or went to far" then you'll be using it correctly.

Photonegative YES ("everything but *that*") is required when putting very, very specific ideas into someone else's brain. As far as I have experienced, a technically specific idea cannot be inserted into Oscar's brain in any other way. And, the only way to screw up the PNY is to *not even notice* Oscar's *incorrect* choices, which is a kind of error we humans hardly ever make.

In fact, the way I teach the PNY is to teach my clients how to "choke." Choking off your Yes string at the moment Oscar went too far is essential to this skill. I teach teachers to literally say "yesesuguckck…" which is a word that brings about an immediate and very accurate reversal in Oscar with a million fold improvement in results when compared against the word "NO."

Choking can be expressed through voice, through body, or even through the writing of the words "and yet." Miniscule gaps in a sea of yeses are all that's needed because Oscar will interpret the gap in communication as a need for a corrective adjustment on his/her part, like repositioning oneself to get a better cell phone signal. *Can you hear me now?*

Conversely, saying "No" is always constricting. Use of "No" teaches Oscar to try less often. But an absence of Yes is always useful information, if used sparingly. The absence of a Yes becomes an implicit No but not an actual No. PNY adopts the *function* of the word *No* without any of the risk or the detrimental effect of judgment and abandonment of Oscar. The Photonegative Yes is like the Approval skill's skeleton key. It will get you out of any and every tight jam.

A regular "Yes" is used to *widen* the scope of Oscar's exploration, and then Photonegative Yes is used to *narrow* the scope of Oscar's exploration, while the exploration itself remains intact and fully functional. Photonegative Yes is the best teaching tool available for fine detail work. It removes entire choice component categories and also achieves more specificity. It's akin to both adding and removing clay when creating a sculpture.

Note: try not to scare Oscar by trying to help them. If "momentum itself" is an overwhelming experience to Oscar, or if your PNY voice itself is a somewhat frightening sound, you can always dial it back by fluctuating your tone a little, but do continue to use a metronomic rhythm to maintain the "wallpaper of good." I call this "two-tone PNY for the temporal phobics." Hi hi high (tone), lo lo low, hi hi hi, lo lo lo, hi… It's like a sign wave used as a steady message. The undulation makes it more lulling, safe sounding, and less jackhammer-like.

6.6.d Try Not to "Panic & Chase"

Just like the kaleidoscoping fractals of mathematical geometry and snowflakes, Oscar's exploration paths can always get exponentially more complicated. Just like the ever-branching branches on a tree, Oscar can always find a way to be nuttier, and s/he can also always figure out how to do less than half of what s/he did before. Try not to chase Oscar's wayward actions down the rabbit hole into Crazytown. Never say No, but just *don't say Yes* to any of… whatever went astray.

Still, you are human. So some of or maybe even much of what Oscar experiments with or starts to reject outright might make you nervous, cringing, or downright scared. And when social animals who perceive a crisis (you) feel uncomfortable in these ways, they/we tend to find safety in numbers.

So I've noticed that any teacher who panics this way will instinctively, and without thinking, try to *follow* Oscar in order "to help." They will chase Oscar down a rabbit hole of technicalities that seems to go on forever. You'll find yourself approving of smaller and smaller choices that lead into tighter and tighter dead-ends and back eddies. Like chasing a ghost, you won't even remember how you got in so deep and so lost.

When you get swept up this way, you obviously now have to back pedal. But it feels like every situation with Oscar's experimentation, no matter what s/he's experimenting with, is so different from every other fractal bit and dead end street. You'll think you're losing your mind with frustration because you can't help Oscar find her or his way out of the hole.

And yet, it's not Oscar who has gotten lost on the map; it's you. You've not noticed that you've been approving of things that are in no way related to the overall concept of your original goal. And you've been doing so out of anxiety, panic, and feeling that Oscar will be forever lost if you don't chase after them to keep up with their nonsensical brain.

The real issue is that many people don't even know that they've gone down a hole at all. But knowing you've gone down a hole is very important information. The Boss, Mr. Springsteen, said, "like a river that don't know where it's flowin', I took a wrong turn, and I just kept goin." The "wrong" pathway is still a path, and any path, like any river can always be tracked upstream back to the source, and you can find the point where the wrong turn happened.

If Oscar's choices seem to be slipping through your fingers every time you think you've got her/him pinned down, it's because you are chasing. Plain and simple. The better choice, always, is to let Oscar experiment with their wayward idea, let them find out that all they hear down in that hole is crickets (and not your approval Yeses).

If you wait one more moment, you'll see Oscar climbing himself or herself right out of that dead-end hole. Oscar will have learned not to bother with that whole dead end street. Oscar may even feel slightly embarrassed for not paying closer attention and for going that far astray. Just pick up where you collectively left off, and leave that fractal foray of erroneous exploration behind you.

6.6.e Oscar's Glassy-Eye Stare

When someone does a piece of what we want, but not enough of what we want, all too often we don't try to shape it into something more. Instead we often condemn them for being "wrong" overall. An offering is not enough for us. We get angry with them for doing the right thing when they don't do it the right *way*, our way.

Listen again to that first part. *We get angry at them for doing the right thing.* This leaves Oscar pretty confused, and Oscar's brain goes into a holding pattern mode as it tries to do the math on our "logic." Oscar's body goes quiet and the eyes begin to stare blankly. Confusion has been followed by fear more than once in Oscar's past, so what you are seeing here is a slow motion onset of fear.

But do not presume that Oscar's mind is blank or disinterested. Also, do not presume that Oscar is scheming you. The glassy eye stare you sometimes see in Oscar is not usually scheming; it's only trying to comprehend. Give it the space it requires to do so. [The glassy-eye stare is not to be confused with the "dead stare" or Clint Eastwood's "make my day" look that an already angry and over-the-edge Oscar uses to say, "don't mess with me again because if you do I *will* attack you for reasons of my own self defense.]

If Oscar is staring at you with a blank stare, or is staring off into space, or staring especially far out over the distant horizon, then what s/he is actually doing is merely like rewinding his/her own short-term "memory tape." Oscar's memory tape bounces between rewind and replay a bunch of times. There is an unmistakable uncomfortable silence when someone is "rewinding and rewiring" neurons in the brain, but an improved choice is now extremely likely to pop up "out of the blue" if you wait a minute for it.

So during this Glassy Eye Stare processing moment, it is an extremely bad time to change the conversation onto some other topic. Just expect that you will be hearing some radio silence for a bit. Let it happen with no comment from you. Appreciate a blank stare for what it is, instead of what you fear it might be; it's not disrespect or ignoring or passive absence or lack of brain cells.

6.6.f Hear Oscar's Will

Go out onto your driveway or onto the sidewalk or into a field, any place outside that's also fairly empty. Ok. Go out there (when no one is around who will peer through the window to judge you as crazy.) With your hands in your pockets, walk in a straight line. Now, let only your imagination tell you to turn. Let it pick the direction, how far you turn, and let it pick how long it takes you to straighten out.

Sometimes, the voice tells you what NOT to do, but just as often, the voice tells you about opportunity: what you CAN do. And as you learned from Operant Conditioning or from here in Chapter 6, since YES causes all good things to happen, and since NOT / NO is not capable of causing anything good to happen, then which of those styles of the "voice" do you think is more effective at getting things done? Opportunity is a many-splendored thing. Here is an email from a client, written the day after she did this driveway homework:

"At 2 or 3 o'clock this morning I woke up 100%. I was having a conversion with someone in my head. At first, I didn't recognize this voice. Seriously, I didn't, and I wasn't even trying to listen. Then I get it. It was me talking to me.

I just didn't recognize the voice because it was me being present, and I have never heard me being present. I think the doormat in me was trying too hard to override me, forcing me into obedience. I realized last night that I don't want to tell anyone anything, just me. I just want to hear myself, for a change."

I routinely put this same "driveway" challenge to my "learn how to ride horses better" clients. Some clients are beginners, some are near Olympic level, but all have the same set of imagination problems. I say: "Arc to the left. Now, do not decide when to arc to the right, and do not let the horse decide when to arc to the right. Let the universe decide. When the ground starts to spin left underneath you, you will have gone right on the say so of the physics of the universe, merely as part of the mechanics of the whole conjunction."

What happens next is only one of two opposite things: either a) the most well balanced turn of the rider's life, which feels like a Porsche 911 skidding through smooth peanut butter, or b) the turn of a sputtering VW bus on three metal rims and a donut, with additional transmission trouble. The problem becomes obvious to anyone watching: either the rider can imagine the ground turning opposite them, or they can't. We work on it until they can, in both directions, which usually takes between two and five hours.

When listening for the "universe voice" (the voice of your imagination- heard while you're milling aimlessly in a driveway) imagination is not about a plan. It's about having *no* plan. A part of you, the "output you," will still be stuck planning the next plan for your plan to plan so that the plan will be planned by the plan. But there is, also, an "input you" who can switch to a different action simply because s/he imagined it. This version of you doesn't need to do any planning at all. And this universe voice you can now imagine will be the directly audible/perceptible voice of your own Will.

Some people describe the voice of the will as a visual thing, as in varied colors or as in light verses dark. Some describe this "perceived input" as an architectural/gravity thing, as if it's a mirage in the desert. Some describe it as an audio thing, like a voice or like a silent rumble. But it always gets described as "sensory input," and *not* thought. It is something that is *not thought.*

Personally, "the voice of will" for me, is not something I hear or see. It's more like little low pressure density spots in the air, like the weather is changing right around "opportunity," which is usually right around a specific part of Oscar, because that's what/who I'm usually focused on. Imagination is not a communication between me and Oscar; it's a communication between me and me. It will be a communication between you and you. It is a communication between Oscar and Oscar.

Imagination is not the seeing of a "carbon copy or facsimile" of reality, or an "image" as the root of the word would have you believe. Imagination is the first actual step in the sculpting of a real creation. Imagination is the actual seeds of the actual reality tree. Imagination is as real as the thumb on your otherwise fingered hand.

You don't have to be able to envision all (or even any) of the details of the answer you want to find or the answer you want Oscar to find. But you do have to be capable of allowing the answer to come in through the front door, or the back door, or the window, or through the ceiling, or through the floorboards underneath your feet. If you do not allow it in, it can't "occur" to you.

I mean it really can't *occur to or happen* to you. It can't happen, *to you*, at all. And if nothing is happening/occurring, then there's nothing around to notice. If you can't imagine a train barreling down the tracks toward you, then you won't even see it as it's running you over. You'll blame your broken bones on "a mystery" or on "bad luck." And that error is an extremely common reason for a Will-or's lack of success in improving their Emerge skill.

The fact is that Oscar cannot save you from yourself. And Oscar cannot stop time for you. You and you alone have the power to do those things. Oscar cannot extinguish your judgment and Oscar cannot create your love again. Only you and you alone have the power to do those things. And do those things you can, and it becomes easier and easier and easier every time you do, because pivoting on your Will quite literally generates a form of grease in your ball bearings. I don't know what the grease is made of, but it's real stuff, real brain chemistry.

And then, by adding grease... imagination grease... the choices that used to sound like twisting steel begin to sound like sputtering, and then some giggling, and then, even when you and Oscar are on the brink of disaster, you'll be able to laugh at your predicament and laugh at Oscar and even laugh at yourself long enough to get your bearings... or get back on your *ball bearings*... long enough to swivel enough to point to something you and Oscar both believe, and that will get you both to a whole new and better place.

6.6.g Communication Is Merely a Series of Gifts

When the crutch that is our verbal language is taken away, or better yet when it's just sent on vacation, we cannot express what we "could have done or should have done or would have done." We have no way to talk about other possible realities; we are confined to the now of our real reality.

When verbiage is not available to us, we are reduced to nothing but our approvals, our disapprovals, and our "next moves." We are forced to communicate our present intent. In fact, discarding language is so good at helping you uncover your true intent that you can actually use it as a systems check on yourself, to discover whether you are aiming to help or in fact aiming to hurt.

Will-based communication is NOT like a negotiation between whether I win or you win. In Will-based communication, novel unprecedented positions on both sides are being created in each new moment. Will-based communication is actually more like a series of gifts, or, for the technically minded, *gifts in a series*. Even individuals who are afraid, disenfranchised, angry with you, hate your guts, or any combination of the above, will still attempt to give you gifts of their truth in an attempt to try to understand your influence and impact on them. But the question is, will you notice those gifts?

Even in a fight, Oscar will be investing this way, even going into the red and overdrawing her/his emotional expenditure account to reach out to you with the truth of him or herself. And when the disenfranchised offer you a gift, by revealing ANYTHING at all about who they really are, you better damn well appreciate it. And when you find out about an Achilles heel of theirs, you can do one of two things.

You can take this insider info and use it against them... or you can take this insider info and use it to help you both. It's entirely your option. They gave you this power to wield when they told you their truth. They gave you the backdoor access that could hurt them, because they want you to have some access to be able to help them.

CHAPTER 7: IN THE OSCAR ZONE - A NEW OSCAR COMMUNITY

OSCAR Therapy helps animals of any background to become whole, integrated members of their community and of your community. Recipients of OSCAR Therapy, no matter their ages, blossom into fully functional, expressive, independent teammates, who are now capable of working fully *with you* on any goal you have. Goals for you, for the team, or goals for Oscar's own well being can now be met with a sense of co-ownership and co-control over the things you all do for each other. We all gain that sense that we've always wished we could have with our animals in our wildest dreams.

Whenever I had a day home from the aquarium, I would use regular old operant conditioning to teach my roommate's smart and eager dog how to do helpful teammate behaviors like: go time herself out on the big boulder if she chased the chickens (that way, she could weigh her own priorities), bark to tell us when the ice cream truck was coming, open the fridge and bring us a cold beverage on the couch, answer the phone when it rang, and hit the red 911 button in the event of an emergency caused by eating ice cream and drinking cold beverages. (It was better to teach that last one with the phone unplugged.)

With OSCAR Therapy, though, you can create even more *amazing* levels of volunteering. Anyone can teach any animal, no matter how troubling its past, to inject themselves with needles, receive eye drops and ocular exams, pack themselves into tight quarters, recoil away from a fight, accept human babies or their own babies, reverse head shyness in minutes, breathe and hold their breath on cue, produce tail actions on cue, yawning on cue, dental work, blindness aids, deafness aids, drive a vehicle, forget separation anxiety, and how to generally be the best pet ever, be the best patient ever, and be the best partner ever.

But once your animals have *become* the coolest partners ever, and once all of the human onlookers have had to blink twice in disbelief about what they just saw your non-human partner volunteer to do... well, that's when you kinda sorta want to meet other people who know what you know, other people who understand the power of OSCAR and it's potential to fix every animal. What's more, my clients also want to meet the other people who are as flat-out frustrated as they are that the rest of the world doesn't yet know, see, or believe that these results are real.

We all want that for everyone and every animal because we all know that there's nothing more rewarding than rebuilding a broken animal; it's just like helping a water-phobic person learn to dive into the deep end, literally. There's no greater accomplishment, and there's no greater awareness to be had, then that of empathy and understanding.

The main purpose of this book has been to make the case for OSCAR Therapy, but its secondary purpose is to invite you in to join us in "the OSCAR zone." Whether OSCAR Therapy is your first step or just your next step, we want to share all of our networking resources, to help you get started with the OSCAR language, so that you and your animals can reap the benefits for yourselves.

Lastly and selfishly, we also want to invite you into the OSCAR community so that you might share your future stories about what you uncover and discover. That way, we can all learn, from each other, about the depths we find inside the heads of our Oscar partners.

7.1 The Better the Solution, the Less of It You'll Need

Some tools you own are just so perfect that you'll never need to replace them or improve upon them. Old machinery that was built to last forever even while being broadly used are these tools that just never die. Hammers and crowbars come to mind. But the worse the quality of the tool you get, the more times you'll have to replace it with something better, something stronger, or something different. And it's the same thing with the tool called information. The worse the information you get; the more times you'll have to go get additional or even contradictory information.

In brainwork, I like to say: the worse the advice you're getting, the more of it you're gonna need. And the better the solution you've found, the *less* of it you'll need. OSCAR Therapy is so effective at recovering the classically difficult and even "incurable" brains, and so quickly, that OSCAR Therapy is hardly even a reliable revenue stream for us practitioners, but that's not because it doesn't work. That's because it works gangbusters.

Because the animal brain learns how to learn, how to seek mental balance, and how to decode and tackle chaos, then the problems that started out as an animal owner's "worst nightmare" ends up being a partnership that never needs to add a behavior specialist into the mix again. And for the pocketbooks of us practitioners, it's even worse than that.

Because not only does OSCAR Therapy solve the right-now problem but it also precludes all of the future or "later on in life" problems that the animal might normally acquire when aging into the normal world. So not only do we work ourselves right out of a job now, but we also work ourselves right out of having long-term clients!

Simply put, OSCAR Therapy prevents future behavior problems from ever developing in the first place. It prevents future physical problems too. When there is no unsolvable stress and friction in the brain, that's when there is much less physical friction and stress on the joints, muscles, organs, the works. And when you're having much more fun with your animal partner, you'll be present often enough to notice and address any tiny problems yourself, before they grow into bigger ones.

Because OSCAR Therapy is such an effective cure for the brain's central core, it makes for a lousy business model; but that's okay with us. The OSCAR Therapy paradigm is built on successful permanent change. It's *not* based on prolonging treatment (and the practitioner's income) unnecessarily.

Still, in OSCAR Therapy, we don't repair just a piece of an animal at a time; we quickly fix the whole 360-degree animal, beginning from day one. The way I figure it, if we just fix all of the house wiring all at once, no one will ever need to blame the electrician.

But that means that we OSCAR Therapists are constantly working ourselves out of a job, and quicker and quicker, it seems. A case that used to take me 20 sessions now takes me 8. A case that used to take me 5 sessions, I can fix in three. The case that used to take a year, still takes a year because the owners get so deep into the amazing landscape of new potentials and new diagnostic clarity, that they never want to let me go.

Even early on, the progress reports that I get by text and email are NOT that animals are "making slow and steady progress..." The messages I get are that the problems are usually just gone. All too soon for my own bank account, most clients just don't need me anymore. And because they don't, people even forget to send updates on their animals until I request them. It seems that people no longer need to focus so much of their energy on their "was dangerous" four-legged family members, as if they hardly even remember how difficult life with that animal used to be, not so very long ago.

When their animals are finally squared away, clients no longer have to focus on their previous animal concerns. They start focusing on their other goals in life. They move forward with the family dream of having a baby or buying a house or going to the competitions and cleaning up. I've been reprimanded more than a few times for insufficiently responding to the photos of new babies, and new blue ribbons and trophies. It's not that I don't care; it's just that I'm not at all surprised. Rebuilt-to-be-perfect brains do perfect jobs at the challenges that are now waaaaay too easy, compared to what this brain's capabilities now are.

Regarding a comparison of the teaching method of the *animal-derived* OSCAR Therapy versus the other "training" methods we humans have invented, well, there just is no comparison. The others are employing a top-down dynamic, and OSCAR is leveraging the opposite dynamic, more like a bottom-up, "vacuum-based" dynamic. Bottom-up ideas come from the more grassroots parts of us life forms, and not from our adult, mathematically advanced, human brains.

OSCAR Therapy was developed from the lowest common denominator, because those who need it most can't also be relied upon to have any prerequisite levels of awareness, balance, sensibilities, physical health, mental health, common sense, IQ, EQ, or decency. OSCAR was built on (as much as I have been able to gather thus far) Mother Nature's elemental social learning modes. They start not only you but also every other critter and creature equally, on the ground floor.

In the game of life, everyone is playing by their own set of rules. There aren't universal rules; there aren't even universal effects. Whatever you do either helps or hinders or does nothing. You either step on toes or you don't. You either help someone find their better, or you don't. You either get in the way of someone else's game, or you don't. You either break someone else's rules, or you don't.

But as your animal's owner/caretaker, after you've gained a little awareness of what it's like to be Oscar, no hired expert can ever again pull the wool over your eyes about what Oscar is or is not experiencing. Your path with your own Oscar may not be lit up with neon signs reading *This Way*, but after Oscar Therapy, you will notice more readily when other people, or their reasons, or their histories, or even recent events may seem a little... suspishy. Once OSCAR Therapy shows you that you are capable of making your own assessment of your Oscar's state of mind, that's when you may notice that some of your confusion and searching seem to flow away like waves going back into the sea.

7.2 OSCAR Therapy Is Not a Pyramid Scheme

OSCAR Therapy can be used by anyone, regardless of their background, and without need of any other training methodology; OSCAR can get any "training" job done all by itself. In the event that you are already using positive reinforcement, operant conditioning, clicker training, or even the old-timey traditional methods, never fear. If you have come to an impasse, where your current approach might seem to be stuck with no way forward, OSCAR Therapy is the approach that will get your animal's brain past the sticking points, the glitches, and any impasse zones.

And yet, OSCAR Therapy is not a cookbook, where there is a separate recipe using separate ingredients to undo each different kind of problem a brain can have. Such a cookbook list would be thousands of bullet points long because every brain is like a unique snowflake of chemistry sprinkled onto compiled life experiences. OSCAR Therapy is instead using just one single approach that taps into the "whole brain running a whole body" access channel.

OSCAR Therapy knows exactly "what it's doing." Its mere process is what shows you the real, self-evident way forward in that brain. Hence, OSCAR Therapy does not need to be any kind of "earn your level of mastery" scheme where progress is defined by the program designers. (OSCAR Therapy has none). The animals and me and my clients have described OSCAR Therapy, but I can officially state that no one but the learning brains themselves are *the authority* on the matter. We human reporters are not its final authority.

That's just not how we roll in the OSCAR world. We believe that any "better mousetrap" should be accessible to all, both to help save lives and to recover hearts that have been broken. We also believe that learning OSCAR should be largely free to everyone who chooses to learn it, not unlike the open source tools on the Internet. Power to the people. And *empowerment...* to the animals, every last one of us. And to the humans who choose to understand where another brain is coming from, we salute you.

7.3 Will-ing Results, LLC

In the bigger picture though, OSCAR Therapy is just one of the many unexpected byproducts of a new choice-based philosophy I call Will-Mechanics. My gigantic 3-volume "impractical manual" for that philosophy is called *Will-ing.* It's about the –ing part (the active verb) of using your own Will to change the world around you. *Will-ing* is a three volume series soon to be available on as many electronic book platforms as possible and as an audio too.

OSCAR Therapy is just one byproduct of the *Will-ing* method of problem solving. Bich-Fish.com, the "real-time relationship navigator" is yet another byproduct. We eagerly await the other books *Will-ing* will spin off, as it lays the structural foundation for co-authors who want to put the *will-driven system* to good use in their own globe-supporting fields of expertise.

The truth of the matter is that this formalized and encapsulated thing called OSCAR Therapy is just a spin-off, a next generation derivative offshoot of what is the core of my life's work. If you combine all of the ingredients (of Will-based truths) and bake them in an oven of *physical* expression, then OSCAR Therapy is what that end result looks like. The OSCAR oven makes really cool bread; it leverages a physical modality to talk to other species. But here's some of the deeper evolution and context behind it...

Three classes. That's all anyone needs to take/do/experience/mull over.

That's what I found out pretty early on in life, and this same little triad of universal perspectives is what I have continued to teach to this day. Again, the more universal is the information, the less of it you'll ever need. If something seems to be true not only for dogs, biting dogs, horses, bucking horses, champion horses, birds, reptiles, amphibians, fish, sharks, invertebrates, and even for us primate humans, then I figure... maybe I can (we can) rely on that truth.

And yet, life is finite, isn't it... When I was also forced to face my own mortality too early in life, I realized that brains die but pages can last as long as people want them to.

I was asked to write an article once about reversing horse phobias. That article was supposed to be one page long, but it ended up spilling over. I needed a good editor to pare it down because the article kept filling itself out until it was 850 pages long and spanned three volumes. Apparently, when you investigate the essence of choice, and what is shared by every kind of brain regardless of species or backstory, it turns out that there is much to be said. And yet, there was NOT an infinite amount to be said. It turns out that the overall sketch of that kind of will-based physics is finite. The structure of The Will can be scribbled down on the back of a napkin at lunch.

But because everyone's brain is way too overburdened to read these days, I also turned those 3 volumes of proof into an App that literally fits in your back pocket. Tell it what your trouble is, and it will try its best to help you work your way out of that trouble.

If you'd like to try out the fun App, which is in the final stages of contruction as of this writing, go here or contact us at our other websites:

www.Bich-Fish.com

If you'd like to participate in the 3 Primal Will-ing Classes or learn OSCAR Therapy, talk to us here:

www.willingresults.com

www.oscartherapy.com

If you'd like to read the 3 Volume Will-ing Book (hopefully in 2022), go here:

www.will-ing.com   www.willingresults.com   www.willintegrators.com

(But don't say I didn't warn you.)

7.4 The Public Reaction to OSCAR Therapy

A very popular and well-heeled equine journal in the Northeast put out an all call, looking for new equine therapies they could share with their wide audience. I wrote a professional letter introducing them to OSCAR Therapy, and they kindly responded thusly: "We are sorry to relay that we cannot run an article about your new therapy as it is 'too new.' When more people know about it, do let us know."

After getting roughly the same reaction from three other journals and five professional equine journalists, I had to accept that no journal coverage was to be had. Other more progressive journals wanted stories told in 500 words or less, but I couldn't figure out how to tell an unprecedented, education-based case summary within that sound byte limit. And that about sums up why there has been no news coverage of OSCAR Therapy, to date.

When there is a problem that has a known solution, you know which words to look up in the phone book or on the Internet. But when you don't know there's a solution out there to your "unsolvable" problem, and when all of the experts you rely on ALSO don't know that there's a solution out there, then all I can say is I hope you are a good online researcher. My past clients and I are doing all we can to spread the word about OSCAR Therapy in a responsible way, but it's a big world.

And yet probably the main reason why you have never heard of OSCAR Therapy until now is that it presents an opposite paradigm to the one we're all steeped in and accustomed to. Just like the chiral opposite, the OSCAR approach sees and uses the inside out, opposite approach to what the rest of the world sees and uses.

There are even people who watch OSCAR Therapy in action and determine that nothing at all is happening. "If the animal touches the therapist, it's happening by accident," claim they. Besides directing these oblivious, dismissive, and closed brains to unmistakable videos on the OSCAR Therapy YouTube Channel (that convince everyone), there's not much more we can do for these people.

They see what they need to see, they hear what they need to hear, they have a deep need and hunger for being lied to, and their beliefs are being dictated *and directed* by fear, a wolf in sheep's clothing. The funny irony is that these are the exact kinds of brains that OSCAR Therapy would help the most.

We shout it's effectiveness from the rooftops, but some *can't* even *see* what we're doing; their traditional goggles come *pre-programmed* to tune us out. Even many of the operant conditioners, clicker trainers, and progressive therapists haven't yet realized that they are doing too much "unto" Oscar and not letting Oscar *reach out* to do unto the world that they're supposed to be happily learning about.

The fact is that people/humans as a whole haven't yet figured out how to *not touch*. If people actually knew how to "not touch," they would have stumbled onto the OSCAR paradigm eons ago. For better or often for worse, we human are a "hands on" species. When it comes right down to it, the human species more often opts for wielding power over the maintaining of safety. I did too, in my youth. And it took dealing with animals that I *couldn't* touch to figure out how to *not touch* even the ones I could.

In OSCAR Therapy, animal's history reveals itself, not because of any ethereal deducing or guessing, but because they show you where their physical scars are. A famous New England horse trainer asked me to leave her property on day one after inviting me there to teach a weekend clinic. She had banned the use of "something for nothing" on her farm and OC freaked her out. But on my way out the door she said, "You've come all this way, maybe I should have you check out what's going on with this one horse I can't seem to reach…"

After 20 minutes of OSCAR Therapy assessment, I pointed to his Left shoulder blade, making a gesture inward, of the impaling angle of something. Next, the trainer said, "How did you know about that? Did someone tell you about this horse? There is no scar visible there, but he was in an accident and got impaled with a wooden spike right there at that exact angle. How did you know?" "You told me to ask the horse, and I did. If you have no other questions for me, I guess I'll be going."

The overall reaction from many people is that they seem to be embarrassed to learn that there are on/off switches of choices and awarenesses controlling not only their animals' behaviors but also their own behaviors- that they just don't yet see. I try to tell them that OSCAR Therapists are just "brain electricians," but people often blink twice, scratch their heads, and then proceed with life as if they had never met me.

But then there are the people who flat out reject the knowledge. If I may, I'd like to share another word I've fashioned to describe this other common reaction to OSCAR Therapy. My word is "refusant." The person who refuses adamantly a new paradigm, I like to call refusant with an exclamation point. They are "refusant!" As in… some people refuse to learn a thing, but other people are even *refusant to know anything about the existence of a thing they have <u>wanted not to see</u> or experience.*

More often than not, no matter how polite or even curious people are, unless and until they have been up against the choice of using a euthanasia needle on someone they love or respect, they just aren't desperate enough to be able to gaze far enough over the horizon to see OSCAR Therapy for the all-purpose skeleton key that it is.

Even though everyone's local Aquarium has been using similar language since the 1960's, and even though the paradigm is blatantly obvious to all human children, the human adults are hard to convince, even after they've seen the evidence with their own eyes. Belief is belief, and it gets pretty hard-wired. Even the courageous people who have understood it on an intellectual level don't grow into the emotional understanding of OSCAR until a few years in. But once in, most people are *all in, forever after.*

But such is the norm for all manner of human explorations. Every new discovery gets ignored at first, then fought against, and then accepted as if it were always true. I won't live long enough for OSCAR Therapy to be widely accepted, but ya can't have everything… (See my big book *Will-ing*, for all of the emo-logical arguments and underpinnings of OSCAR Therapy.)

For now, maybe our video channel will catch on. And then everybody can feel like they were there at the beginning, along with myself and Lisa and Kendal and Linda and Meg and Dana and JenM and Heidi and Suzie and Michelle and

Hage and Hud and Katie and Julia and Annie and Cindy and Shannon and Candy and Nikki and Leita and Amber and Betsy and Tim and JR and Ernest and others. Where are the rest of the men on this list? Good question.

I was on vacation at a friend's place in Wellington, Florida, home of everything in competitive equine. She was riding every day; I just sat home watching the palm trees rustle, to clear my mind. At week's end, a head trainer in the barn asked to have me assess his own horse. The findings of my exam made the trainer say, "No thanks, but I'll think about it more." By the time my plane hit the tarmac back in Connecticut my phone started dinging with new text messages from my friend. "When can you come back to Florida, 'cus he wants you back." "Why the change of heart?" I asked.

"Well, my dog has always ignored his dog, for years. But today, for the first time, both dogs were playing together. He asked me what had happened to my dog. I told him, 'Well, Casey was at my place so she OSCAR'ed my dog while she was watching the egrets. She just can't help it. It's what she does."

This expert was *refusant* to see it in his horse, but he did see it in the dog. Baby steps.

7.5 The OSCAR Therapy Community

These days, established animal behavior teaching program will teach Operant Conditioning technique to all student animal handlers, and all institutions that house exotic animals (not used for experimentation) use it exclusively. But you'd have to look for an overlap between normal exotics handling and rehab of abnormal domestics, to find any approaches similar to OSCAR Therapy, if they exist at all in other places around the world. And we hope they do.

If you'd like Willing Results, LLC to work on a case, we provide live streaming video chat services, anywhere around the world, for OSCAR Therapy analysis, diagnosis, and problem-reversal treatment for animals *and owners*. Owner–mediated OSCAR Therapy treatment for problem reversal in animals works seamlessly. We use your hands to fix your animal, by use of your favorite real-time video interface.

Got a new species candidate for OSCAR Therapy? Perfect! We are happy to branch out to any species you live or work alongside. I certainly do miss the 750 other species I used to know fairly well in my AquaVet biologist days. My favorite one? Hands down... the Wolf Eels of the Cold Marine Gallery. Part fish, part dog, part snake, and part comedian. No matter if you work in a zoo, animal park, service agency, sports arena, or any other setting where animals need PTSD recovery, phobia reversal, or other spatial anomaly interpretive help, please do give us a call; we will listen to your team, tell you what we see, and help you solve the puzzles and reverse the problems.

Global access by streaming video works just fine as long as we have some kind of overlap in our time zones on live streaming video. For those on the other side of the planet from New England, USA… that can be a sticky wicket, but it's not impossible. Your animals will have to stay up very late or get up pretty early in the morning! We will too.

Foreign languages also pose no barrier. As long as we have a good English language translator in the mix, we can see the Will's choices inside any body equally well. No matter what verbal language is used to do the speaking, *the wills we integrate all speak the very same language.*

Websites

www.oscartherapy.com

www.willingresults.com

oscartherapy1@gmail.com

Social Media (in the works)

"OSCAR Therapy Channel" on YouTube

"OSCAR Therapy Connections" Facebook/Meta Group

"OSCARTherapy" on Instagram

eBooks

Will-ing, The Manual, Volumes 1, 2, and 3

Introducing OSCAR Therapy

Human Cases

OSCAR Therapy is a new approach; hence there exists no formal licensure. Willing Results, LLC may require a licensed, professional primary case manager to be the interface between human cases and us. We can teach experts who work with any kind of brain how to apply OSCAR Therapy in their own fields, regardless of species, age, medical status, or brain state. OSCAR Therapy shares similarities with but is still very different from Feldenkrais, Alexander Technique, and EMDR.

7.6 Certification

Anyone who has any level of success with OSCAR Therapy may quickly find themselves inundated with owners of moderately difficult animals seeking help and problem reversal treatment. But even skilled practitioners may not know if they are ready to tackle certain complex and/or dangerous cases, and the owners of those animals may also wonder if that OSCAR-equipped person is actually experienced enough to safely help others.

Some practitioners have requested that I consider designating different levels of certification; I thought hard about that. One could imagine something like a green badge for the therapists of the safe animals and a red badge for those who know how to tackle the dangerous cases. But in any such structure you'd have to have gradations of all the skill levels in between. It would be all too easy to start making assumptions about what OSCAR users knew and didn't know.

And yet truly, according to the animal (the final judge and jury) there's no such thing as levels of OSCAR Therapy. You are either someone their brain can understand or you're not yet. No matter the level of difficulty of a case, any human individual is either doing OSCAR Therapy in a way that improves Oscar or they're not. And it's very easy to tell the difference. If you don't know or can't tell whether someone is or isn't, just send me a video, and I will tell you what I see. The sole reason for using this therapy should not be in order to achieve a status or to earn a badge. There should only be one reason: to help a brain that needs help.

So in that vein, I personally have no problem at all with anyone of any age stating or claiming that they use OSCAR Therapy. As has been stated many times throughout this book, every person at every level of animal management could and should have the OSCAR tools at their disposal because having an effective language at the ready is never a bad thing.

But beyond that, who am I to suggest that a person with decent OSCAR knowledge is not fit or skilled enough to tackle a difficult and dangerous case? Especially when that person is the only option standing between that animal and euthanasia, whereupon all options will be gone, then who are we to judge?

Even a child with a lot of time on their hands, some good sense, and a little luck can do wonders even for the angriest of beasts. I started down this path at 12 years old. It took me a long while but it worked. This book exists to help anyone and everyone to shorten that timeline. If reading is not for you, you can even spend a bunch of time on our YouTube channel and absorb a lot of the language that way.

There is no way to slice and dice and worry about different levels of fire-fighting skill when you're the only fire fighter at the fire. You either know how to proceed safely or you don't yet. We are always here and available for consult, but the only way I can recommend that a particular practitioner would likely do a safe and effective job on a case is if I have personally observed that they have met the requirements of our OSCAR Therapy Practitioner Certification. When I/we designate you as OSCAR certified, that is my/our only stamp of approval.

This is all to explain why OSCAR Therapy will only have one level of certification, designated by me, signified by our big brass ring and a certification logo the practitioner can use on their own website and media. All OSCAR Therapy Certified Practitioners will also be listed on our website, so that you can know that their knowledge base has at least passed muster with me. It will stand for the likelihood that said practitioner probably won't make things worse before things get better. First, do no harm.

Regarding everybody who has not sought certification, *and that will be most of the users of OSCAR Therapy*, these people should feel free to use, discuss, apply, and teach as much OSCAR Therapy as they know to anyone and everyone they can get their *hands NOT ON* ! You all have my blessing, because grass roots are always the strongest roots. And the more OSCAR roots that can sprout up in their own locations, the more animals and relationships will be helped.

As of this writing, OSCAR Therapy has already been adopted by people from vastly different species interest, vastly different disciplines, vastly different sports, vastly different religions, vastly different politics, vastly different verbal languages, vastly different age groups, and vastly different finance levels. The variety of cultural backgrounds of the human participant doesn't seem to faze OSCAR at all. In fact, on the only thing these people seem to have in common is that they realize that a human being is just another animal, just another species, trying to make a bridge to the other brains in their midst.

If you'd like to become certified in OSCAR Therapy, we do have a certification process. Every practitioner must apply for certification status. Direct learning from us is not necessary, but video or real-time confirmation of your OSCAR Therapy skillset, specified in the list below, is what is required. If you can do it, we will know; OSCAR Therapy is very hard to fake.

OSCAR THERAPIST CERTIFICATION 2021

RE-CERT IS NOT NECESSARY (as of 2018)

NORMAL WR RATES APPLY, NO CERT FEE

CASEY DECIDES ALL CERTS - LOGO AWARDED

All steps must be completed to teacher satisfaction.

CERTIFICATION PROCESS AND CHECKLIST:

- OSCAR CLINIC GRAD
- OSCAR X, Y, Z AXIS MAP KNOWLEDGE
- TAKE CLASS 1 (Language) AND CLASS 3 (Disengage)
- TAKE CLASS 2 (Presence), WITH DIAGNOSTIC TESTING
- BE 1-12 X, Y OSCAR BALANCED, KNOW & EXPLAIN LIMITATIONS
- FENCE-SAFE ACCESS OSCAR ON VIDEO

- VIDEO OF R&L CASEWORK, 2 SPECIES MINIMUM. ANY TWO NON-HUMAN SPECIES ARE FINE

- VIDEO OF OSCAR THERAPY IN MOTION

- 1 ESSAY DESCRIBING A "RED CASE REHAB" YOU REVERSED YOURSELF. BEFORE & AFTER DESCRIPTIONS, BULLET THE STEPS YOU USED.

7.7 The Future of OSCAR Therapy Looks Like...

Who knows? *We* certainly don't.

But for starters, all domesticated species rescue and rehabilitation organizations, groups, and efforts would be wise to add OSCAR Therapy methods to their programs. There is no faster recovery for animals that quickly need to become safe for/in their new adoption homes. The animals who keep cycling back through the rescue system are prime candidates. They don't need therapeutic euthanasia; they need the help of OSCAR knowledgeable humans, to quickly convert them into the normal animals that they maybe used to be and could be again.

Secondarily, all animals and all humans who are working and learning in animal husbandry programs, at universities, through extension programs, at veterinary schools, and at veterinary technology programs would benefit tremendously. By incorporating the OSCAR awareness into their daily activities with the animals they're trying to learn from, students could also learn so very much more about the impacts of their work, even directly from the *animal's* perspective.

All of these education-based programs exist to disseminate information about not only the physical and environmental needs but also the *social and emotional* needs of the animals who live and work together with us. For the "normally reared" and the abnormally reared animals like, OSCAR can teach our animals to also *purposefully* partner with us, the success rate of our ultimate goals for and with them takes on a skyward trajectory.

Although the animals that are destined for release back into the wild should not be overly socialized to humans, most species do still require the social skills they may have missed in an unnatural rearing setting managed by humans. But since ours is more like a self-discovery process for individuals, if the human smells and visuals could me removed from the system, I can imagine that OSCAR Therapy might even help these populations to be more socially equipped when they return to the wild. Who knows?

But for the backyard masses, the neighborhood farms, the summer farm camps, the after school programs, the humble animal guardians, and for any individual who adopted *or who was adopted by* an animal in need, OSCAR Therapy is not only *for you*, but it also originated *from you*. I was one of the many well-intentioned animal folk who was also up against a wall of traumatized animal trouble that the experts couldn't solve.

Love was not enough to conquer the challenge but my dedication to never stop working the puzzle *was and continues to be* the answer. We at Willing Results, LLC work towards a future where OSCAR Therapy can continue to take on a life of it's own, in assistance to caring individuals the world over.

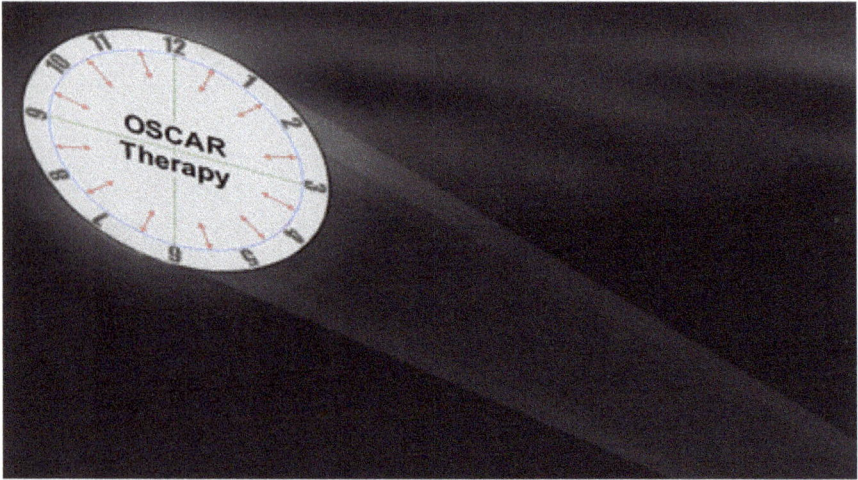

Figure 23. Whenever you learn of any animal in need, you can share this OSCAR Therapy Bat Signal (even anonymously) with the owners; you can find it on our websites. If they see it attached to their own story, maybe they'll be curious enough to look us up. And if they do, we will do our best to help!

Conclusion

The last pre-flight bit of advice to be aware of before you embark on learning OSCAR Therapy for yourself is the fact that you will be judged. Not by me, but by plenty of people. You are going to stumble some in the learning process, and people watching you out of the corners of their eyes are sometimes going to see you bombing out. Even when your forward progress is achieving leaps and bounds, "others" are at worst going to be *suspect,* and at best going to be *confused* by your OSCAR activities.

At some point or another, even the people you know well are very likely to be suspicious of new concepts. Most people, even good people, really do not accept very easily those who stand apart from the rest. And heaven help you if you're already a professional. Because the professionals are the people who are not really permitted by any culture of society to show that they are still learning... enough to alter their stance on something... amazingly enough.

There's not much you can do to change any of that (not yet anyhow), and if you were in their position, you would most likely make similar judgments. You've probably been suspect of new ideas on this very day, and maybe you haven't even noticed. But it's OK. In fact, it's a gauge. If people do not take notice that you are doing something differently from most of the other people around you, then you probably aren't.

So as you begin, expect that you will be questioned and even warned "for your own good." You will be watched closely with the side-glances, peripheral vision, and head on stares of other people who are curious, just as you may have been. It's OK. Just let it come. Let the suspicious ones be a footnote in *your* story, not the other way around.

Onlookers may even try to protect you... because they observe, correctly, that you are "being affected" by your new routes of exploration. It is true that some degree of emotional impact is unavoidable for most individuals who experience OSCAR Therapy, because these merely technical changes usually cause one or more central "adjustments" to your core belief system.

The work can feel very brain consuming in the beginning, because most people aren't accustomed to a morphing of their own beliefs. I suggest you take nothing on faith, and continue to ask as many questions of this book as you can. And don't forget to thank those onlookers for their caring, every time it comes up.

Choosing to experiment with tackling old problems in a new way requires moxie, and yet having moxie takes a toll; it can be exhausting. So to manage the stress of self-realization and change, learners often find it most helpful to remember to think of this new information as purely technical information. OSCAR Therapy aims to both *widen* your communication *input* channels and specifically *focus* your communication *output* channels. The conversation will feel a little vague at first, but it will make sense much sooner than you think.

We were taxiing up to the runway recently, and wouldn't you know, a guy with a certifiable but untreated fear of flying had managed to buckle his seat belt while still clinging to the seat in front of us. My traveling companion was talking to him about Valium dosages, and I was describing how turbulence is like hitting potholes in the road. The pill-popping fidgety man said, "But up there, there is NO road."

Just because you don't see a road doesn't mean there isn't one. If there weren't a road, giant hunks of aluminum and steel would never be able to launch into the atmosphere. We are never aware of the well-traveled roads, the self-fulfilling prophecies, and the *self-propelling* processes happening all around us. Until we are.

Afterword

Appendix 1

OSCAR Competitions!? ...It's Time to Change the Game

Want an opportunity to have an *unprecedented* blast?

Sometimes life is just more fun when you can one-up your neighbor, when you can strive for an event on the calendar, when you can bring your A-game of unprecedented partnership and skill, or when you can laugh your butts off at yourself and at each other in the process! Whether at live events, or virtually on the web, one-upping the other team is something OSCAR Therapy was born to do. Like our clients say, "There aint no party like an OSCAR party 'cus an OSCAR party... *invites the brains of ALL the different species,* and that's no joke."

Unlike the stuffy horse competitions I competed in as a kid, below is what we now imagine an OSCAR competition (for horseback riders) might look like... *Just imagine...*

Rockin' Horse!

...it's time to ROCK the ARENA !

Will the *OSCAR Riders* Please Step Up ...to the *DANCE FLOOR!*

<u>*Imagine the DIFFERENCE... !*</u>

...to a competition where over-bearing riders could never pass the qualifiers!

...when backyard owners can compete against professional riders on the same field!

...when the dexterity of Dressage combines with the 'horse independence' of calf-cutting!

...when the teamwork of 4H trail class is ramped up to the high speed of a video game!

...with an equine challenge favoring mental flexibility & creativity over focus & precision!

...in an arena where your mount's self expression is actually required!

<u>*Imagine the FUN... !*</u>

...of a horse sport where audience hoots & hollers are compulsory!

...of the opportunity to challenge your competition to a throw down!

...of a safe sport that's as entertaining for the audience and the horses as it is for the riders!

...of a riding event where neither money nor whips & spurs are allowed in the arena!

...of being on the cutting edge of a new sport... like the California surfers of the 60's!

...of the YouTube viewers watching you *rock out* on your incredibly *cool... Rockin...Horse!!*

<u>*In the Riding Arena AND in the Liberty Arena :*</u>

Morning Round 1: *Technical Qualifiers: Tempos, compass, gaits, changes, transitions, elevation, bounce, creations, and furniture.*

Qualifying Levels Assigned.

Afternoon Round 2: *Prepared demonstrations: Two songs prepared at home and displayed in Round 2. Riders will be grooving to one fast & one slow tune and making it look GOOOOD!! Beach Boys, Rolling Stones, Motown, Funk, Disco, Joan Jett... You pick the tune!*

Evening Round 3: *Jukebox Challenge! You and your horse will groove to a familiar song SELECTED at RANDOM!! Limit: two challenges per pair.*

Final Exhibition: Rockin' Horse Throw Down! Two *top* dancers square off!

Rockin' Horse Competition RULES:

- ✓ Songs will include past and present Top 40 hits ONLY. No classical music allowed!
- ✓ Access to the Juke Box is provided only 2 weeks before the competition date, which is just enough time to solidify the songs in your own head. Every competition date changes the Jukebox play list.
- ✓ Scoring: 10 points each for difficulty, technical, story telling, artistic, and applause. Top score is 50 pts
- ✓ Every ride must end in dismount so that raucous applause and cheering doesn't frighten horses when riders are up.

Hosting a Rockin' Horse Competition: Requirements

- ✓ OSCAR's stamped Brass or Metal "Carousel Rings" awarded to winners
- ✓ All additional prizes are provided by the Host.
- ✓ Rockin' Horse Points Awarded, permanently recorded by Willing Results, LLC
- ✓ One competition arena, emptied of all furniture and obstacles
- ✓ Completely closed arena for protection of AT LIBERTY performance horses
- ✓ Low Dust Footing, mandatory for video quality and healthy lungs
- ✓ Audience bleacher seating recommended.
- ✓ All audience seating is outside the arena dirt, for the safety of the audience
- ✓ An arena-wide sound system with Digital input that plays custom-mix media
- ✓ Available Parking for horse trailers
- ✓ Restroom facilities for visitors
- ✓ Equine videographers recommended, professional or amateur

Appendix 2

Acknowledgments

Without these individuals, this book would not exist:

Heather Ramsay Elliot, Melissa Potopowitz Green, Elaine Solarz, Tammy Scaplen

Wally Bjorn, my High School Guidance Counselor

June Sugarman, Linda M. Sugarman, Richard S. Sugarman, Tracy A. Sugarman

New England Aquarium, Vet Services/Animal Care Department

Howard Krum

Lisa Samoylenko

Frank Lishing

The Hagemann Family

Special editing thanks to: Deb Heminway, Nikki Kagan, and Janeen Rose

Chronology

1990 to 1994 Sugarman volunteered for MM Dept, at New England Aquarium

1994 to 2004 Sugarman was part of the New England Aquarium Vet Dept

2004 OSCAR Therapy was named Partnership Engineering and Willing Results

2005 OSCAR Therapy was first used for blind horse case Johnnie

2016 Gracious response from Caroll Spinney

2018 OSCAR Therapy name was trademarked in the US

Casey Sugarman, Will Integrator

Let's be honest. Third person bios are designed to appear as if they are written by a third party when, in truth, they are usually written by the author. So here goes, full disclosure...

Casey Sugarman's (my) insights stem from my perspective on the task at hand—the task of needing to solve impossible animal-mental-health emergencies before the euthanasia clock runs out. From a young age, I have been a self-proclaimed student of interspecies conversational dynamics, and what I call "The Mechanics of Will." From raising a dangerous, PTSD horse up to age 33, to the cephalopod and sensory biology labs at Boston University and the Marine Biological Laboratory in Woods Hole, MA, I have been gathering unique experiences as a translator of cross-species intention for over 30 years. Extrapolating out, I am fascinated with applications of these *identical dynamics* in the human-to-human relationship realm. Spending 14 years in exotic aquatic animal management, eventually as a senior veterinary biologist at Boston's New England Aquarium, I was co-constructor of its Aquarium's Medical Center: A Live Working Exotic Aquatic Veterinary Hospital Exhibit. Alan Alda's *Scientific American Frontiers* PBS show came calling in 1998. Showing what we humans have in common at a visceral level with aquatic "alien" species promotes global conservation. After the aquarium, I hung out a shingle and went to work on the brains of the impossible individuals among the working animals, farm animals, and family animals. I have been among the first to apply whale training techniques to the psychological rehabilitation of domesticated species, but mainly the individuals who have become dangerously violent in reaction to traumatic accident, injury, history of abuse and/or social neglect. Experiential learning dynamics that apply to all species from snail to shark to human have led me to develop an applied behavioral modification technique for application in human education and training, medical management, both physical and psychological rehabilitation, and even sociological and administrative strategy. But be warned that I am just as likely to quote a lobster in a seminar, as I am to quote your boss. In addition to teaching animal owners and the professionals in animal industries, I am excited to teach the distilled essence of Choice/Will Integration to educators, coaches, associations, and companies. I live in East Lyme, Connecticut, but no matter the taxa, species or where you and they are around the globe, I am eager to work your collective puzzle and figure it out. Let's help *every* brain *choose* to work toward the best goal for all.

www.ingramcontent.com/pod-product-compliance
Lightning Source LLC
Chambersburg PA
CBHW052010030426
42334CB00029BA/3159